EXPLORATIONS
into the
ETERNAL

Also by Ramesh S. Balsekar

Consciousness Speaks
Duet of One: The Ashtavakra Gita Dialogue
Experiencing the Teaching
The Final Truth: A guide to Ultimate Understanding
From Consciousness to Consciousness
Pointers from Nisargadatta Maharaj

(See also at the end)

EXPLORATIONS
into the
ETERNAL

Forays into the teaching
of Nisargadatta Maharaj

By
RAMESH S. BALSEKAR

Edited by
Sudhakar S. Dikshit

The Acorn Press
Durham, North Carolina

First American edition published by arrangement with
Chetana Pvt. Ltd., Mumbai, India, 1989.
Reprinted 1996, 2006.

ISBN 0-89386-023-9
Library of Congress Catalog Card No. 89-81300.

Preface

It was towards the end of the year 1983 that a young Australian student telephoned me for an appointment, and later came and saw me. He had read *I am That* and also *Pointers From Nisargadatta Maharaj*, and wanted to talk to me about Maharaj and his teaching. He said he and some friends of his were staying at an Ashram some forty miles from Bombay.

He sat with me for more than three hours that morning, and his hunger for information regarding Maharaj and his teaching seemed insatiable. My wife offered refreshment which he accepted gratefully thus confirming my suspicion that he had had nothing to eat since he had his breakfast at the Ashram quite early in the morning before leaving for Bombay - the journey by the overcrowded bus and local train took him more than three hours. Before leaving he asked if he could see me again soon and bring some friends with him. I said I would be happy to see him and his friends as often as they wanted because, ever since Maharaj had first authorized me to talk about his teaching-and later, just two days before his physical death, commanded me to do so-this has been the most satisfying thing in my life: writing and talking about Maharaj and his teaching, both of which seem to happen effortlessly and spontaneously.

Thereafter he came three or four times with his young friends. Then he had to return home to Melbourne, back to his studies on ophtamalogy. His friends, however, continued to visit and

Two or three of them were Canadians, some others were Australians, most were Americans. The talks with these young, enthusiastic visitors have been the inspiration for this book. It is one of my firm beliefs-*which I feel in my very bones*- that nothing is "coincidence", that every event is a link in the network of events that constitutes "life", that the totality of everything that happens is at each moment the "living" itself, and that therefore there really is no question of anyone consciously changing anything or "becoming" something. Everything that happens is as it should be. From the viewpoint of totality the question of right or wrong, proper or improper does not arise, for these considerations arise only in the split-mind of the illusory individual entity. I do, therefore, feel that the visits of these young men and women served a dual purpose-one, the clarification in my own mind of the significance of the many queries they raised; and two, the analysis of the queries itself produced this clarification which in turn resulted in the emanation of Maharaj's teaching into spontaneous answers to all the queries and problems. As I said before, it is surely out of these talks-which covered a wide range of topics and situations-that this book has emerged. The two who visited me more often than others are Ed Nathanson (Ananta) and Kent Brocklehurst (Sanak). It goes without saying that in every item of this book all thought, treatment and interpretation has been inevitably based on the Nisargadatta teaching.

At one juncture during these talks it seemed to me that there was a constant repetition of the basics of Maharaj's teaching. When, however, I voiced a hesitant apology, my young friends quickly assured me that this repetition was extremely useful, that it served not only as a reminder but, more importantly, it brought out the essential nature and the constant element in the basics of Maharaj's teaching. Moreover, they affirmed, the repetition gave them the opportunity to see, in depth, the interconnection between mind, thought-word, idea and knowledge. There are certain moments when the whole subject-and its strange significance-seems absurdly simple and clear, though by no means easy to communicate. What we are endeavouring to see in duration-with one sentence following another in the relativity of time-could really be apperceived only *sub specie aeternitatis*, its essential nature seen only under the aspect of eternity. Therefore the essential nature of the basics which had eluded one earlier might suddenly flash itself in consciousness when repeated the umpteenth time-and this could happen only if each repetition was given *total attention every time*, and not treated as a mere formula. It can well be imagined that this is the real reason why almost every master keeps repeating himself. And, I have had personal experience of it several times when listening to Maharaj's talks. The reason for this phenomenon is perhaps the fact that while trying to understand what some one is saying, what we are in fact doing is trying to understand ourselves. And, in this actionless activity of trying to understand ourselves we suddenly find ourselves in possession of THE MASTER KEY which opens all doors of enquiry.

The Master Key? It is simply this: *From the view point of the illusory individual entity, problems never cease. From the viewpoint of the totality of phenomenal functioning, problems never arise.* Why is this so? Because, consciousness is all that exists and everything else is an appearance therein, including the individual. As I have understood the Master's words, this is the thread which goes through the entire Nisargaddatta teaching. This is the Master Key which I have received from my Guru. With humility and Love I offer to you this Master Key which will open the door to the peace that is joy, the joy that is freedom.

But wait. Who is there to offer what and to whom? The Master Key is the understanding which Maharaj meant when he repeatedly stated: UNDERSTANDING IS ALL-the true understanding that comports the realization that there cannot be any entity to understand anything or to do anything. All "do-ers" are illusory dreamed characters in the dream-play of this *Lila* that is the totality of the phenomenal functioning. True understanding is impersonal, noumenal: We can only be the understanding.

One of the most important things I have picked up from the Nisargadatta teaching is that whatever is created-music or painting or writing or dance or scientific invention or whatever-is part of the totality of the phenomenal functioning, and the "who" connected with such creation is totally irrelevant as the creator, he is relevant only in so far as an appropriate psychosomatic apparatus was needed for the purpose. There is an interesting anecdote concerning this point, that Truth is to be recognized not by "who" utters it because truth, as Maharaj used to say, becomes untruth-a concept-as soon as it is verbalized; words can only point to it. A Tao Master one day read out for his monks a text not familiar to them. When asked who the author was, he replied: "If I tell you that this text is of the Lord Buddha, you will venerate it and prostrate before it; if I tell you that this text is written by a patriarch, you will ponder it with great respect though not with the same veneration you would accord if it were from the Buddha himself; if I tell you it is written by an unknown monk, you will not know what attitude to take; and if I tell you that this text was written by our cook, you will laugh and mock at it".

There is another anecdote which, I think, illustrates the very core of the Nisargadatta teaching. Houdini, the renowned magician, had an act which was believed to be his masterpiece-to be tied up in chains or sealed up in sackcloth or imprisoned in other ways, and he would free himself in a matter of seconds. On one occasion, however, in Italy, he could not come out of a jail for several hours. When he finally did, he was tired, frustrated and terribly angry as he came out. He complained most bitterly: "Not fair, not fair at all. They fooled me and they tricked me. In spite of all my efforts all these hours, I could do absolutely nothing, and I finally fell on the lock in utter despair-AND THE DOOR OPENED: IT WAS NEVER LOCKED." As Maharaj would say, there is no lock on truth, and therefore no key-no effort is needed to open it. He once told a visitor in answer to a query that he could show him truth in one moment. He picked up a metal cigarette-lighter, threw it on the ground, and sat in intense concentration with his eyes closed. He repeated the procedure. Then he said,"there, that is Truth-when the sound ceased, where did it go?"

The ultimate question that the discussions with the students brought out is: If there is no lock, what is the use of the Master Key? How does the Master Key work? If nothing really has happened and the phenomenal manifestation is merely a mirage or a sound that has appeared and would finally merge in its source, how is one to live one's normal life? Life, Nisargadatta Maharaj repeatedly said, is like a dream, like a stage play where the various actors play their respective roles while never really being unaware of their true identity. The expert actor playing the role of a king is never for a moment unaware of the fact that he is really a pauper; he *lives* the role of a king and never while acting does he *think* of the hardships of being a pauper. In life, thus, what we are expected to do is to live our roles naturally and accept whatever life brings in its course according to the grand design of the totality of phenomenal functioning. All that one is expected to do-and indeed all that one *can* do-is to live according to the inherent nature of the psychosomatic apparatus, and let the deep understanding of our true nature work such changes as are considered necessary, without any thinking or volition on our part. Any attempt at controlling our inherent nature can only result in supression and its adverse consequences. All that is necessary is the witnessing of whatever happens in life, including the thoughts and acts of the "me" while being *passively but continuously* aware of our true identity (such awareness is indeed the true understanding). Then, there is no wanting to change the "what is" to what the "me" thinks "what-should be" because the understanding comports the realization that all the "me's" concerned in life are *together* truly the eternal, subjective "I" expressing itself objectively as the phenomenal manifestation in its totality.

The clock now shows 4.30 in the morning, the time which is traditionally known as the "Amrita-Ghatika"-the immortal time, the eternal moment, the HERE AND NOW, the infinite intemporality, the "I" in the absence of the "me". Let us BE this Amrita-Ghatika".

I may add a few words about the information contained in this book, which covers a variety of aspects relevant to the essential subject. This information was gathered over a period of years through several books among the many which happened to pass through my hands (the many coincidences in this regard would mean a different story altogether). The notes I had then made were purely for my own edification. There was not then the slightest intention of using them any other way: there was never any intention to write a book. The point is that I am not now able to give specific credit either to the relevant book or to the author. And the book has no bibliography at all. However, I do acknowledge my debt to these various books and their authors. If this book, or any of the others, could be of similar assistance to others in future, it would be a gratifying fact. Some of the views I have expressed (based on my own personal experiences and deepest convictions) may not only not be acceptable to some but will undoubtedly raise a number of traditional eyebrows. One hopes, however, that the discriminating reader, the seeker with an open and receptive mind, will on occasions feel an intuitive tug at his heart that may make him leap in sheer joy that is the eternity.

Bombay

January 1986

Ramesh S. Balsekar

Introduction

A small compact physcial frame, a dark-complexioned face with large luminous eyes, and an astonishing aura of the utmost physical and mental relaxation — this is my indelible impression of Nisargadatta Maharaj, an impression I had formed on one of my earlier visits to Maharaj and which has since firmly remained. On this particular occasion, I had arrived a little earlier than usual and found myself almost alone with Maharaj. I was proceeding towards the rear of the room where one found safety in numbers and a certain protective anonymity, when Maharaj beckoned to me to sit nearer in front of him. As I sat down, he smiled and asked if I had any questions. As I looked at him smiling benignly at me — just the Master and me — I found all my questions literally disappearing into thin air, and I instantly found myself, unbelievingly, answering that all questions had disappeared, that it was as if no questions had really existed, and that I seemed to want absolutely nothing; and almost in the same breath came the thought: now I am going to have to face his wrath in full measure; he is going to shout at me whether I had suddenly became a Jnani that I should have no questions to ask. But what had happened was totally spontaneous and unpremeditated and there was nothing I could have done; I could certainly not have taken my words back nor did I wish to. Maharaj then bent forward, looked straight into my eyes for a moment or two that seemed like eternity to me, and then leaned back with what seemed like a grunt and an almost imperceptible nod of his head. Somehow, thereafter, whatever Maharaj said seemed to have deeper significance, seemed simple and straight enough to hit the target — and yet, with neither the speaker nor the listener nor the target.

At one stage Maharaj had seemed to speak in riddles or had even appeared to evade questions with a counter-question like "But why don't you ask youself: Who is asking the question" or "Who wants to know". But suddenly, doubts like this vanished and were replaced by a reaction like "Of course that is so"!

Maharaj said: "Intellectual understanding is useless because it is a temporal phenomenon with a triad of the speaker, the listener and what is said. It concerns intellectual interpretation that can vary from person to person, but intuitive apperception is immediate without any interpretation because it is the Truth". And one wondered — without realizing that, that itself was a temporal phenomenon — whether Maharaj was only playing with words! But at a certain unspecified moment of time, it suddenly became absolutely clear that Maharaj was NOT playing with words. It was with tremendous amount of compassion that Maharaj was almost urging his listeners to absorb the true meaning of his words. The word itself was merely the product of temporal conceptualization and had therefore only a limited usefulness. It can only point, it can only suggest, it can only indicate. Word can only describe the mango, it cannot give one the taste of the mango. That is why Maharaj used to say repeatedly that the listener must absorb the meaning and, more importantly, the intention and the purpose behind his words, and then throw them away. Then, there was the point of duration: the meaning must be absorbed spontaneously and instantly, and that would be of the nature of intemporality; intellectual discussion would necessarily be at the level of conceptualization and temporality. The *manana* (reflection) that Maharaj recommended was not to be about the words and their interpretation but on the meaning already absorbed, and when all doubts had disappeared, there would be *nidihyasana* (concentrated absorption and remaining in the source).

Maharaj laid great stress on spontaneity - whatever was spontaneous was correct because it was untainted by temporality or duration which was the base of conceptualization, and thus, of the separation and the ego. Spontaneous understanding led to spontaneous action, and therefore to free living or noumenal living where there is no thought, no conceptualization, and therefore no separation of "me" and the "other".

Maharaj often said that the quickest and perhaps the only way for enlightenment *to happen* was for the disciple to listen to the Sadguru with an open, free or vacant mind: preconceived notions and pet concepts were insurmountable obstructions in the path of the arrow of the Sadguru's word towards the target of the disciple's heart. Maharaj repeatedly asserted that a full and sincere acceptance of the truth could instantaneously result in awakening, but most disciples were so densely conditioned by conceptual knowledge and notional concepts that they were just not ready for it. In his own case, Maharaj used to say, it so happened that the Sadguru's word hit the bull's eye because when he visited his Sadguru he carried "no luggage" (of preconceived ideas and theories in his mind). His Sadguru told him, "If you dis-identify youself from the body, and firmly remain entrenched in that animating consciousness which gives you sentience and the sense of presence - I AM -, you will have peace and freedom from bondage this very instant". And this is the "knowledge" which he was now passing on to his listeners. Deep understanding and full conviction was all that is necessary. Any further action as such would indeed be not only not necessary but could actually prove to be a hindrance and obstruction.

Many of Maharaj's visitors found it almost impossible to accept his definite view that no personal individual effort was necessary for achieving elightenment. They would try in many ways to get him to give them advice on what they should "do". In doing so, however, they would show that they had not really and truly understood the very basic point in Maharaj's teaching: wanting the personal and individual attainment of enlightenment, and wanting to make a personal and individual effort is wholly incompatible with the essence of enlightenment, which is the annihilation of the ego, the "me-notion". It is for this reason that Maharaj asked people to eschew the desire to understand at what he called the intellectual level because such understanding clearly indicated an individual "me" who would understand it. He repeatedly asked people to understand that perceiving and conceiving are twin elements in the process of concepetualization which lead to action in the temporal mechanism whereby we create bondage for ourselves. Any further positive action can only strengthen the ties of this bondage. What actually is required, Maharaj would say, is the contrary — to rest in beingness, to KNOW that we are nothing, to BE in the nothingness of the no-mind state, to cease conceptualizing, so that whatever happens would be *not our doing* but the pure functioning which we witness passively. In other words, all thought, all conceptualizing, all action is in duration. The very realization of this fact is all the action that is necessary to take the illusion of an objective "me" in temporality into the subjective "I-I" of intemporality. All action is in reality *the functioning* in totality that the split-mind of the conceptual individual construes as the action of a personal actor.

Any personal effort, as Maharaj clearly saw it, was through the identification with the very same illusory separate individual, from which one was seeking escape. Surely, therefore, all personal effort would only make the bondage even more strong.

Also, personal effort could only be in duration which again is the very concept from which liberation is sought into intemporality. Therefore, said Maharaj, all that is necessary is the clear realization of what we are, of our true nature which is obnubilated, clouded and darkened by a conditioned reflex which identifies the subject *that we are* with the object (the individual) *that we think we are*. Such realization cannot need any effort. It can only be sudden and spontaneous through immediate apperception.

What is meant by "personal effort" needs some clarification. For instance, Maharaj would ask someone to practise meditation while to someone else he might say that meditation could be an obstacle. When he recommended meditation it would generally be to those who complained of an overactive mind always flooded with too many thoughts much as he might have suggested regular doses of castor oil to someone suffering from chronic constipation. But those who prided themselves on their regular meditation at fixed times for long periods as a means of achieving enlightenment, were warned by Maharaj that their meditation was an impediment and an obstruction for enlightenment to happen. The difference was clear: the intent and purpose behind the meditation. In the latter case, there was an individual "meditator", meditating with the specific intention of "achieving" enlightenment for "himself". To such meditators, he would say "all right, you meditate and go into Samadhi for 10 hours, or 10 days or 10 years or 100 years - but then What? you would still remain in the framework of space-Time". He would give the instance of a Hatha-Yogi who asked his attendant for a meal, and then went into Samadhi; he resumed normal Consciousness again after 10 days, and promptly asked the attendant: Where is my meal?! Maharaj would therefore warn such meditators that meditation of this kind could be a definite hindrance apart from being useless because it could bring in certain Yogic powers at the meditator's command which could easily bolster up his ego and make him swerve away from his original objective which though misguided was nonetheless laudable. However, when someone explained that he did meditation whenever he felt like it, but without any specific purpose, not meditating on anything in particular but as a means of mental relaxation, and emptying of the mind, Maharaj certainly did not discourage him.

There was an interesting case of a visitor who assured Maharaj that he had been listening to him with total attention and had thoroughly understood what he had said, that listening to

Maharaj was a wonderful experience, but that he was at a loss to know what he should "do" in the daily routine of his life. The visitor insisted that there must be something he had to do in order to practise what he had learnt from Maharaj, and also in what manner he should exercise his choice and take action in daily life when business and other matters demanded his attention. In such a situation, Maharaj would only smile and ask "who is asking this question? - find out". If the visitor felt that Maharaj was evading the issue, he would make another try by a different approach, and then Maharaj would say "Do whatever you like". The visitor would then perhaps laugh, but deep down he would no doubt feel that it was not fair that Maharaj should give such a cavalier answer! It is astonishing that many people could covertly sympathize with the visitor without realizing that in the circumstances that was the only answer Maharaj could give. Maharaj would repeatedly assert that he was not talking as one individual to another, and that if someone listened to him as an individual, they would be talking at cross purposes. The visitor wanted to know what he should do as an individual in his daily life while the very basis of Maharaj's talk was that as the individual is an illusory entity, he cannot and does not live according to his sweet will as he thinks he does, but actually is "being lived". The attempt of such a "lived" puppet and that of a "dreamed" puppet to lead his own life are identical in as much as both are reacting to impulses generated by psychic conditions over which neither has any real control. The apparent sentiency of both is merely a movement in consciousness. Therefore, Maharaj said, "Do what you like", meaning that whatever happens is independent of the volition and the choice that the individual thinks he is exercising! All that happens is that by the acceptance of the concept of doership, a further concept of guilt and bondage is created.

What Maharaj asks us to do is simple enough: The only way enlightenment can happen is by transcending conceptualization; the only way to transcend conceptualizing is by avoiding purposeful intentions because without intentions there is no "me-notion" since "Will (intentions)" and "Ego" are synonymous terms. Without intentions, there cannot be conceptualizing, only noumenal action.

As Mahraj repeatedly used to say, "Understanding is all, and enlightenment is the realization that enlightenment is not something to be attained". Enlightenment is not an object and therefore it cannot be attained. Enlightenment is "not to be attained" also for the simple reason that we ARE that enlightenment. The question of attaining or not attaining something arises if that something is different from what we are. And what we are is the eternal subject "I" without the slightest touch of objectivity. Enlightenment or illumination is, therefore, the realization that what the seeker seeks is himself, that therefore in reality there is neither the seeker nor the sought nor the seeking. It is only in temporal conceptualizing that this triad of seeker, sought and seeking exists, and when conceptualizing ceases the seeking too ends, and all that remains is the eternal subject not aware of itself.

If the specialist doctor tells the patient that he does not have the wasting disease that the patient thinks he has, that he has conducted all the necessary tests and in his expert opinion he is convinced that the patient is perfectly healthy, the patient may accept the doctor's diagnosis and be happy, or not accept it and visit other doctors. If he has faith in the doctor's expertise and accepts his verdict, does the patient have to "do" anything thereafter?

In the same spirit in which Maharaj assured his visitors that all they have to do is to have faith in him and accept his words that a deep understanding of "What-is" is all that is necessary, Ashtavakra in his Gita (or Samhita) tells his disciple King Janaka:

"You do not belong to the Brahmana caste or any other caste. You are not concerned with any of the four stages of life, prescribed by the Scriptures (student; householder, retired life of *Sanyasa* or renunciation). You are not perceptible to the senses. You are the unattached, formless being, the witness of all and everything. "BE HAPPY".

If there were other religions prevalent in Ashtavakra's time, he would no doubt have added with equal authority: You are neither a Hindu, nor a Muslim nor a Christian, nor anything else. Ashtavakra says, "Be Happy". Maharaj says, "Understanding is all". Ashtavakra does not say "do what I tell you to do and you will be happy after 10 years or 20 years or in the next birth or after you are dead". He says: understand that you are that which is imperceptible to the senses, that unattached, formless being (ness), the witness (ing) of all and everything. BE HAPPY now, this instant, because whatever causes unhappiness does not - cannot - affect you. The idea of, and the desire for, personal liberation comports the idea of the need for personal effort, and instantly obstructs the simple realization and acceptance that we always have been free. When there is deep impregnation of this simple realization, everything becomes benignly clear, including the ineluctable fact that there is no thing like an individual who can possibly be expected to make any effort as such, because he is only an appearance in consciousness which, through his sentience, is able to perceive and cognize other appearances in consciousness.

Editor's Note

Explorations into the Eternal, the third book of Ramesh S. Balsekar's proposed Nisargadatta Trilogy, is not just another work providing an interpretative insight into the teaching of Sri Nisargadatta Maharaj. It is much more, much much more.

His first book *Pointers from Nisargadatta Maharaj* contained the teaching of Maharaj in its entirety and the author kept himself in the background except for occasional appearances where the context demanded his presence.

His second book *Experience of Immortality* contained the application of Maharaj's teaching to the main theme expounded by Sant Jnaneshwar in his Amritanubhava, namely "the identity of the noumenon and the phenomena, the perceiver and the perceived". In this work the author is not in the background as in the case of *Pointers.* His active presence is seen throughout the book as an humble devotee serving two sages — Sant Jnaneshwar and Nisargadatta Maharaj. He even erects a broad pedestal for the two sages to sit together and he stands at its base conveying to the readers in his mellifluous language what the sages say.

In the present work, *Explorations into the Eternal,* the third book of the trilogy the author assumes for himself the central role, the role of the explorer. His guru, Sri Nisargadatta Maharaj is there of course, but as an invisible though a dominant presence throughout. Maharaj's presence in this book reminds me of the concept of *skambha,* as visualized in the Atharva Veda. Skambha is represented in the Veda as the primal framework of the entire creation, even more, it is the transcendental ground on which stands everything, where the plurality of the manifold aspects of manifested reality can be seen as the Supreme Oneness of the unmanifest.

In *Exploration into the Eternal* Maharaj's teaching is the *skambha*, the transcendental ground from where the author makes his forays into different directions and different realms of knowledge — philosophical, mystical or scientific. He has his encounters with saints and sages — Mukundaraja, Lao-tzu, Hung-jeen and others. He takes plunges into the Yogavasistha, Tripura Rahasya and other spiritual classics. He surveys the theory of relativity and the quantam theory and, in company with the modern physicists, studies the behaviour of quarks, atoms and sub-atoms. He explores many different spheres where human mind can reach and at times his findings are strikingly similar to his personal experiences as reflected in the incidents and events of his own life.

Explorations is indeed a unique book in the sense that it traverses over a vast expanse of human thought and reaches a point where science and spirituality merge together into the Supreme Truth. Few such books are written these days, for there are few who can write them.

As the editor of Chetana's publications I was in the privileged position to become the first reader of this book. And I deem it my privilege to introduce it to seriousminded readers who are in quest of the truth.

Bombay   Sudhakar S. Dikshit
May, 1987   Editor

Contents

The Grace of the Guru

There is a verse in the Bhagavadgita, where the Lord says:
Is it not astonishing that only a rare one will show any
interest in this (great philosophy of unicity). Is it not a
matter of further astonishment that (among the few who
have studied and deeply understood the philosophy)
hardly anyone would speak on the subject, and almost
none to hear it, let alone someone who would not only
apperceive it but actually experience it in practice? Is this
not the greatest wonder in the world?
Nisargadatta Maharaj was one of those rare sages who, after
enlightenment had happened, was easily accessible to those who
felt the need of guidance to go very deeply into the meaning and
purpose of existence in this manifested world. What kind of a
person was the usual visitor who took the trouble to locate Maharaj's humble residence in a humble locality, and thereafter attend
his talks as often as he could? The average visitor was a seeker who
had made many efforts and had ultimately landed at Maharaj's
feet. In fact, as is stated elsewhere*

"Maharaj often says that very few of those who come to
him are novices in spiritual knowledge. Generally they are
those who have travelled far and wide in quest of
knowledge, read many books, met many Gurus and have a
certain idea of what it is all about, but rarely a clear vision
of what they have been seeking.
"Many of them do not hesitate to acknowledge that all
their efforts proved unrewarding and they felt frustrated
and disappointed. And there are some who even wonder
if they have been chasing a mere will-o-the-wisp.
However, inspite of all their frustration and dejection,
they do seem to know that life does have an ultimate
meaning. Maharaj feels deeply concerned for such visitors
and takes personal interest in them. But he totally ignores

those who come to him out of an idle curiosity or with the
object of talking about him at a weekend party with a
holier-than-thou attitude or perhaps with
condescension.

In many cases, the visitors concerned felt quite bewildered by
the extraordinary combination of circumstances and events that
led to their arriving not only at Maharaj's residence but even land-
ing in Bombay. It clearly seemed that the meeting between the
Guru and the disciples could not possibly be chance events. And
the situation becomes even easier to understand if we look at this
relationship not as between one individual and another – as one
would usually be inclined to do – but as part of the totality of
functioning of manifestation as such. As Maharaj used to emphasize, the individual really does not exist as an independent entity,
that when he talked to a disciple, it was consciousness talking to
consciousness (and not one individual to another), and that unless
this fact was clearly understood and constantly kept in mind, nothing worthwhile would emerge from the talks.

It was not denied that the Guru would be regarded in the beginning by the disciple as the embodiment of Truth in the form of
a human being who has known and experienced reality, who is
able to remove the disciple's doubts and difficulties; and in the
process the disciple is bound to develop a personal feeling of love
and respect towards the Guru.* The point that Maharaj was at great
pains to emphasize all the time was that the disciple should not let
that love and reverence for the person of the Guru be an impediment to the clear understanding that the Guru is not an individual,
that the Guru himself, being identified with Reality, sees others
also, including the disciples, as pure consciousness, and that,
therefore, unless the disciple too is ready and prepared to see the
falseness of his own individuality, the relationship between the
Guru and the disciple in relativity would not fructify into Reality.
In this fructification the knowledge that was perhaps not unknown intellectually to the disciple, but was still hazy in its application, suddenly comes into sharp focus, and into that focal
point merges the disciple's individuality.

It is just as well that we have plunged ourselves right into the
middle of the Guru-disciple relationship; but, broadly speaking,
there would be four aspects of the matter – (a) Why does one seek a
Guru at all? (b) Does every seeker find his Guru? (c) What does the
Guru actually do? and finally (d) Is a Guru really necessary? All

* Author's *Experience of Immortality*, Chapter 2, "Homage to the Guru", Chetana,
Bombay-1984

these four aspects are in fact interrelated.

(a) Why does one seek a Guru at all?.
This aspect of the matter is really concerned with the question of what we expect out of life. Basically and essentially, what the average person in the world wants out of life is just one thing : happiness. The word "happiness" may mean different things to different people at different times, but the fact remains that the common man has one basic aim in life, and that is, to find happiness. It is in this quest for happiness that he goes through life, day after day, in the firm belief that he can find happiness in and through the material objects in the world. What does one mean by the word "happiness"? In this frantic search for happiness, what is one really interested in? The answer must necessarily be that what one wants is SATISFACTION, the fulfilment of what one at the moment considers as one's need, whether the need be better living conditions or social service or whatever. Basically, therefore, what one is after is the satisfaction of a need or desire, whether it be in the form of food, shelter, sex, social service or power or status or whatever. There comes a time, however, when man gets utterly tired – physically and mentally – of this constant search because he finds that *this search never ends!* Either the very basic objects of this search are not obtainable, or more likely, as soon as one object has been achieved there is desire for another. He comes to the inescapable conclusion, perhaps the startling discovery, that no kind of pleasure can provide lasting happiness, that every kind of pleasure has *within itself* the roots of pain and torment. At this stage, man's search takes a turn towards that kind of happiness which would be true, lasting. He *knows* that there does exist this kind of happiness because in certain lucid moments, during his frantic search for pleasure, he has had glimpses – brief glimpses – of a happiness which did not depend on any material object of sensual pleasure, and indeed was without any ostensible reason Pure Joy. It is in search of this deep, constant, lasting, pure joy that man seeks the help of someone who is already immersed in such joy and happiness that has no relation to pleasure or pain. Such a "someone" is the self-realized Guru. And such a "someone" was my Guru Nisargadatta Maharaj.

(b) Does every seeker find his Guru?
The answer is YES, depending upon the sincerity of the seeker, the intensity of his need, and the capacity of the seeker to receive guidance from the Guru. When asked whether a person could have more than one Guru, Maharaj used to point out that there is only Sadguru, and that is the consciousness which every sentient

being has on his own, the knowledge "I am", the sense of being alive and *present*. Subject to this Sadguru, it is possible, he would say, and even sometimes necessary to have more than one Guru according to one's circumstances, according to one's spiritual development and according to one's inherent tendencies. But the essential point to remember is that, as Maharaj often pointed out, from the point of the Guru, there are no disciples as such because he does not regard any one as being outside of himself; it is only from viewpoint of view of the seeker that there is a Guru. The grace of the Guru is like an ocean – it is entirely upto the disciple how much of the ocean he wants and how much he can carry! And even this is only a concept. Truly there is no duality of Guru and disciple, and this realization brings the search to an end.

The problem, however, would seem to persist from the point of view of the seeker inasmuch as several questions remain unanswered. For example, how is a seeker to recognize his Guru from the numerous spiritual teachers he may come across? Or, assuming that a seeker decides on a particular person as a competent Guru by the peace of mind he felt in his presence and the respect he felt for him, what would be the position if that person turned out not to be suitable as far as that particular seeker is concerned? Presumably, the fate of the seeker in such a situation would be decided according to the degree of his own preparedness and merit. There is also the point that whilst the seeker himself saw no improvement in himself despite his following the Guru's instructions, it may well be that there had actually been considerable improvement though it was not apparent to the seeker. And then, of course, who is to decide upon the suitability and competency or otherwise of the Guru? Finally, there remains the question: Who is to be accepted as a Guru? In the traditional sense of the word, a Guru is one who has been "invested" with the authority to initiate disciples and prescribe a routine discipline for them; and in this sense a valid investiture would seem to be necessary to lend authority to him as a Guru, whether or not he is truly self-realized. There is, ultimately, the most interesting statement of Bhagavan Ramana Maharshi when a reference was made to the fact that he himself had no Guru as such. Ramana Maharshi said:" It depends on what you mean by the term GURU; he need not necessarily have a human form, and I might have even had such a Guru at some time or other; and also, did I not sing hymns to the Arunachala hill?"

The point of the whole matter is that questions will never cease if the matter is considered from the viewpoint of the individual, while questions will not even arise if it is considered from the viewpoint of the functioning of manifestation as a whole. The individual is, after all, only a small part of the totality of the manifestation, and anything viewed from his viewpoint would necessarily be in a very limited framework. The question of enlightenment is generally viewed from the point of view of the individual. The fact, however, remains that the individual as an autonomous or independent entity just does not exist. The individual is merely an appearance in consciousness like any other objective phenomenon. How can there be enlightenment for an appearance? The matter of "enlightenment" – or what goes with that label – is seen in perspective if it is viewed as an event or occurrence within the totality of functioning in order to maintain the normal equilibrium in the total phenomenal manifestation. Whenever such a phenomenon of enlightenment occurs, it is only the other individuals who consider that a certain name and form has become enlightened. The individual concerned has in fact disappeared as an individual entity *before* enlightenment could have occurred: indeed, enlightenment cannot occur so long as there is any identification with a particular name and form as a separate entity.

What then should be the attitude of the seeker in search of a Guru? The answer would seem to be astonishingly simple: all he need do is to keep firmly in mind the one essential fact that the human being has no separate existence other than as a part of the total manifestation, that he himself as an individual has neither the initiative nor the choice to be in the circumstances in which he finds himself, and that therefore it does not seem right or proper that he should strive or make any effort other than keeping this basic fact in mind. In other words, all that he really *can* do is to keep free from all sorts of concepts which could only act as obstructions in the working of the total manifestation. In its own good time, this totality of functioning would do whatever is necessary in its working and if it includes what is known as liberation, the necessary events including the meeting with the Guru must naturally take place. Such an attitude will prepare the necessary ground for the Guru's word to take root and blossom into enlightenment.

(c) **What does the Guru actually do?**
The straightforward answer to this query would be that the Guru not being any individual but pure consciousness, actually does nothing other than merely watching or witnessing the advice being given to an individual phenomenon and that advice being received according to the receptive capacity in each case. As Nisargadatta Maharaj used to say "All I do is to present a mirror in which to see your true self" Thereafter, to what extent the seed of

the Guru's advice takes root, flowers and blossoms into enlightenment would depend upon the working plan of providence or Prakriti or Prajna!

It is necessary to go deeply into this question of what the Guru
is actually supposed to do, because quite often the seeker goes to
the Guru with the hope, the belief and perhaps even the conviction that once he has been accepted by the Guru, it is the responsibility of the Guru to provide him with liberation' or awakening or
enlightenment or whatever. This is an entirely erroneous notion,
this expectation that the Guru would provide him with an object
called liberation (misconstrued as unalloyed pleasure or happiness) which he would be able to enjoy perennially. Such an expectation is likely to cause great frustration leading to a search for
a more effective, more "powerful" Guru! In fact, enlightenment,
far from being something to be enjoyed by an individual, is an
event, a movement in consciousness which bridges the relative
manifest with the absolute unmanifest, which by its very nature
signals the total dissolution of the very entity that wished to "enjoy" it.

Once again is thus seen the misconception in trying to consider
the role of the Guru from the point of view of the individual
seeker. In the traditional sense, the word GURU is used as the
"dispeller of the darkness of ignorance". (GU = the darkness of
ignorance, and RU = the dispeller). The immediate question, from
this definition, would be: Can the Guru actually dispel the ignorance of the disciple? All that the Guru can do is to point out to the
disciple what his true nature is. He cannot dispel the other's
ignorance; otherwise the Guru would be expected to dispel the
ignorance from all his disciples, irrespective of the capacity of each
disciple. The pointing by the Guru to the Truth is like the pointing
at a destination by someone who has traversed along the road and
KNOWS   that the road leads to the destination, and from this viewpoint is certainly not only important but necessary. But the error
lies in expecting the Guru to *carry* the disciple to the destination.
What the Guru would do is to recognize the capacity of each seeker, and while he may direct one to take the high road, he may well
suggest to another that he take the lower road. To many others the
Guru would certainly suggest that they would not reach the destination if they intended to carry heavy baggage on their shoulders – such baggage being the pride of intellect and learning, or
the pride of having done a number of *yatras* (pilgrimages) to a
number of sacred places, or of being able to recite from a large
number of scriptures, or of having done an enormous amount of
social work, and various things of this nature. Exactly what is

meant by words like a seeker's "capacity" or "faith" would be almost impossible to define. The essential requirement, however, would certainly be not too strong a presence of the "me", the very "me" who wants liberation!

At this stage, a clear distinction needs to be made between a Guru like Nisargadatta Maharaj and the religious Gurus who lay down do's and don'ts about one's behaviour and conduct. Whenever a question was asked about the morality of any sort of behaviour or the correctness or otherwise of any action, Maharaj would at once point out that all norms were based on duality whereas he was not concerned with ethical or moral values. Once the seeker had truly apprehended his real nature and the nature of the manifestation as such, all problems about social, moral or ethical behaviour would sort themselves out spontaneously. There have been many religious leaders in the past hundreds of years, Maharaj used to say, but has there been the slightest change in the basic nature of either the elements or the human being? A Guru like Nisargadatta Maharaj is not concerned in changing the world but only in taking the disciple back to the source of manifestation (of which the human being is a part) and presenting a clear view of "What – is", of the Truth.

(d) Is the Guru really necessary?

Before this question can be answered, it is necessary to examine the question itself. If the question refers to the need of the seeker, the answer is simple enough. Even in the case of technical and other academic subjects, inspite of all available books, personal instruction by experts in the relevant subjects is considered absolutely essential. How much more then would the Guru be necessary in a field which is totally beyond the scope of the mind and intellect – in which mind and intellect must yield to feel and intuition? The question, however, assumes real significance from the point of view of the totality of manifestation. Viewed from this standpoint, both the Guru and disciple would be equally necessary to bring about the phenomenon known as enlightenment.

Broadly speaking, there would be three types of people from the point of view of the need of a Guru. At one end will be the man who has no interest in the Guru in regard to his spiritual development; he is so deeply concerned in the material benefits of this world for himself that he would be interested in the Guru only if he could get something for himself – money, status, fame or power or whatever – out of such an association. In the middle will be the man who is interested both in this world and in the hereafter: he wants the best of both the worlds; he wants the goodies of this world and is also interested in ensuring a decent place for himself

in the other world or in the next birth or whatever. At the other
end will be the man who realizes, either intuitively or because of
some traumatic experience, that life is not a bed of roses but one of
thorns, and seeks some way to get away from it all. Each of these
three types will act according to his inherent nature, according to
his psychic make-up, which itself would depend a great deal on
the genes or chromosomes, and to a certain extent on the circumstances which have brought about the conditioning he has received
since his birth. The essential point is that the process of evolution
would take care of the weight of each class of the people at any one
time and the speed with which the number of people would move
from the lower class to the higher class (the Vedantis would label
these three classes as the *adhamadhikari* meaning the lowest, the
madhyamadhikari, the middle class, and the *uttaamadhikari,* the
highest class). The evolutionary process itself would be part of the
functioning (in duration) of the totality of the manifestaton (in
space), like the orderliness of the movements of the stars and
planets in the universe. This functioning is called Prakriti or Pra-
jnya or whatever, and the phenomenon of enlightenment together
with the interrelation between the Gurus and the seekers would
be part of this impersonal functioning of Prakriti. When this impersonal functioning of manifestation as such is ignored or forgotten, all kinds of problems arise. For instance, instead of viewing
the evolutionary process of the stream of psychosomatic apparatuses from one class of people to another class (from the lower to
the middle, and from the middle to the higher, and then on to
enlightenment) as an impersonal phenomenon, the process is
viewed as the passing of the individual soul (whatever it may be)
from one body to another, and thus is created the concept of rebirth and its consequential problems.

It is only when the evolutionary process is seen as the impersonal one that it is, that the relationship between the Guru and the
disciple comes into perspective. The enlightened Guru like Nisargadatta Maharaj does see the relationship as an impersonal evolutionary process but the disciple, when he goes to the Guru, does
not. The disciple goes to the Guru as an individual seeking enlightenment as something which he can enjoy as an individual.
The enlightened Guru, then, gradually and systematically, explains to the disciple that the individual entity has no independen-
dent existence other than as an appearance in consciousness *within the total manifestation,* and that the clear understanding of this
fact itself is the enlightenment or awakening that he is seeking,
because such understanding demolishes the bondage of dualism
created by the disciple's mistaken belief that he is an entity sepa-

rate from all other people and all other manifestation

To come back to the question of the need of the Guru from the individual seeker's point of view: Why do I go to the Guru at all ? The direct answer is because I am unhappy and I want happiness. I do not exactly know what I want; I may have been told of enlightenment or I may have read about it, but whatever it is, I am seeking it, I am wanting it, and I believe that the Guru can provide it for me. In the awareness of my deep sorrow, my deep unhappiness, I believe that the Guru will provide the means for the escape. What the Guru does is in fact to point out to me that what I am trying to do is to escape from sorrow and that there is NO ESCAPE, that the only way to deal with this sorrow is to turn back - to reverse, as Nisargadatta Maharaj used to say, and find out *for myself* exactly what this sorrow is, to find out what has caused it, the source of the sorrow - and then to cut at the root of it. This is why the Guru is necessary. When I meet the Guru, what in fact happens is that the seeking, the searching, the escaping stops. Then I deal directly with the sorrow. He is *not* the enlightened Guru who helps you along to escape from your sorrow by prescribing some procedure or method for you because any method has the innate fault of becoming a mechanical exercise, of turning into a deadening drill. The only effective method – if it can be called a method at all – is that which has no mechanics involved therein but requires you to face your sorrow, analyse it, understand it so thoroughly and so intimately that in that very understanding, it disappears.

This brings us to the manner in which the Guru makes the disciple understand the problem of his sorrow. Just as people could be broadly divided into three main groups according to the intensity (or the lack) of their need for the Guru, so also they could be divided into various groups depending on their intuitive and intellectual capacity to understand the problem. Nisargadatta Maharaj used to say that the direct and the quickest method was that of self-enquiry: What is this "me" who seems to be suffering ? But not everyone is endowed with the capacity to absorb this kind of teaching. For such people of limited intellect he was obliged to ask them to count beads, to repeat God's Name, to do *Bhajan* etc. in order to improve their psyches. Here again there comes up the question of evolution that was mentioned earlier. There may be a question: Would such a method get for such an individual the enlightenment he seeks ? If the nature of the process of evolution within the totality of functioning is clearly understood, it would be quickly perceived that the question is misconceived because no individual can exist as a separate entity with autonomous and independent beingness. The only answer that can be given to such a question is that enlightenment through what is known as Bhakti can certainly happen in those cases which fit in with the plan of the totality of functioning (of the totality of manifestation) or the Prakriti or Providence or God or that which may be known by any other name. The process of evolution is continuous and it is for this reason that the Lord in the Bhagwadgita says: "When their Bhakti is deep and sincere enough, I give such bhaktas the deep intuitive understanding to apperceive my true nature".

Then there is what is known as Raja-Yoga, the aim being to cultivate certain qualities which would make the seeker a good citizen and rid him of the psychological conditioning, and thereafter to sit in quiet meditation so that the psyche may be purified. Here we would be concerned with the question of what really constitutes meditation and what such meditation would achieve. Here again, the danger, as Maharaj used to point out, is that meditation could easily degenerate into a drill and at the same time a hazard because of some of the attractive consequences which the deep concentration of mind could bring about. As Maharaj would say, meditation is useful to the extent that it would purify the psyche, but true meditation is constant witnessing of whatever takes place as movements in consciousness. Meditation, in any other sense, could at best be a waste of time, a temporary escape from suffering, and at worst could be a definite hazard. "You may sit for 10 hours or 10 days or 10 years or 1000 years in meditation, but when you are back in space-time, what then?"– Maharaj used to ask –"Are you any nearer to finding your true nature or the root of your suffering?"

2

Sentient Being is Sentience,
Not the Being

It has been the fond hope of the scientist over the past several centuries to prove that living organisms and sentient beings are nothing but the total of their material components, by producing in the laboratory from inanimate materials the rudimentary proto-plasmic cell. The scientist has been well aware that once such a proto-plasmic cell has been produced, he could depend on evolution to do the rest. But this has not happened and there does not appear to be any chance of its happening in the foreseeable future.

The gap between the living and the not-living, between the sentient and the insentient, between the thinking and the not-thinking, continues to be as unbridgeable as ever before. As one scientist has put it, the pebble and the chestnut, though similar in colour, weight and size, will continue to be basically dissimilar inasmuch as the pebble will remain a pebble for hundreds of years whereas, given favourable conditions of soil, moisture, light and heat, the chestnut in course of time will become a magnificent spreading tree. As Nisargadatta Maharaj would say, this difference is symbolic of the difference between conceiving the universe as the total of its material components and the universe in its entirety. This difference between the pebble and the chestnut represents the fundamental difference between life and death, between life and mind on the one hand and matter on the other; it is in a way the problem of the relationship between body and mind, or body and consciousness.

It has, of course, been established that the working of the nervous system is subject to mechanical laws and processes, and that the stimuli passing along the nerve fibres and providing the necessary data to the brain that enables the senses to perceive, are electrical in nature and can be timed and measured with precision; within the brain itself there are electrical activities, closely connected with thought processes, that can be recorded by the Electro-encaphalograph (EEG). But all this refers only to the outside impulses and their transmission to the brain, and therefore to perception, and is very much on the surface. It does not go deep enough to tell us anything about the consequence of perception in the conscious mind, about the interpretation of the sense-data in the brain, or about anything apart from the mechanism of perception. In other words, all the sciences put together cannot do what a single grain of wheat does, that is, germinating in suitable conditions; nor can they explain anything at all about the creation of new ideas or the processes of reflection and decision, which clearly arise from within, independently of any related thoughts or experiences. As Professor Eccles has put it, we are compelled to consider the behaviour of the individual particles of matter in the active cerebral cortex as something "outside physics". What all this amounts to is that we are still asking the question that Aristotle was asking two thousand years ago: how is the mind attached to the body? It would seem that scientists have not only not solved the problem of the relation of mind to brain but that they do not have even a clue about a basis for its very beginning.

Could it not be that the endeavour to discover the nature of thought is *basically misconceived* because that which is thinking and this which is thought about are one and the same; because there can be no subject-object relationship in such a quest: because that which is sought is this which is seeking. In the absence of a mirror, how can the eye see itself?

The development of a new-born infant is a fascinating thing to study: a single cell, during the period of nine months has progressed through the successive embryonic states and has culminated into a human personality. The process of development automatically continues without interruption even after birth. In the course of the next few days, weeks and months the infant rapidly increases its weight and develops the other capacities gradually, including the mental capacities which create in the infant the sense of the exercise of will and volition. This development of the infant, like that of a plant, is not really through an outside source but *its own inherent energy* contained in that single cell which has thus developed. This inherent vital force within the growing embryo contains the self-regulating properties which ensure that the end-product will be according to norm inspite of any accidental hazards that may arise during the course of the development. *It is the chromosomes of the fertilized egg which determine the potential of the new individual.* This fact was repeatedly stressed by Nisargadatta Maharaj·

One is so thoroughly identified with one's body that one would think the person is daft if he were to ask, "apart from your name and form, who (or what) are you ?" We are all accustomed to think of our body as that solid, material stuff with a certain volume and weight which is susceptible to pain and pleasure and ultimate decay and death. But *is the body really solid* ? However solid the body may appear to be, the established fact remains that it is from a single cell that the body has been developed. The electron-scanning microscope, with a magnification of several thousand times, shows the human body as a sort of phantasy, a seascape as different from our perception of the body with our eyes as could possibly be imagined. The pores of the skin open like ocean caves; a bundle of nerve fibres curving its way across a section of muscle tissues appears like a "sea serpent lying on a giant walrus"; what appears as thousands of tadpoles swimming furiously against the current are, unbelievably, sperm cells struggling for survival against incredible odds, – the whole presenting a monstrous sea spectacle. However, underneath there is still apparent solidity because the magnification that could penetrate this solidity is not yet available. But an intelligent projection, based on what the electron microscope has so far revealed, would clearly indicate the "solid" flesh dissolving into a sort of condensed vapour, muscle fibre assuming a distinctly crystalline aspect showing that it is made of long spiral molecules interconnected and held in place by imperceptible waves pulsing many trillions of times a second. Within molecules would be atoms, their interiors veiled by vague clouds of electrons; then the shell dissolves and it is all emptiness. Deep, deep within that emptiness, the sub-atomic physicist tells us, is a nucleus which, being an oscillating field, begins to dissolve, showing further organized fields, protons, neutrons and even smaller particles, each of which also dissolves into nothing but the rhythm of the universal pulse. This is surely what the mystic has perceived intuitively! In considering the question of what the body is made of, the ineluctable conclusion is that *there is no solidity at all either at the most sublime level of the body, or at heart of the universe.* This would seem less astonishing if, as Nisargadatta Maharaj said, we would remember that the characters in a dream appear equally solid.

The compact nucleus at the very heart of the atom, then, is nothing solid but rather a dynamic pattern of concentrated energy throbbing and vibrating perhaps at a speed faster than 10 raised to over 20 times – a veritable frenzied dance, the Dance of Shiva, in which creation and destruction take place continuously and almost simultaneously. This is what prompted Sir James Jeans to call the universe mental rather than material, – *chittamatra* (mind-stuff only) or *vijnaptimatra* (representation only) as Nisargadatta

Maharaj would say.

The astronomer also presents us with the same beguiling transparency that in the final sense seems to constitute what are apparently solid objects when he tells us that *when galaxies sometimes meet head-on, all they do is pass through each other like two summer clouds.* The human body, like all living objects, has its own electro-magnetic field, and therefore, we are affected to a varying extent one way or another by the pulsating fields that criss-cross one another throughout space, not only by the nearer events like the turning of the earth on its axis, the tides and the seasons, but even by the distant solar flares known as sun-spots. It would seem that there is very little doubt that, as the Eastern mystic has always held, *each one of us is in direct or indirect relationship with all that is.* It is through the senses that the various organized fields of rhythm (that apparently constitute the totality of an individual entity) are connected with one another and with the rhythms of the entire universe.

It would thus seem that there cannot be a separate personal identity if every human body is nothing but emptiness, a concentrated pattern of energy. But the wonder that *nisarga* or nature is, hàs so contrived that each emptiness, each individual body and each personal identity has an essential characteristic that distinguishes it from all others. Personal identity is, in fact, the very basis of human relationship. The botanist tells us that every leaf on a tree is in some way or another atleast slightly different from all others. The chance of two fingerprints being identical has been computed at less than one in sixty billion. Brain wave patterns are observed to be clearly distinctive. An effective voiceprint definitely identifies the speaker through the recorded voice frequencies, and a new born baby's breathing pattern is said to be as distinctive as a finger-print! It would seem therefore that the evolutionary process itself has ensured individual variations within each species by means of a series of rhythmic wave functions composing a personalized inner pulse that synchronised in varying designs with everything else and everyone else in the world. It is perhaps this inner pulse and the extent of its synchronity with the other person or thing which produces instant attraction, revulsion or total indifference.

The all-in-one-ness of the Eastern mystic has been now clearly accepted by the modern scientist, but he finds himself, along with the layman, facing seeming absurdities in the quantum theory conclusions. He must however accept them because the theory works! A formulation made by the physicist J.S. Bell – Bell's Theorem – particularly emphasizes that "no theory of reality com-

patible with quantum theory can require spatially separate 1
events to be separate". This means, simply, that distant events are
interconnected. What is more, it already implies that each electron
must *know* what every other electron in the universe is doing in
order to know what it itself has to do every moment. It further
implies that each sub-atomic particle within is in touch with all
that IS. The mystic intuitively understands the problem and the
solution that is contained in the problem: all there is, *is* the primal
ENERGY   which is nothing other than   CONSCIOUSNESS   which
has produced on or within itself the   MIND-STUFF   of the universe
(chittamatra) as a representation only *(Vijnaptimatra)*. In other
words, all there is, is   CONSCIOUSNESS   which in the case of
sentient beings may be called   SENTIENCE,   an aspect of consciousness which enables him to cognize other sentient beings.
This is indeed the core of the Nisargardatta teaching.

If the body is scientifically seen as emptiness, a throbbing energy, the question would arise : What then is a "sentient being"?
Perhaps the question answers itself. In the sentient being, if the
being is merely emptiness, then the being that is sensorially perceptible must be a mere appearance like a mirage on the sands,
and the "sentient being" must be what remains: SENTIENCE.   If
the physical being is merely an appearance, an object, a phenomenon, it is quite obvious that it cannot be expected to perform
any action as an independent entity on its own initiative. The fact
is illustrated by the Chinese Master Chuang-tzu's oft-repeated
story of the sow who died while her piglets were suckling — the
little piglets just left the inanimate body because their mother was
not there! The body became inanimate because the animus was no
longer within. This animus, the sentience in the body, regarded
by the Eastern mystic as the consciousness (or the "Heart" or the
"Mind") which is not the personal element in each sentient being
but the universal, primal energy which pulsates in all sentient
beings, and indeed in every particle in the entire universe. This
impersonal or universal consciousness is, therefore, what the sentient being really is. And, indeed, all there is, all that exists, is
nothing but the universal consciousness.

This impersonal consciousness, in its static state of rest, is the
Absolute unmanifest subject. When movement arises in it, it becomes conscious of itself – I am – and in that first split-second of
awareness the universal consciousness concurrently comes into
manifestation by objectifying its pure subjectivity into the duality
of subject and object. The mystic, who intuitively understands this
split-second of awareness, would perhaps give a smile of understanding to the physicist astronomer who sees that split-second as

the "big bang" of the manifested universe. When the manifestation occurs, the universal or impersonal consciousness becomes
identified with each object, and thus arises the concept of the
egoistic "me" in human beings because of which the phenomenal
world appears to be "real". This process of identification of the
consciousness with an individual object and considering that object as "me" in the subjective sense (as apposed to all other objects)
means in effect the objectivizing of pure subjectivity, thereby
creating an apparent separation, between "me" and the "other". It
is this "me – concept" or self or ego which is the "bondage" from
which "liberation" is sought.

Whatever appears to be done by a sentient being can only be
conceptual because a sentient being, objectively, is only an
appearance, an illusory dream-figure. All actions in the framework
of space-time are dreamed by a dreamer that can have no objective
existence – the universal consciousness in movement. Sentient
beings may imagine themselves as causative instruments but they
are only an integral part of the hypothetical emptiness of the universe, one of the multitude of manifestations. It is universal consciousness which produces within itself the totality of the manifestation. The sentient beings are illusory objects from the point
of view of the phenomenal manifestation, mere dreamed figures
and therefore "nothing". But they are also "everything" because,
·noumenally, anything dreamed can be nothing other than the
dreamer. The dreamer is the subjective aspect of consciousness
while all manifestation is its objective aspect. The sentient being,
therefore, dreams the manifested universe - including himself (as
in a personal dream) – by objectivising it. And it is as this subjective aspect of consciousness that the sentient being can be said to
BE. As the phenomenally present illusory object, the sentient
being is nothing; but, as the phenomenally absent – and noumenally present – he is everything.

There is a very beautiful Sufi story that is rather relevant to what
the sentient being really is. A banquet is being given in honour of
the King. All guests are assembled, seated according to rank, and
only one chair remains vacant, awaiting the arrival of the King. At
this point a raggedly dressed Sufi walks in and occupies the chair
reserved for the King. The chief minister is extremely upset, and
approaching the Sufi, he asks: "How dare you sit in that chair reserved
for the King? Are you an important minister?"

> Sufi: No, I am not an important minister, I am more than
> that.
> Chief Minister: Are you the king?
> Sufi: No, I am not the king. I am more than that.

Chief Minister: Are you the Prophet?
Sufi: No I am not the Prophet. I am more than that.
Chief Minister: Are you God?
Sufi: No, I am not God. I am more than that.
C.M. (Horrified): How can you say that? There is nothing more than God.
Sufi: I am that "Nothing".

The sentient being comes into manifestation along with the rest of the manifestation which is a process of objectivization necessitating a duality into two elements – a subject to perceive and an object to be perceived. Phenomenal existence, therefore, is the correlation between the cognizer and that which is cognized and obviously neither could have any independent existence without the other: both exist only in consciousness in which objectivization takes place, and it is this consciousness which we all are (but not as individual sentient objects). The cognizer considers himself as the subject of all that is cognized, but truly both the cognizer and his object are objects in the totality of manifestation.

We mistakenly attribute the sentience (which represents what we are noumenally) to the operational centre, which makes the psychosomatic apparatus a "sentient being", but it has no more autonomy or volition than any physical organ. The operational centre is necessarily psychic just as the liver or the heart is somatic. It is this centre which directs all functioning through the perceiving and cognizing by the senses and thus acts as the "subjective element" in the psychosomatic object. But it must be clearly undestood that this "subjective element" could not possibly be anything other than an object. It is only a communication and control mechanism, a mere switch-board and not the power-station. In all the phenomenal manifestation neither the apparent perceiver (and cognizer) nor the perceived (and cognized) is an entity in its own right, and cannot therefore, have an independent nature with autonomy and volition.

In other words, we are conditioned to think of ourselves as independent entities with volition, and therefore think – and believe – that we possess or experience sentience. The fact of the matter, however, is that sentience is not "something" and that "we" can neither possess nor experience it. Sentience is a manifestation of what we noumenally ARE. If we must think in terms of "possession", as Nisargadatta Maharaj said, it is sentience (that-which-we-*are*) which possesses the physical body (that-which-we-*think*-we-are)

3

Human Conflict and Unhappiness

There cannot be any phenomenal manifestation except in duality for the simple reason that manifestation necessarily implies the observer observing the observed object. The subjective noumenon cannot objectify itself – manifest itself or express itself in the form of the objective universe – except in the framework of space-time duality, again, for the simple reason that an object with its tri-dimensional volume needs space in which to manifest itself and time (duration) in which it could be observed. To this extent noumenal unicity which is subjective and the phenomenal duality which is objective cannot be separate: *Phenomena are nothing but noumenon extended in space and time.*

Dualism (as distinct from duality) which is the basic cause of human conflict and unhappiness is an entirely different concept and needs to be thoroughly analyzed and understood. Such clear understanding is itself the solution to the problem of human unhappiness. Such understanding relieves man from the double-bind in which he finds himself in his relentless pursuit of happiness, in his search for unalloyed happiness. *Duality is polaric, inter-related and therefore not separate, whereas dualism is opposition, separation and therefore conflict.*

Manifestation of that-which-we-are is a process of objectivization which basically requires a dichotomy into two elements – a subject which perceives and an object which is perceived. This process is known as duality; and all phenomena that are sensorially perceivable are the correlation of a subject (object-cognizer) and the object (the object-cognized). This process of duality makes it evidently clear that without such a process there cannot exist any phenomenon, and that neither of the two phenomenal objects (neither the cognizer nor the cognized object) has any independent existence of its own – the existence of one depends upon the existence of the other. In other words the totality of the phenomena is an appearance in consciousness in which exist both the cognizer and the object cognized. Indeed, nothing truly exists except consciousness which is what we *are*. When it is in a state of rest we are not aware of our own existence; it is only when consciousness is in a state of movement (and change), that we manifest ourselves *as the totality* of phenomena in duality. There can be no manifestation unless there is an observer and that which is observed, both being integral parts of the total manifestation in the conceptual or imagined framework made up of "space" in which the phenomenal objects can be extended tri-dimensionally, and "time" or duration to enable the appearance of the phenomena to be perceived. This is the concept of duality which forms, together with the associated concepts of space-time, the conceptual framework in which consciousness creates phenomenality within itself, and perceives it through the millions of psychosomatic apparatuses known as sentient beings.

This duality is purely conceptual inasmuch as noumenality and phenomenality are separate only when so conceived. In reality, however, they are the inseparable unicity because phenomena are nothing but noumenon extended in the conceptual space-time framework, the objective expression of the subjective noumenon. When this is clearly apperceived there is no question of either any Samsara or any bondage for any individual for the simple reason that the "individual" is merely the psychosomatic apparatus, the instrument through which the process of perceiving and cognizing takes place. Our unhappiness, our conflict, our bondage arises as the effect of the identification of what-we-are (consciousness) with the object-cognizer element in the dichotomy of the whole mind (consciousness) into subject and object in the process of duality. This identification or entitification as an independent entity (as the pseudo-subject) is the dualism – the Maya – which results as the practical application of the principle of duality. It is this illusory entitification that causes all the conflict, all the suffering, all the unhappiness that is collectively termed "bondage". Indeed, bondage is only the bondage to that concept because in fact there is no entity to be bound! What-we-are is as much the subject-cognizer as the object-cognized neither of which has any kind of volition or personal choice or independence of action as they are both interdependent concepts in consciousness. If the subject-cognizer is thus merely a concept, obviously the suffering and bondage can have only a conceptual structure, the result of conditioning. Obviously too, the only way to get rid of the suffering and bondage is to apprehend profoundly the nature of either that-which-we-*are* or this-which-we-*are-not* – or both. And the crunch comes in the fact that such apprehension or apperception can come about only in the functioning of what-we-are as soon as the misapprehension of what-we-are-not drops off. There is nothing of any independent nature to be "achieved".

The immediate cause of the entitification or identity with a spurious entity is the fact that consciousness chooses to ignore its essence as the sentience of all sentient objects and to identify itself with the fictitious operational centre of each sentient object – the whole process being the working of Maya or Lila or the dream-play that this life really is. It is interesting to see in practice this dream-play in action, this dualism in its everyday functioning. To begin with, it can be noted that the animal as distinguished from the man, may be "unhappy" because of physical pain but he is not unhappy in the sense in which the word is used in regard to the unhappiness caused in man by an inner conflict within him. The animal is as much a sentient being as the man because it is the same animating consciousness which pervades both. As Nisarga-datta Maharaj pointed out, the difference lies in the fact that it is because of the existence of intellect in man that he can *observe* the functioning of that consciousness whereas in its absence the animal cannot.

The essence of all phenomenal manifestation is continuous change from integration or birth towards dis-integration or death. As soon as a sentient being is "born" – whether it is an insect, bird, animal or man – the animated consciousness infuses in the creature the will to live, not to yield to disintegration, and this is the ego, the identification of the individual organism with the will not to let go of the integration that it is.

In the absence of intellect while the animal's ego is certainly aware of the irreconcilable opposition between the "me" and the "not-me," between the outside world divided into friends and enemies, between integration and dis-integration, between consonance and dissonance, between pleasure and suffering *the animal cannot "think" or "feel" this duality;* the animal can distinguish between pleasure and pain, but it cannot be intellectually conscious of the two opposing states in the absence of the actual physical circumstances. *An animal with its hunger for food or sex satisfied, cannot "think" about these physical needs, but man can and does "conceptualize"* — think and compare and judge and plan — about the past and the future satisfaction of these physical needs. It is this element which creates a feeling of conflict, disharmony and unhappiness in the man but not in the animal. This is one part of the double-bind. The other part consists in the fact that while the animal has no feelings of guilt in his efforts to maintain and preserve its own integration or existence, intellect in man gives him the clear perspective that mere persevering to exist is not his real objective. Intellect enables him — or rather, compels him — to see at least intellectually that he is something very much more than his physical organism, and therefore to seek his true identity, which he intuitively knows as infinity, intemporality, immutability. The double-bind consists in the fact that man thinks of his true nature only in terms which his intellect can understand, that is to say, man imagines his true nature within the framework of animal affectivity in the form of a state where happiness will reign supreme with limitless good food, unbounded sexual vigour, unrivalled physical and intellectual capacity etc.!

The significance of this "desire" of man to "attain" the perfect affective life needs to be clearly understood in order to go to the root of the problem of human conflict and unhappiness. As Nisargadatta Maharaj used to point out, the fundamental fault in such thinking – man's desire for perfection in the frame work of phenomenal living – is in forgetting that the entire phenomenality is an appearance in consciousness, an apearance which is based on polaric dualilty in which happiness and unhappiness are inseparably interdependent. Indeed, the bondage consists entirely in the "desire," to want something, to "attain" something, to "become" something; and the liberation therefore can consist only in apperceiving that any desire – whether for some material benefit or even for spiritual enlightenment – is itself the only obstruction. In other words, man wants absolute harmony but he wants it in terms of living this life; he understands the fact of disintegration or death, but he thinks of it in terms of life, hoping an after-death state of undiluted happiness in those terms which he can understand. He thus understands that there must be a "being" at the end of this "living", but he can only think of *that* "being" in terms of *this* "living" without its sorrows; he simply cannot comprehend the fact that to arrive at the "being" which he already is, all that he has to do is to give up his "living" *as he knows it.* Man wants to continue his "living" and yet demands his "being". Man will not give up war but needs and wants and demands peace! Man will not give up what he now thinks he has in order to get something which he does not know; he is not prepared to give up his *"reality"* in the hope of getting something that he considers ephemeral; does not know that it is his apparent "reality" that is ephemeral and that true reality is forever shining as soon as the covering of ephemeral reality is abandoned. Man is not prepared to let go – and that is the real problem. *Man wants to wake up but will not give up the dream.* Man intuitively knows that he is unicity but is not prepared to give up the dualism that he practices as a phenomenal object in the duality of manifestation. Man forgets that the ultimate goal of his life – if such it can be called – is not "becoming" something but "non-becoming" or "non-living" – a letting go of his phenomenality which would bring in noumenality.

When awareness arises in the noumenon as consciousness of its beingness – as I AM –, concurrently arises the manifestation in consciousness as phenomena; consciousness thereafter identifies itself with each sentient phenomenal object, in the duality of the functioning as subject/object, observer/observed-object. When the sentient object is an animal, consciousness in its identification finds itself entrapped by the organism and it is for all practical purposes the organism itself. In the case of man, the appearance of intellect permits him to disassociate himself from the psychosomatic apparatus to the extent that he calls it *his* body, *his* mind. But such disidentification with psychosomatic organism is only partial in the sense that he identifies himself thereafter with the operational centre of the psyche-soma, without which he cannot in fact be a sentient being. Such identification with the operational centre means in effect being released from the finite bounds of the physical body to the mathematically (not metaphysically) infinite, that is, indefinite bounds of intellectual conceptualization and objectification. The fact of the matter is that while our sentience is noumenal in nature, the operational centre is only psychic like the heart or any other organ is somatic in the psychosomatic apparatus. This centre directs the activity of the organism through the five senses, and therefore seems to be the subjective element in the phenomenal object. But actually, this centre, with which man identifies himself as a separate entity with independence of choice and action, is not the subject of other objects but merely a part of a phenomenal object (another psychosomatic mechanism) which becomes the fictional "me" or "self" in opposition to the "other" and immediately thereby considers itself to be in bondage and seeks deliverance. In fact it is this separation between the fictional "me" and the rest of the world that is the cause of all human conflict and unhappiness; and, unbelievable as it may seem, man seeks salvation from this imaginary unhappiness not for himself but for this illusory "me"!

The basic and dominant point about the difference between animal and man brought about by intellect(thought-word)is that this difference is nothing more than an illusion. While the animal is perfectly content and happy so long as the needs of his physical organism are satisfied, thinking makes a man restless inspite of his physical needs being reasonbly well satisfied. When a visitor came to Nisargadatta Maharaj, he was generally allowed to talk for a reasonable time to explain his circumstances and give a general idea of his daily life. After a time, when the visitor brought up the question of his personal difficulties that had brought him there, Maharaj would suddenly interrupt him and ask him: "Who is this 'I to whom all this has been happening? What was he a hundred years ago? What will be the position a hundred years later? Think deeply on these questions."

When we talk about man's conflict and unhappiness, we must be clear about who it is that is in conflict and therefore unhappy. It is clear that it is the operational centre or organ in the body that is referred to when one refers to "I" BUT IT IS REALLY THE "ME-CONCEPT" WHICH IS IN OPPOSITION — in a condition of dualism — to the "other" which in practice means the rest of the phenomenal manifestation in varying degrees of friendship which may itself vary from time to time and in different circumstances. It is interesting and instructive to study the mechanics by which this "me-concept" comes into existence. The existence of this objective operational element or "me-concept" is based on the assumption of an entity separate from the rest of the manifested phenomena; and obviously therefore it cannot hope or pretend to coincide with the totality of the manifestation. The very acceptance of a person as a separate   entity brings in at once the dualism of the "other". Such dualism, therefore, is based on the rejection of the polarity or interdependence of the opposing concepts like the subject and object: It is the polarity or interdependence of the opposites which constitutes the harmony of the manifested universe, and as soon as that polarity is abandoned in favour of the separation of a pseudo-subject *vis-a-vis* the object, the only result can be disharmony, conflict and unhappiness. To expect harmony and happiness in the framework of the dualism, for the fictional entity — which regards the rest of phenomenality as a menace to its pseudo-reality — is ridiculous. What is more, the "me-concept" as the pseudosubject then proceeds to extend the pseudo-reality of those objects which it considers congenial and friendly to its own reality; this friendly circle, of course, expands and contracts at various times according to circumstances, leaving the rest as the menace that causes all the conflict and unhappiness.   This   dualism   created   by *each* "me-concept" (which considers itself as the "I-reality") is what causes the conflict, and it should be obvious that as long as the "me-concept's consider themselves independent and autonomous subjects *vis-a-vis* all other objects - and therefore the only Reality - so long must conflict and unhappiness necessarily exist in the framework of dualism.

It is important to realize that when the "me-concept" sets itself up as the subjective realilty, all that actually happens is that it considers itself an independent entity. It is not concerned with the rest of phenomenality and does not have any aggressive intention towards it; all it is concerned with is the protection and perpetual continuance of its own "reality". When there is conflict the "me-concept" considers that it has been driven into this conflict by the "other" which threatens its position! It is not concerned with victory over the adversary but merely wishes that the "other" should let it remain in peace and happiness, and should therefore be driven away for good so that it would no longer threaten its security and well-being. All that the "me-concept" is concerned with is that there should be no enemy to threaten its security. And the joke is that each "me-concept" thinks exactly in terms of a separate, independent entity – terms which are synonymous with dualism. The abandoning of polarity in the opposites means separation which brings about the fear of the "other" and this fear manifests itself as human conflict and unhappiness.

Thus it can be seen that the operational element in the organism, while setting itself up as the subjective reality, is not basically concerned with the "not me" or the "other". It is only concerned with the continuance of its own existence without any temporal limitation and will not accept the fact that in so setting itself up it has itself created, along with its own fictitious existence, the existence of a fictitious enemy which, it fears, will challenge its existence. The image which this pseudo-subjective entity has created, quite unwittingly, is an enemy that keeps on persecuting it and challenging its existence, its "reality". Whatever the conflict in life – whether it is the struggle for the basic necessities of life or a struggle to amass riches or acquire fame – the real struggle is to save its existence as the reality against the enemy forces of disintegration which intend to attack this reality and reduce it to nothingness. All this struggle is within the framework of temporality and dualism, whereas true reality has nothing to do with space-time; but the fictional entity, itself a·creation of intellect in the context of space-time cannot apprehend this. The reality conceived by the "me-concept" is nothing but a belief in personal absoluteness in temporality, a complete misapprehension in itself. The more this "me-concept" endeavours to protect itself from annihilation the more it increases the strength of the bondage and the farther it gets away from Reality. An understanding of this fact will make it clear that each "me-concept" – each man – believes that all the "others" (excluding those within the "friendly circle" existing at that moment) intend to destroy his temporal security which is his reality, and therefore, all our affective relationships are one great misunderstanding based on the non-apprehension of the polarity or interdependence between all sets of opposites. We are our own enemy.

Reality can only be that unicity wherein the very idea of separation is unknown. The "me-concept", born in dualism (not merely duality which is the necessary prerequisite for phenomenal manifestation), irreparably splits this unicity of Reality and makes a Sartre say "Hell is other people". All people – "me" and the "others" – are merely phenomenal appearances in consciousness, all are objects of the one absolute subjectivity. Whatever the "me-concept" may believe, the fact remains that the pseudo-subject is only a phenomenal object, and identification with it as a separate entity brings about conflict, the basis of which is fear and hope, which bring in its wake various affective manifestations. Even after a victory over "the enemy" has been achieved, the fear of the future is never overcome although it may be masked as anger or frustration or revolt. Man is constantly afraid that the happiness achieved at one moment may not last for long, and hopes for constant, changeless joy. He does not realize that constant change is the very essence of phenomenal manifestation, and that so long as he thinks and speaks and acts as an independent entity, he will be constantly subjected to the lacerations of temporality. *The dread of insecurity and the hope of aid from a superior power against the enemy, drives man to the concept of the supernatural.* By whatever name or nature conceived, this superhuman element is considered to have complete power and control over all destiny. Whether this powerful element is given any form or name is immaterial because the relevant point is that it is considered as an extraneous force capable of overcoming any unknown quantity or imponderable factor like chance or luck. In believing in such a super-power, man forgets that it is only a concept in his mind, an objectification, a mental fabrication. Indeed he forgets that the "me concept", which seeks security and in aid of this search creates the concept of a super-power, is itself a concept. This is precisely what the Zen Master had in mind when he said "If you meet the Buddha on the road, kill him at once", or "If you see Buddha on your way, do not stop but proceed to where you do not see him".

The answer to the problem of conflict and unhapppiness lies in the problem itself. What has brought about the problem is the conceptual separation between man and the rest of the manifestation, between man and man; the separation is brought about by conceptualization, the basis of which is dualism and the "me-concept". As Nisargadatta Maharaj put it, the answer is to recognize the cause and abandon it; if there is acidity in the body and the cause is located in the intake of certain foods, the obvious remedy is to give up those foods. The question in the case of human conflict may arise: how can the separation of subject/ object, observer/object-observed be given up when duality is the very basis of phenomenal manifestation? The answer is that this duality is polaric in nature and is totally different from the dualism in which man identifies himself with the functioning element in the body as a separate individual entity and thereby separates himself from the rest of phenomenality. The fact of the matter is that noumenality and phenomenality, non-duality and duality are really not separate; they are separate only when so conceived, but unconceived–in–Reality they cannot but be inseparably un- ited. Why? Because phenomenality is nothing but noumenality extended in space and time merely as an objective expression of the subjective noumenon, so that the phenomena may be per- ceived; and the objects are endowed with sentience so that they may be perceivable to one another. In other words, the space-time duality of observer and the object observed is merely a medium, an instrument through which the perceiving may take place. The significant point in this analysis is that the observer and the object observed (which are inter-changeable) are both objects, neither of which has any autonomous, independent existence.

Noumenon and phenomena, the unmanifest and the man- ifested, are what might be called the original interelated or polaric opposites – the one conceives the total potential and the other the totality of what is manifested and sensorially perceptible. They include each other and they are not opposites except in interrela- tionship; they are the opposite aspects of what would remain in their mutual negation of what is conceived – That which was prior to the conceiving process or prior to the arising of consciousness, the awareness of presence I AM , pure subjectivity. Nisargadatta Maharaj used to say that the clear apprehension of this unity be- tween the duality of phenomena and the non-duality of noumenon is itself all the emanicipation that man hankers after. The polaric duality is the medium which is necessary in order to project the phenomenal manifestation of the subjective noumenon, an expli- cit duality expressing an implicit unity, and is entirely different from the dualism which is the cause of separation between man and man resulting in conflict and unhappiness. It has been seen how the operation of dualism causes separation. On the contrary, the operation of duality — the interrelationship of opposites — not only brings about the manifestation of objective phenomena , but virtually maintains the totality of manifestation in balance. It is the principle of duality which presents a view of the universe as an organic and relational whole — "A multi-dimensional network of jewels, each one containing the reflections of all others *ad infinitum*"— that has been in principle accepted by modern physics. According to this organic view there is mutual interdependence and inter-penetration of all events and phenomena in the universe, and the whole universe is implicit in every phenomenon; every point — every sentient being — may be regarded as the centre of the universe: "pick up a blade of grass and all the worlds come with". There cannot be any thing or event except in relation to other things and other events, what science calls "field". The observer and the observed object are not independent opposing things but are intimately concerned in the relationship of observing.

A clear apprehension of the difference between duality and dualism leads to a diminishing of the sense of anxiety and conflict and gives a fullness to life that never existed before, because such an apprehension comports the understanding that it is utterly futile to expect only a part of what living means since in any case man does not have any volition as he is an intrinsic part of what life is all about; and even if man did have full volition, he would find a life of continuous happiness without any fear and hope an intolerable bore without the struggle which provides zest to the living!

In dualism, the opposites, like the positive and negative, life and death, light and darkness, good and evil, are at war with each other. As far as metaphysical duality is concerned, this is as unthinkable as an electric current without both positive and negative poles. Dualism means pursuing happiness to the exclusion of all unhappiness, pursuing triumph to the exclusion of all defeat, pursuing what is good to the banishment of all that is considered evil – in short, health, wealth and happiness to the absolute exclusion of sickness, poverty and pain. The principle of polaric duality, on the other hand, means the willing *acceptance* of the interrelated opposites as the very basis of both the universe and life therein. Life then becomes an art, holding the two interrelated opposits in balance. As Lao-tzu puts it, "knowing the male and keeping the female, one becomes a universal stream; becoming a universal stream, one is not separated from eternal virtue". Male and female, of course, refers not so much to sex as to the dominant characteristics in the masculine and the feminine. The interrelated opposites, in other words, are like the opposite but inseparable sides of a coin, the poles of a magnet, or the pulse and interval in any vibration. To quote Lao-tzu again,

When everyone knows beauty as beautiful, there is

already ugliness;
When everyone knows good as goodness, there is already
evil.
"To be" and "Not to be" arise mutually; difficult and easy
are mutually realized;
Long and short are mutually contrasted;
High and low are mutually posited;.....
Before and after are in mutual sequence.

While the exercise of volition and personal effort in the separation of dualism results in turning life into one mad hectic rush, a
real understanding of the polaric nature of duality gives life a
cyclical serenity, as illustrated by the Taoist story of a farmer
whose horse ran away. When the neighbours gathered that evening to console him about his bad luck, the farmer said "may be";
the next day, the horse returned to the farm and brought with him
half a dozen wild horses, and when the neighbours again got
together to congratulate him on his good fortune, the farmer again
said "maybe"; the third day, his son broke a leg when he tried to
saddle and ride one of the wild horses. To the expressions of
sympathy from neighbours, the farmer said, "maybe". The following day the conscription officers came to the village to recruit
young men for the army but the farmer's son was rejected because
of his broken leg. Again, the neighbours arrived in the evening
and said how good it was that everything had ended so well. The
farmer said, "maybe". According to the principle of the polaric
duality of opposites, not only does life mean a continuous cycle of
good and bad events which prevents any monotony and makes
living a wondrous affair, but nature has very conveniently provided our psychosomatic systems with alternating states of sleeping and waking, forgetting and remembering.
    When the Genesis refers to the fall from grace of Adam and Eve
because they gained the "knowledge of good and evil", the meaning clearly is that their fall was due to a discrimination between
"good and bad", "useful and useless", "acceptable and unacceptable", due to a concern about what is of advantage and what is
not in the prevailing environment. In other words, man brings in
unhappiness for himself when he shows an obsessive preoccupa-
tion with security and survival. On the other hand, an understanding acceptance of the polaric duality, on which life and nature is based, would mean a oneness with the universe that enables one to live out one's life with a serenity that would increase
the chances of security and survival for the very reason that there
is no anxiety that could hamper and curb the free movements in

whatever one would normally be doing. Without the oppressive anxiety to survive and win there is a calm confidence that provides greater physical and mental power. What this really means in effect is that man's conflict and unhappiness is based on two interrelated misconceptions: one, that he is separate and distinct from the rest of the manifestation and two, that in the functioning of the manifestation he has independence and choice of action in determining the results and events. What we *really* are, however, is nothing objective which can suffer any experience, positive as happiness or negative as suffering and unhappiness. As Nisarga-datta Maharaj said, it is only thinking that makes it so because what we are is consciousness, the sense of being present – presence of presence when there is consciousness, and presence of absence when the consciousness holds itself in abeyance as in deep sleep or under sedation. What we are phenomenally is the functioning – seeing, hearing etc. – and not the "me"'s that we think we are who see, hear etc. In other words, there is no entity as an individual either to exercise free will or to suffer destiny. The functioning – seeing hearing etc. – is done, or rather happens, through the psychosomatic mechanism; and therefore it should be obvious that "we" do not really live our lives, but that living happens through the various psychosomatic mechanisms.

When man believes that he thinks and acts, such thinking and acting takes place through a split-mind, the two parts discriminating between apparently irreconcilable independent opposites like good and bad (not the interrelated opposites which vanish when superimposed), and such thinking and acting is not natural or spontaneous or non volitional. Man's true nature, conciousness, cannot be split ("Like the sword that cuts but cannot cut itself, like the eye that sees but cannot see itself".) It is noumenal and subjective. The illusion of the split arises because the thinking mind assumes the dualism of the subject and the object, wanting to be *not only itself but also its notion of itself.* The only way to stop this illusion of right and wrong, happiness and suffering, bondage and liberation etc., is by the mind ceasing to act upon itself, by ceasing its objectivization (in Maharaj's words, "sitting still, doing nothing"), letting things happen naturally and spontaneously, merely witnessing what happens.

The spontaneous or natural action has a peculiarly subtle element in it inasmuch as any effort to be spontaneous would at once make the action not spontaneous and, more subtly still, any effort not to try to be spontaneous would make matters worse still: "You cannot get it by taking thought; you cannot seek it by *not* taking thought"!

It is for this reason that Nisargadatta Maharaj used to say that all that is necessary is a clear apprehension and utter conviction of the basics of phenomenal manifestation, the identity of noumenal unicity and phenomenal duality. He would assure his visitors that all the necessary action would thereafter be natural and spontaneous because it would be pure, not vitiated by any thinking of the split-mind. This is so because the clear apprehension of the basics would comport the understanding that there just cannot exist any independent individual entity with supposed volition and choice, and therefore, in the absence of identification with any fictitious entity, all action through the psychosomatic apparatus must necessarily be non-volitional, natural and spontaneous. It is needless to say that such action, whatever the results and consequences, would carry no sense of guilt or responsibility.

It is rather a curious fact that each man craves for certainty and security as an intrinsic part of happiness but he really does not have a very clear idea of what this "himself" is. This "himself" (or "myself") is in effect an   identification between the mind and the image which it has about itself, an image which is really an abstract of memories of events over the past. Indeed, it is this censored and edited abstract that is considered as the individual; it is more concerned with the past than the present, and the future happiness that he desires is related to the certainty and security which is based on the past. Just to give an instance, a man makes financial and social investments after making certain calculations based on past experience together with a judgement regarding the future prospects based on conventional standards. However it is not at all uncommon to find that inspite of all his calculation and past experience and future predictions, his investments turn out to be a ghastly failure, whereas it turns out that someone else who has certainly not ignored his experience but has not disregarded the "hunch" has done remarkably well.

Nisargadatta Mahraj attached great importance to intuition and spontaneity. What actually happens in life is that man attaches undue importance to past conventions, to conscious thinking, to communication by linear signs and mathematical symbols, and not nearly enough to the intuitive "feel"; far more to the central spotlight vision and not enough to the peripheral vision; far more to the analytical data and not enough to the "gut-feeling". It is absolutely essential to understand that it is not at all a question of one *against* the other but really a matter of one complementing the other. What happens now most of the time is that the conditioning of conventionality is so powerful that it smothers spontaneity; and this unfortunately is clearly to be seen in the education of a child, where the stress on abstract, linear thinking combined with social conventions sometimes reaches such a degree of repression of the child's inherent spontaneity of expression that it could do positive harm to the child. What is necessary is certainly not a surrender to a mad urge of caprice, but a rational recognition of an intelligence that does not base itself on the too orderly working of reason and intellect, an intelligence the actual working of which can be clearly seen in our bodies by the way we are able to move our limbs and take our breaths. As someone has put it, "men are afraid to forget their own minds, fearing to fall through the void with nothing on to which they can cling". Man is afraid to rely on the spontaneous functioning with which he is naturally endowed, but which gets blocked when restrained in its natural working by any efforts to understand it in terms of conventional techniques:

The centipede was happy, quite,
Until a toad in fun
Said, "Pray, which leg goes after which?"
This worked his mind to such a pitch,
He lay distracted in a ditch,
considering how to run.

The identification of the mind — the split mind with its own image of "onself"—results in a kind of paralysis, as it is never certain what it should or should not be doing at any time, because the image,, based on the abstract of the past events, tries to im-agine itself in the contemplated action. In other words, constant thinking and objectivizing the future in terms of the past, results in perpetual contradiction and conflict and tension. The only answer is to realize that the conscious thinking process, the ego, is a creation of the split-mind. It is only when the mind is let alone to function in its natural way, which is the integrated spontaneous way of the whole mind, that man can witness its working resulting in a special, undefinable effectiveness and power, which the Chinese philosophy of Tao calls "Te" that can only be loosely defined as natural and spontaneous virtuosity. Such a state of mind, in which its functioning is "non-active", is called "no-mind" or "fasting mind". It is by no means a state of idiotic vacuity; on the contrary it is precisely the opposite of it when the mind, undisturbed by any intruding thoughts or objectivizing, is at its most alert. This state comes about when the split-mind gives up the impossible task of controlling itself beyond a certain limit and surrenders itself in the sense that it realizes the futility of the perpetual operation of the dualism of thought and action, and lets the whole mind take over. In other words, split-mind ceases to think, and act, and think on the action, all at the same time. This kind of blockage occurs also in the dualism of action and feeling, for example not just feeling happy while enjoying music or food or whatever, but also wanting to feel oneself feeling the relevant feeling! It is precisely for this reason that it is said in Yogavasishtha that the *janani* not only enjoys whatever comes his way but that he is a "super-enjoyer" *(mahabhogi)* – *the janani* gives full attention with the whole-mind to whatever he is doing at the moment without any distracting thought of comparison or con trast with a previous experience or future expectation.

The non-action in the no-mind state is not generally apprehended in its true significance; on the contrary, it is misconstrued as idleness in a society where what is approved and expected is a furious competitive spirit in order to achieve a particular goal. But what is forgotten is that all such thinking and acting is in dualism and even the apparent success "achieved" thereby is so loaded with an inherent depth of guilt that very soon it seems empty and ephemeral, and the split-mind goes ahunting for more and better success, leading to ultimate frustration and a sense of having wasted one's life. This is the basis of the Eastern concepts of *dukkha* and the world being *anitya* (not merely "impermanent" but more importanly, "insubstantial" in the sense that worldly success cannot really be grasped). Indeed, it is only when the significance of these concepts or doctrines of *dukkha* and *anitya* is firmly apprehended that mind ceases to grasp itself, that mind achieves its pristine purity and becomes what is known as "unborn" mind or the "whole" mind, and the action that is in reality "non-action" *results* (not deliberately but spontaneously).

Nisargadatta Maharaj constantly stressed this very point when speaking on spontaneous action. A perspicacious visitor would ask him a very pertinent query: While I am fully convinced about the severe handicap under which a divided mind (or split mind operating in the dualism of thought and action) must necessarily work, it is impossible to prevent the dualistic thoughts from arising – how then can the whole-mind operate in wholesomeness?. Maharaj would at once reward the visitor with a warm, flashing smile, acknowledging at once the justification of the query and the insight of the questioner. Maharaj's explanation was that thoughts – and even desires – arise in the mind not only of the ordinary person but also in the mind of the jnani (because that is the nature of mind) but there is a most significant difference: While the ordinary person gets involved in them (either in trying to hold them or to reject them) the jnani does not pursue them; he lets them alone. The point of course is that any attempt to stop thoughts from arising (apart from the futility of the effort) divides the mind into that which does the stopping and the mind that is stopped, and creates conflict. Thoughts arise because of the continuous conditioning that takes place and the mnemonic impressions that are thereby created. To try to erase them consciously and deliberately is like "washing of blood with blood". *Thoughts arise but being without substance they promptly vanish if they are not accepted and pursued as effective reality.* If thoughts are let alone and no attempt is made either to hold them or to discard them, they disappear by themselves without doing any harm. Mind cannot be used to control mind. Any positive effort to control mind or to let go of oneself only strengthens the ego. In other words, spontaneity and intention (or purpose) are contradictory terms: "You cannot get it by taking thought; you cannot seek it by *not* taking thought." This situation is precisely what is indicated by the classic instance of the effectiveness of the medicine depending on *not* thinking of a monkey while taking it; the condition itself becomes a mnemonic impression of the monkey which promptly arises whenever the medicine is about to be taken. The very thought of spontaneous action makes it not spontaneous. This is the kind of double-bind in which man finds himself almost every moment if he thinks and acts as an individual entity.

This is precisely why Nisargadatta Maharaj repeatedly used to urge his visitors not to think in terms of "what am I supposed to do.?" To this question his answer invariably was: "Nothing – let the understanding turn itself first into deep conviction and then into apperception, and whatever action *results* thereafter will be spontaneous, natural noumenal action because then no individual entity will be concerned in it". An indication or symptom of such apperception would be a distinct feeling not of frustration (only an ego entity could be frustrated) but of utter freedom. As a Zen Master put it: Nothing is left to you then but to have a good laugh. It has been known that such a feeling of total relief and joy has so destroyed the separation between the Master and the disciple that they have sometimes ended up by rolling on the ground in uncontrollable laughter, unreasonable mirth and joy.

What happens at such a time is that the walls of the prison of dualism suddenly collapse and one finds oneself in an altogether different world inasmuch as there is a sudden realization that it is indeed spontaneous action which has been happening *all along* and that the effort at spontaneity was only an illusion. It is as if one has all along been in the stream of life, being carried along the current, as if the effort of trying to swim against the current was not only ineffective but wholly unnecessary; indeed it is as if the dualism between the self and the other, between the observer and

the observed disappears in the knowledge that both are objects
being lived in the dream play that is "living". Here is what the
Arabian sage Monoimus says about such realization:
    Learn whence is sorrow and joy, and love and hate, and
    waking though one would not and sleeping though one
    would not, and falling in love though one would not. And
    if thou shouldst closely investigate all these things, thou
    wilt find God in thyself, one and many, just as the atom;
    thus finding in thyself a way out of thyself".
    All dualism is illusion, all action is spontaneous and all volition
is an illusion. Once this is realized one ceases *to try* to be spontaneous. *Seeing the illusoriness of volition makes all action automatically spontaneous.* By the same token it must also be clear that it
needs no effort as such through any disciplines or practices or
devices, such as any repeated affirmations of any formulas or
thoughts or words, in order to see something which is already
there. The Chinese philosophy calls all effort to realize the Tao as
"putting legs on a snake" because "everything is Tao". It is interesting to note that Nisargadatta Maharaj referred to such efforts
in similar terms.
    Maharaj repeatedly used to say, to the utter confusion of many
of the visitors, that the final proof of apperception of Truth is that
all thought of Truth disappears! You may discuss the matter with
others but then it is only for the sake of what he used to say,
"time-pass'. He would explain the statement by the example of a
man who works hard with concentration at his daily tasks, but
never has to remind himself during that period about his personal
identity and particular circumstances. Similarly, in any game or
sport once the basics have been grasped, success depends almost
entirely on the extent to which these basics do not enter the mind
in the actual performance. It is precisely from this point of view
that Maharaj would asseverate again and again that the understanding must be allowed to flower and blossom by itself without
any interference (i.e. instruction) from the intellect. He would say
that persistent and constant raising of problems and questions is
like scratching onself at a particular spot and *thereby* raising an
itch! The fish swims in the water but is he mindful of the water?
The bird flies in the wind but knows not of the wind. The teaching
of Tao or Vedanta is like a thorn that is used to remove the notion
of desire for material security that is like a thorn in the skin, but if
that teaching is used to seek spiritual security for the individual,
one thorn gets replaced by another. Therefore, pure understanding is all; apperception is not the means but the end; to seek life it
must be destroyed: the "one" must die.

4

The Nature of Self-inquiry

I went to Nisargadatta Maharaj as an individual in a state of utter spiritual exhaustion and intellectual frustration wanting to know what it is all about: this phenomenal manifestation which appears so very real and lasting and yet disappears totally when I am in deep sleep; and what is this "I" who intrudes all the time with demands and desires when awake, and disappears altogether in deep sleep until I wake up again?

Maharaj's answer was simple and direct:
This phenomenal manifestation is the objective expression of THAT which is pure subjectivity, which may be called NOUMENON, unknown and unknowable as substance or thing because it *is* in itself. You — and the billions of all other sentient beings — are part of this totality of phenomenal manifestation. Therefore, all the "me"s — and the "you"s— are merely appearances or mirror-images of that subjective Unicity without name (because it is pure subjectivity) but which EXISTS as "I", the Infinite, Intemporal BEING.

This answer, so direct, so spontaneous and sudden, was like a tremendous blow into the solar plexus, and stunned me into a senseless vacuum in which the intellect was not only hopelessly inadequate but wholly irrelevant. For some time I could only sit there with my eyes closed, drowned in the depth of that numbness. When I came to, I found Maharaj smiling benignly. *Without uttering a word*, he made a questioning gesture with his right hand; I could only join my palms together in silent reverential obeisance as an answer. I think we sat there for some time without a word being uttered.

I noticed later from experience that Maharaj did not use such a knockout blow too often, but he did hit you with a fairly hard, direct answer; and it was for you to gather the various pieces from his subsequent talks and to put them together in order to arrive at

the full picture. He took good care, however, to see that you did
not let yourself go astray; he gave you several pointers about the
way you should listen to his talks. Thus, he warned you repeatedly
that he talked to you not as one individual to another (because an
individual did not really exist) but as consciousness to consciousness, and therefore, nothing would be achieved if you listened to
him as one individual to another. Further, you were supposed to
understand that words were really quite inadequate to convey
spiritual truths; and there must therefore be such concentration
(not tension) in the listening — and such a type of receptivity —
that the meaning behind the words would convey itself like the
point of an arrow piercing the target. In other words, care must be
exercised that too much attention is not paid to the words themselves; words must be used like stepping stones, lightly and with
nimbleness, because if you stepped on them too heavily you invited the danger of falling into the intellectual mire of logic and
reason. It was not for nothing that Truth has been likened to a
razor's edge. Without consciousness a body is nothing but a car-
cass, and mind is the content of consciousness; Maharaj, therefore,
certainly did not mean that the mind must be forsaken or shut out
when listening to him, but that the mind-intellect must have the
keenness to realize its own strict limitation, and therefore not to
intrude unnecessarily into the listening as such. Mind had to be
treated as the servant, not as the master.

Nisargadatta Maharaj attached great importance to the fact that
listening to the Guru must be done with the full realization that
the absolute or noumenal state cannot be described because that is
the source of all thought (and of the "word" which is vocalized
thought), and the shadow cannot know the substance. All that the
word can do is *to point* towards That, and the irony of the matter is
that this direction must necessarily be *away from itself*. In fact,
Maharaj repeatedly reminded his visitors that all that the Guru
himself can do is to give pointers, and no more; he cannot *erect* a
tree but only plant the seed : the result would depend upon the
nature and the quality of the soil. All that the word can do, therefore, is to point; and even in this limited objective the word will
not succeed if the basic intention is not strictly honest: if the
intention is to *achieve something for oneself,* and not the reaching of
a very deep understanding or apprehension *as such.** If the listening is pure and devoid of any egoistic taint, it lends itself easily to
the direct apperceiving of the Truth to which the Guru's words

* For an extraordinarily perceptive analysis of this sbject by the sage Jnaneshwar
see Chapter 6 "Invalidation of the word" AMRITANUBHAVA — the author's rendering
in English as *Experience of Immortality* Chetana, Bombay, 1984.

have pointed.

We can understand how different Maharaj's teaching is from the conventional or traditional view regarding God and religion if we remember that the basic precepts of all the important organized religions of the world — Hinduism, Judaism, Christianity, Islam — have their basis in a search for God by an individual entity for its own personal betterment in this world or the world beyond. They prescribe the progress of the entity from a lower plane of existence to a higher one in an ascending scale at the top of which is God, the highest entity who eternally controls the manifest universe. Such a scheme naturally envisaged the progress from the lower plane to the higher plane only through hard, intensive personal effort until the entity reached the very top, close to the supreme entity, the creator and ruler of the entire universe and all that exists therein. Everything is associated with a divine entity, prayers are personified and His grace is considered essential for material and spiritual prosperity.

During the course of this spiritual history there were occasional rare instances throughout the world — but more so in the East and especially in India — when an intuitive approach to the Truth produced a radical vision of transcendence wherein Reality became transported into a different dimension wherein the manifested apparent was seen as illusory and the absent unmanifest was perceived as the Reality. Such were the sages who instinctively understood that what they had experienced was truly exceptional and could not possibly be understood by the average person who was too deeply involved with himself. Such a separate entity could not possibly have even a glimpse into the mystery of transcendence and unicity that for some reason the sages were privileged to apprehend. Indeed the sages perhaps found that any inclination they had of sharing this mysterious knowledge with others would not only be an exercise in futility but could get them into serious trouble both with the religious leaders and with the law of the realm! So it was that these sages either continued to live their lives quietly without any fuss among their neighbours and some even preferred to live as hermits away from human society. However, whenever they found kindred spirits on the threshold of this transcendental knowledge needing their guidance, they did their utmost to help them; and those who received such help would naturally regard the helper as being so superior a person that they would consider him as the very personification of Truth. It is perhaps in this way that the extraordinary relationship of the Guru and the disciple came into being in India and which is beyond the logical comprehension of the Western people.

The basis of the transcendental way is the very antithesis of the traditional religion inasmuch as the individual entity is considered to be non-existent, the "knowledge" which such an entity is supposed to acquire is considered not in the least different from ignorance since both knowledge and ignorance are interrelated opposites of a polarity, and finally, the ultimate attainment is the realization of the unicity which is tantamount to the total annihilation of the separate entity that was doing the seeking! This view of Reality has undoubtedly prevailed under different names, of course in a very limited way, over the last several hundred years in different parts of the world —the more well-known being Advaita in India, Chan or Tao in China, and Zen in Japan. The essential characteristic in all of them may be termed "Self-Enquiry" or "who or what am I" or something similar. The basis of such self-enquiry naturally is the understanding that "I" am not the psychosomatic apparatus, the body which is generally considered to be the symbol of man's individual existence, and *ipso facto*, the image of God as the supreme entity has had to undergo a revolutionary change. Xenophones, in the sixth century B.C. criticized and ridiculed the prevailing tendency of presonifying God in man's own likness, of considering the essential beingness not as the infinite intemporality but as a projection of his own ego: while the Tracians would give their gods blue eyes and red hair, the Africans would make their gods snub-nosed and give them a black complexion. As C.M. Bakewell has cited in his Source Book in Ancient Philosophy, Xenophones said, "If oxen and lions had hands,and could paint with their hands and fashion images as men do, they would make the pictures and images of their gods in their own likeness; horses would make them like horses, oxen like oxen".

It was undoubtedly in order to wean man away from this anthropomorphic representation of God that lord Buddha is supposed to have ignored and even discouraged questions about God; though, of course, because of this there has been a misconception through the ages that the Buddha was an agnostic. Actually all that the scriptures could do was to point the way to the existence of the Higher Power or the Self or Atma or Tao or any other name, and so various myths and symbols have been used to make this process of pointing easier. But unfortunately this fact has generally been ignored and the pointing signboard — the symbol — has been mistaken to mean God; the map has been mistaken for the territory. Nisargadatta Maharaj's teaching was uncompromising Advaita, but considering the overall spiritual level of his visitors, Maharaj would sometimes enjoin absolute

THE NATURE OF SELF-INQUIRY

faith in and total surrender to "God", though, of course, the real basis of his Advaitic teaching was that God as such is merely one of man's concepts. In fact, however, there was no inconsistency —the inconsistency, if any, was in the understanding. For someone who could conceive of the essential unicity as the totality of the unknown potential from which arose the totality of the manifested known (and which would ultimately merge with the potential) it was easy to apprehend that God as an entity, even though all-powerful, was merely a concept; whereas someone who found it impossible to conceive such a unicity because he could not disassociate himself from his identification with a separate embodied entity could only be given the pointer to the higher power as God, the creater of the universe, in whom he must put his faith and to whom he must surrender. The ultimate goal in any case is the annihilation of the ego, of the identification with a separate entity, either through intuitive understanding or through intellectual surrender.

Self-enquiry is essentially an enquiry into the nature of man because, whatever man may think of the world outside, whatever man may conceive of God as the creator, all of it would be conjecture and conceptualization. The only thing of which man can be certain, the only thing he KNOWS is that he exists, that he is alive. In deep sleep, he is quite unaware of the world outside or of the creator of that world, and yet when he wakes up he again KNOWS not only that he is alive but that he was alive even during the period of his sleep. This is the basis of the Nisargadatta teachings.

It is the Guru who guides the disciple in the latter's enquiry into the nature of the self. This knowledge of the Self is beyond that knowledge which is the polaric counterpart of ignorance; it is the kind of knowledge which has existed from time immemorial, indeed since before time ever was; in fact that knowledge is itself BEINGNESS-HERE-NOW.

As the Guru's introductory advice to the disciple concerning the nature of self-enquiry, it would be difficult to find anything more inspiring than that offered by Mukundaraj, one of the greatest sages of Maharashtra who lived in the twelfth century.* Mukundaraj addressed the disciple as follows:

I shall now tell you how to acquire that basic secret knowledge, without the apprehension of which there cannot be anything gained, in which one must keep one's mind concentrated, that knowledge in which the Yogi keeps himself constantly immersed.

I shall convey to you clearly the very essence of this knowledge like the nectar churned out of the ocean or butter from the milk so

* *Paramamrita* by Mukundaraj (in Marathi).

that you may give up the various practices that are based on mere concepts and which are therefore only an exercise in futility so long as there has not been a clear apprehension of the significance of the sublime pronouncements of the *Mahavakyas*. Who can understand the extent of the seeker's misery so long as he has not clearly apprehended — and experienced — the true nature of the Absolute? Those poor souls who have accepted the shackles of physical penances and mental disciplines have in reality entangled themselves in doubt and indecision. How can they ever hope to cross this ocean of Samsara? Worship, pilgrimages, charities, sacrifices, mantric and Tantric practices can only provide timebound results. Prayers and penances cannot bring about liberation unless there is self-knowledge.

Pure knowledge —Reality — cannot shine forth until the basic unity of the individual phenomenon (Jiva) and the Absolute noumenon is clearly realized, and there is an unblemished understanding of the nature of illusion or ignorance (Maya) which is the cause of the *apparent* difference between the two. How can there be any question of liberation so long as the identification with the body as a separate entity is not lost through a proper understanding of the terms "Thou" and "That" in the *Mahavakya* "That Thou Art" ? So long as the stigma of considering others as different from oneself has not disappeared and discrimination has not come about, there can be no question of liberation.

How can there be liberation without a clear apprehension regarding —

(a) the significance of the three terms "That", "Thou" & "Art", (b) what is beyond "Aum"; (c) what is perishable and what is not perishable; (d) what is beyond both the perishable and the not perishable; (e) the terms "Sat", "Chit" and "Ananda"; (f) the relationship between cause and effect?

How can there be liberation unless there has been (a) instruction on Vedanta from the lips of the Guru, (b) meditation on the Guru's words, and (c) total absorption in the Guru's teaching?

Rules of conduct laid down by the Shastras are only meant for the smoother working of the social structure. The seeker should seek instruction from the Guru regarding the essence of Vedanta. Thereby one would realize that state of liberation which is prior to thought and word; and when in that state of liberation there is union of Jiva and Shiva, the state of duality disappears.

Mukundaraj thereafter proceeds to explain to the disciple the significance of the *Mahavakya* "That Thou Art" as under:

When the Absolute subject with the help of the primordial energy objectivizes itself, the noumenon expresses itself as the multifaceted manifestation; the aspect of the creation, maintenance and destruction of the manifested universe takes place in consciousness. Whatever has form and shape and is therefore perceptible to the senses is to be rejected, and that which is unseen and remains as the witness is to be recognised as the Reality. Know that to be Reality which is prior to the arising of consciousness which is termed the all-knowing, all-controlling principle.

That Reality is the witness of everything. It cannot be measured by any criterion, it has no specific place of abidance; it is all-pervading, limitless, unknowable. That Reality is what remains when everything impure, that is illusory, is rejected, and is itself pure knowledge, pure joy — self-evident. That reality is prior to the arising of consciousness and all that is reflected therein as the totality of manifestation.

That reality is all by itself, the original fullness of potential, prior to witnessing of all that is created, maintained and destroyed. The Absolute Reality is totally apart from all aspects of manifestation — Brahma (the creator), Vishnu (the one who maintains the universe) and Rudra (the destroyer) and the primeval power (consciousness). It is pure Brahman. It is only in this perspective that Reality is to be apprehended —it will not be comprehensible by any means and practices based on ignorance and duality.

The physical form could be classified into four segments —(a) the physical body associated with the waking state, (b) the subtle body associated with the dream state, (c) the causal body associated with the deep sleep state, and (d) the super-causal body associated with the Turiya or the super-conscious state. Having disassociated from the individual entity, the one which remains as the witness of the four types of body and the relevant states is the pure Brahman.

The superficial meaning of the term "Twam" (Thou) is conveyed by that which is governed by Maya (the physical form with its four bodies and their respective states). The true meaning of the term "Tat" (That) is pure Brahman (which cannot be apprehended except after due discrimination). A clear apperception of the true meaning of the term "Tat" is indeed liberation itself. The same sight in both eyes, the same sound in both ears and the same word in both lips —similarly, when one sees the same meaning in both "Tat" (That) and "Twam" (Thou), the state of Brahman is attained which is beyond duality. Just as the difference between the space in a pot and the space in a house disappears when both the pot and the house are broken up, so also the duality disappears when it is realized that the difference between the individual consciousness and the universal consciousness is merely illusory.

The apparent difference between the two is only because of the illusion of Maya. As soon as the false is seen as false, only Reality remains.

Then Mukundaraj goes on to show to the disciple that he is not the body in any of its aspects. Nisargadatta Maharaj considered the body-mind-intellect as one apparatus and reiterated that the identification with this apparatus was what produced the supposed bondage, and left it at that. Only occasionally, would he go into the details of the four aspects of the physical form. His was a more direct approach. Mukundaraj, however, goes into a fairly detailed analysis to impress upon his disciple that the identification with the body is the basic fault that must be removed for Reality to prevail. He proceeds on an analysis which would perhaps be of some interest to readers:

The knowledge of the self is Advaita, that is non-duality, but it is to be acquired in apparent duality so that the duality disappears in due course when one remains firmly in that knowledge. Instead of looking ahead as one usually does, one must look back and seek the source in order to realize one's true beingness. ("Looking back" —as Nisargadatta Maharaj would repeatedly suggest —is to be interpreted in the sense that the eye can see the objects in front but it cannot see itself; if one wants to see one's own eyes, it can be done only by the mind, the mind can be seen only through intellect, and it is consciousness which can witness the intellect).

What one sees from this transformed view is nothing tangible but an all-pervading oneness, where there is an absence of Maya and non-knowledge —something immeasurable which one can know only by experiencing it. That knowledge of Brahman I shall now proceed to expound —listen attentively. That knowledge is self-effulgent, like a solid mass of profound happiness, the realization of which means the end of the *conceptual* cycle of birth and death (because such realization comports the end of conceptualization).

I shall tell you how to acquire that knowledge by which you shall have perpetual peace and contentment. But one must first find out precisely who or what it is that *is doing the seeking;* only thereafter can one seek Reality. One must first understand who is seeking what? First, understand the means by which you can proceed to acquire that knowledge. The only thing you KNOW as a matter of absolute certainty is the fact I AM. But you do not know who this "I"is. My friend, why have you forgotten your self? Who are you, and where have you come from? Indeed, have you really gone anywhere or come from anywhere? You have never even thought of considering the matter on these lines.(This is precisely what Maharaj used to say).

Are you the body, or is it you who have the body? Does the body know you, or is it you who know the body? You are the subject and the body is your object. Only a little thought would make you see that it is you who have the knowledge of your body and indeed that you wear this body like a garment. Although you have acquired this body as a covering made of five elements, you have identified yourself with it and you strut about as an individual. Be clearly aware that this body is an object, that you who can see the body are quite apart from it, and thus give up the mistaken identity with the body.(again, the very words that Maharaj used).

You are aware of the constitution of your body, that (a) the hair, skin, veins, flesh and bones —the solid part of the body —represent the earth; (b) saliva, urine, blood, marrow and semen —the five fluid materials — represent water, (c) hunger, thirst, indolence, sleep and sex represent fire; (d) movement, running, resisting, relaxing and contracting - the five kinds of activity represent air, and (e) desire, anger, grief, greed and fear —the five qualities —represent ether. The physical body, with these twentyfive parts, qualities and activities, has six natural changes: it is conceived, delivered, grows, matures, becomes old and finally dies. You know the colour and the form of this body, and the name it has been given. How then can you identify your beingness with the body that is something other than you? You as the beingness —or consciousness —are formless, whereas you can see the form of the body. Fire is latent in the wood, but is it wood? Similarly, you pervade the entire body and you are aware even of the tip of a hair but the body does not know you. Therefore "you" are neither male nor female. In the waking state it is consciousness which acts through the body and has the various experiences through the senses. The feeling that you have a particular name and form belongs to the mind, and *you as the knower of the body and the mind, are apart from both.*

You hear through the ears, experience touch through the skin, see various forms through the eyes, taste through the tongue, smell through the nose, use words through speech, give or take things by using your hands, use legs for walking, and sex organs for sexual pleasure; and you evacuate through the anus. But it is your beingness which gets these organs to act, and you are something other than these organs. Hearing, touching, seeing, tasting and smelling are the five senses of knowledge; and sound, touch, form, taste and smell are the respective objects. The organs which are used for talking, giving and taking, going and coming, sexual pleasure and evacuation are the action organs. It is you who are aware of the position and working of the five aspects of breath or the air, - *prana, apana, vyana, udana and samana* *

Although you are apparently seen as the manifestation of the psyche *(antahkarana)*, mind, intellect, concentration and ego, *nevertheless you exist prior to the manifestation of these five constituents of the subtle body.* The psyche has little memory; from it — or on it — arise the various passions and emotions, and the one who knows the psyche, the timeless one, must surely be prior to it. It is wrong to consider that the awareness came after the passions and emotions; it is consciousness which is there first — spontaneous, self-effulgent. The one who is aware of the rising of passions and emotions is the mind and it is the intellect which discriminates and decides; that which purposefully concentrates on the decision of the intellect is the Chitta or the operational centre; and the one who accepts the doership of actions is the ego. It is you who are aware of this five-fold analysis of the psyche because you are the self-awareness or witness or Atma. The thread is made out of cotton though it is different in appearance. Similarly, mind, intellect, discrimination and ego may appear to be different but all arise from the same source — Beingness or conscious Reality.

The thread is a thread only so long as the twist is there, but irrespective of the presence or absence of the twist, what exists is cotton and nothing else. If there is a ripple on the surface of water, the ripple is only water, and when the ripple disappears, its water mixes with water. When the ripple settles down there is nothing other than water; when mind settles into quietude it merges into consciousness. The breeze is the cause of the ripple on the water, and the twist is the cause of the thread; similarly, Maya is the cause of the appearance of the subtle body. When the cause is removed both the ripple and the thread disappear, similarly, with the arising of self-knowledge and the removal of ignorance, Maya becomes exposed, and disappears. When the ripple and the water, or the thread and the cotton, unite the duality disappears; similarly, when mind merges into consciousness, the sense of duality disappears.

Let us for the moment leave the question of how a concept arises in consciousness, and keep aware of the fact that the psyche is the subtle body and that the relevant condition is the dream state which is based on desire. Mind works through the senses, and such desires which remain dormant in the mind manifest themselves in the dream state as objects and desires which have been

* for a detailed discussion on this point, see Chapter 11 — "The Play Goes On" — in *Pointers from Nisargadatta Maharaj*, Chetana, 1982.

experienced earlier. The manifestation of the dream world occurs because of that very speck of consciousness which illumines the psyche, just as the heat which heats a metal in sunlight is the quality of the sun. If consciousness were not present, would you have been able to use any of the senses? It is this consciousness which has made manifestation possible. *If consciousness were to disappear, there would be no manifestation to perceive, and you would be in your original state of the fullness of potential joy.* If you ponder upon it, you will realize that you yourself are the inspiration for all phenomenal manifestation and that it is you yourself who are the consciousness and all that is reflected therein. You must understand that you are that self-effulgent principle because of whose light the psyche has its inspiration or illumination.

Do understand that it is because of this reflected awareness which is your consciousness that all phenomenal manifestation appears before you as an illusion. And when this consciousness disappears —and along with it the illusory manifestation —your original state of reality remains in its fullness. If you reject as illusion without any substance all that you see and experience in your consciousness, then you will be immersed in what remains as reality. If all that is reflected in consciousness is rejected, only consciousness will remain merged within itself without movement. Reality is the original self-effulgent state the reflection of which is the consciousness, just as the lamp illumines itself by its own light. *Reject whatever is perceived or experienced as an illusion or a mirage -and then ponder deeply who you really could be.* (One might well wonder if this could not be Maharaj talking to his visitors.)

Having thus clearly shown to the disciple that he could not possibly be either the physical body or the subtle body, Mukundaraj then goes on just as relentlessly to show that the disciple is not even the causal or the supercausal body. Now he is, as it were, taking his disciple by the hand and guiding him towards the higher cliffs of Advaita or non-dualism. He tells the disciple :

The shadow shows the shape, form and parts of the original body but is actually without substance; similarly the one who says "I do not know" is, like the shadow, an illusion. There is the prior one who knows or witnesses the other one who says "I do not know". Strictly speaking, self-knowledge is always there, but ignorance prevents that self-knowledge from being known. There must be prior knowledge because of which the ignorance — "I do not know" — is itself known. The fact of not-knowing was known not to ignorance but to knowledge. That knowledge to which the not-knowing was known is the ATMA. Make no mistake about it. The reason for the confusion is that although one does have the primal knowledge there is an impression that one is ignorant. Even if one believes that one does not have self-knowledge, this very fact could not have been known in the absence of knowledge. Therefore, ignorance as such is an illusion. As soon as there is realization of the nature of ignorance, ignorance at once becomes illusory. That basic knowledge which has known ignorance is the light of Atman. *If you* KNOW *that you do not know why do you unnecessarily involve yourself in the concept of ignorance?*

Do understand that you yourself are the self-effulgent Atman and that ignorance is an illusion. Once you dispel this illusion, you remain as the ever-present reality. This ignorance, about which I have talked so far, is itself the causal body of which the physical body and the subtle body are the instruments.

Listen now to the symptoms and the quality of deep sleep. The state in which the mind deals actively with the outside world is, of course, the waking state. Various concepts, based on the events in the waking state, arise in the mind and reflect themselves in the dream state. But when consciousness, which is the substratum for both the waking state and the dream state, suspends its operation then comes the state of deep sleep — total non-knowledge. This NON-KNOWLEGDE-IS-TRUE-KNOWLEDGE (because it is the absence of both knowledge and ignorance which are interrelated polaric opposites), but we do not usually realize this because we are enveloped in ignorance. When consciousness re-emerges into movement, this deep-sleep state forgets its true nature and again identifies itself with the individual entity and accepts the world as real. When, however, ignorance gets discarded, Reality shines just as gold remains in its purity when the impurities are destroyed in the fire.

The individual who uses his consciousness to acquire knowledge of worldly matters will face the obstacle of ignorance. When, however, as directed by the Guru, ignorance is destroyed the individual consciousness begins to know itself; this state of the psyche is known as the super-causal body. After ignorance has been demolished and self-knowledge has come about, that which sees the physical, subtle and causal bodies as a witness, is the super-causal body. That state which witnesses the three other states is known as the Turiya state. The super-causal body is so called because it creates the working bodies (physical and subtle bodies) and the causal body. When through self-knowledge the working bodies and causal body are demolished, how can the super-causal body itself survive? When the effect is destroyed, the cause also gets destroyed.

That changeless state where one is aware of one's self-existence is Parabhrahman, Liberation, Reality. Meditation along these lines results gradually into firm conviction, and then one experiences the hollowness of the world. That witness of the conviction "I am the pure Brahman" — who, other than you, can it be? *When both knowledge and non-knowledge disappear, then will dawn that Knowledge which is the Absolute Reality.*

One must recede into the source whence springs all knowledge. That source is reality, the immeasurable potential into which conciousness ultimately merges itself.

Mukundaraj has thus brought the disciple to the stage where consciousness merges into its source, the state where conceptualization ceases and duality ends, the stage where the basis of all duality which is the polarity of interrelated opposites gets demolished into what would phenomenally seem to be a void. Mukundaraj, therefore, proceeds to show to the disciple that what seems to be a void cannot really be a void but the plenum, the fullness of potential. If the source itself is to be considered a void, he says, how could one have a concept about it, give it a name and have knowledge about it? How could something which is a void know itself? He therefore, proceeds to explain that what appears phenomenally as a void is in fact the fullness of reality:

That reality which is self-effulgent is subjectivity and therefore cannot have a seer to see it as an object. That reality remains after ignorance has been demolished and knowledge has submerged itself. Therefore, in the absence of consciousness, Reality is not aware of its own existence. But, for this reason, can it be called a void? That which is aware of everything! It is only in consciousness that the nature of the void can be conceived and that consciousness finally merges in reality (together with all concepts). Reality, therefore, is not a void: It is neither consciousness nor manifestation nor ignorance but the fullness of pure knowledge, the limitless potential beyond comprehension.

That self-knowledge is reality, where the "void" can assume a form (when reality objectivizes itself into manifestation), where ignorance has been demolished, and which is subtler than the subtlest. You are that reality, the Absolute plenum (the fullness of potential) which has gobbled up even the concept of the void, that self-effulgent source of everything. It is this Reality that you should imagine yourself to be : independent, pure, the witnessing principle whose clear image it is impossible to visualize. You are that primordial state of total freedom, that fullness of pure joy, that concentration of light which is the witness of everything. You are that reality where all that is illusory has been absorbed, where the duality of a "Thou" cannot survive; and so the terms "That" and

"Art" also become superfluous. But now that you yourself have lost this greatness of yours how will you rest in you natural state? On this question, Mukundaraj provides an assurance to the disciple that he would provide both the answer and the method. He tells the disciple that this advice is the very core of the *Mahavakya* "That Thou Art", and exhorts him to listen to it with a pure heart and to put it into practice diligently. Mukundaraj then inspires supreme confidence in the disciple by assuring him that if his advice is clearly apprehended and diligently followed, "You will have a conviction about your real nature, you will apperceive Reality, and will thus be always calm and peaceful." Mukundaraj tells the disciple :

First, convince yourself about your true nature as has been expounded so far, and then adopt the regular practice as follows: Find a quiet spot where the mind will not be restless; then quietly check the outward flow of thoughts, and sit calm and relaxed. With an attitude of renunciation towards all that is manifest, the mind should be turned inwards, away from the sense objects, to the core of the heart (The great modern sage Ramana Maharshi was very clear that for spiritual purposes the heart should be conceived as located a little to the right of the centre, not in its physical place at the left). Then give up gradually your identification first with the gross physical body and then with the subtle body and causal body, and let your mind be one with space (so that the mental space becomes united with the physical space). Release your attention, smoothly and effortlessly, from the gross senses and let it merge with the total mind or consciousness. Whenever the attention is found to have strayed, it should again be brought back into the vacant mind smoothly and gradually, so that with patience the period of concentration (not tension) becomes longer and longer. If the mind gets attracted to a particular object, do not pursue that desire but bring your attention back to consciousness which is your real nature in duality. Whatever object the mind gets attracted to, let your discrimination reject it as illusory and worthless. It is only in this manner that the mind will soon give up its flights of fancy and remain in quietude.

When by discrimination the identification, with a separate entity gets gradually discarded, then the mind will also give up its tendency towards self-identification and will finally merge into consciousness. Until the mind naturally remains in consciousness (having given up its affinity with material things) persistent (but gentle) persuasion is necessary to make it drop whatever it is involved in and return to its source. *As you keep watching your mind and discover yourself as the witness, how is it possible for any-*

thing else to appear on the screen of your consciousness? Two things cannot occupy your mind at same moment.

When you understand that anything with a shape and form is, by its very nature, a hollow shell without any substance, and that what is real is formless — the light of consciousness — you will be immersed in the depth of reality. After a heavy flood everything gets submerged in water and nothing is perceivable except the expanse of water;similarly,when mind gets absorbed in consciousness all objects disappear from the mind. Mukundaraj at this juncture issues a warning to the disciple that if one were to pursue self-knowlege whilst being firmly identified with the body as a separate entity and without proper guidance from the Guru, there is danger of losing one's mind. It is the mind through which the self-knowledge must be pursued, but the fact is that it is the mind itself which has been in the delusion of ignorance and which now pursues self-knowlege. Mind, therefore, finds itself surrounded by all kinds of doubts, and wails that it cannot understand what self-knowledge is all about. This is like a person coming from the outside glare into the semi-dark house and finding himself unable to see anything inspite of perfect eyesight. Mukundaraj tells the disciple:

Do not put yourself in the position of the person who suddenly wakes up in the deepest dark of the night and thinks he has become blind. Do not get yourself enveloped in the darkness of ignorance. In the state of ignorance whatever you conceive in your mind would seem to appear before you, but give up your ignorance, see all manifested phenomena as an illusion, and remain peacefully in reality. Consider the mental state of a person who is talking to himself or giving advice to himself : his thoughts then have no shape or form or direction. Delve within and find out where thoughts arise; seek the source of all thought —*it is this source, the consciousness, which must seek and acquire the self-knowledge.*

Imagine for a moment that everything that is now manifest, including one's own body, has suddenly disappeared. Where precisely is it that the resulting nothingness would be registered? What has suddenly happened to all the phenomenal manifestation ? All that remains is I consciousness : inside and outside, there is nothing other than the nothingness of the void which is the fullness of beingness, the potential plenum. In this state all ignorance has disappeared, the mind and intellect have set, and the sun of pure awareness has arisen. Just as the gross body (phenomenal manifestation) has been made to disappear in this manner, so also the subtle body must be got rid of. That on which consciousness has arisen must surely be prior to consciousness. When the source of consciousness itself has been reached, consciousness disappears. Understand beyond any doubt that it is this source of consciousness that you are in reality — the source of consciousness and all that appears as phenomenal manifestation in consciousness. It is in consciousness that everything appears including your sentience — the "I AM" sense of presence and the psyche consisting of mind, intellect, discrimination and the ego. Once this fact is clearly seen and apprehended, can anything remain other than self?

Can water give up its nature to create ripples? Can space give up its nature to create breeze ? So also, consciousness cannot give up movement which is its very nature. The ripple can only subside iñ the water itself and the breeze in space; so also any movement in consciousness can only merge in the consciousness. Is it possible to shake off an arm which is attached to the body ? How can you shake off the mind which is the content of consciousness? *The very thought of shaking off something is a movement in consciousness; whatever action you contemplate, the very thought of it arises only in consciousness.* When you think, it is the mind that does the thinking; when the "me" is involved in the thinking, it is the ego; when you are quiet, the very quietude is in the consciousness itself.

Consider this : if you could have remained absolutely quiet, would any mnemonical recollection have sprouted? Would there have been any wish, any desire ? If you could have remained absorbed in the consciousness, would you have been troubled by thoughts ? Then would there have been any cause to identify yourself with the body as a separate individual ? Therefore, my friend, that wherein all ignorance disappears is in a totally different dimension. If there were not something called pure knowledge, the totality of all potential, where could the ego have arisen, which is the "me" concept ? This pure knowledge, this perfect knowledge is neither knowledge nor non-knowledge and is not concerned with memory. *This pure and perfect knowledge is not aware of itself; it becomes a witness only when a movement in consciousness presents some manifestation to witness.* That perfect state of unicity of the full totality of potential has absorbed within itself the sentience (the "I-am"-ness) and the consciousness — and, therefore, it is totally without any quality of knowingness or the lack of it. It is pure subjectivity without even a touch of objectivity — who therefore can understand it? Where is the question of understanding it? There is no one to understand or know anything and nothing to be understood or known.

Mukundaraj winds up this subject of how the disciple should

conduct the self-enquiry under the direction of his Guru by giving an admirable summary of what he has already said and at the same time by re-emphasizing the nature of reality which all sentient beings ARE. He expresses the central concept in one mind-shattering epigram which says : *"That you do not know is known to no one else but yourself — that is itself the reality from which arose this knowledge that you do not know.*Can this source, the potential of all knowledge, from which arises the very knowingness — the animating consciousness and the sentience of the sentient being — ever be non-knowledge or ignorance? "Mukundaraj gives his final advice to the disciple thus:

Giving up your identification with the body if you would remain quietly absorbed in the sense of the totality — in the "I am-ness" — without attachment, you will know all that is to be known. When you thus remain immersed in consciousness, the personal consciousness having lost its power of Maya, will itself take you to its source, which is what you ARE — Reality. In that state there is no duality of any kind, all interrelated opposites being mutually superimposed into nothingness — word/no-word, form/no-form, seeing/non-seeing, self/other, remembering/forgetting etc. All there is, is pure knowledge, pure beingness without awareness. One cannot hold it nor can one drop it; one cannot say it is nor can one say it is not; indeed, it is not something one can experience — it is only something which is no-thing, to be apperceived, to be felt, to BE and to remain in.

Hold on to the sense "I am" to the exclusion of everything else. The mind being thus silent will shine with a new light and vibrate in the totality. When you keep the "I am" feeling in the focus of awareness and watch yourself ceaselessly — *when there is continuous witnessing of all movements in consciousness* — the conscious and the unconscious will for a time play the game of hide and seek until finally the two become one and the one becomes the totality. The person then merges in the witness, the witness in awareness in pure Being — Who is there then to take a measure of that ecstacy?

The way Nisargadatta Maharaj expounded his teaching — even the words he used and the effectiveness with which he used them — was very similar, even parallel, to the manner in which Mukundaraj gives his advice to the disciple. And yet, the astonishing fact was that, while Maharaj had heard of Mukundaraj, he had not, it seemed, actually ' read any of his works! This simply means that each was speaking from experience. When someone, seeking some elucidation from Ramana Maharshi, read out a passage from the scriptures, the Maharishi confirmed the statement in the scriptures because it tallied with his own experience. Sant Jnaneshwar in his Amritanubhava asseverates that what he had stated therein is the Truth, irrespective of whether the scriptures confirmed it or not, and irrespective of whether he himself had said it or not. Truth is Truth, and neither time nor space nor any individual has any relevance to that which is Truth.

The fact that the teaching of Mukundaraj has been given in this chapter in such detail would perhaps need some explanation. I remember that many visitors had mentioned to me that they wished Nisargadatta Maharaj had gone into some more details about certain parts of his teaching. Perhaps Maharaj did not then have the necessary time and the energy to do so; perhaps he wanted the visitors to do some homework. Be that as it may, I had realized that the visitors did feel the need for some details in Maharaj's teaching. Mukundaraj's teaching — which is in essence identical to that of Maharaj — at once satisfies this need and throws into prominence, as it were, Maharaj's unique Mahavaky-as. In any case, the fact of the matter is that Mukundaraj's teaching entered itself into this chapter with an effective spontaneity that could not be denied or resisted.

5

The Image of the Jnani

The curiosity about the appearance and behaviour of the Jnani is so persistent and insatiable that it was a source of constant amusement to Nisargadatta Maharaj. How astonishing it is, he used to say, that the average seeker should listen to all I have had to say on the subject of Jnana and Jnani, and still be so intensely concerned about the appearance and behaviour of the Jnani *as an individual*. Maharaj made it clear that the distinction between the states of the Jnani when he has a body *(jivanmukti)* and when he sheds the body *(videhamukti)* does not really exist for the Jnani, and that the notional distinction is generally made only for the sake of an analytical understanding for the benefit of the student.

Nisargadatta Maharaj would repeatedly stress the fact that it is not only futile but obstructive to think of the Jnani in relevance to his physical form. Ramana Maharshi too was averse to answering questions about the relative state of the Jnani and positively discouraged such questions. He would sometimes quote a verse from Bhagavata which says: "Just as an intoxicated person is not aware whether his upper garment is on his body or has slipped off the body, similarly the Jnani is only dimly conscious of his body and is totally indifferent whether the body exists or not."

An American visitor to Nisargadatta Maharaj once asked me, at the end of a session, why people, on arrival, knelt and touched Maharaj's feet. I had to explain to him that in India the Guru was an institution totally different from that of the preacher or the teacher in the West, that the disciple touched the Guru's feet as a token of his love, regard, respect and devotion to That which has manifested in human form, and that Maharaj was totally indifferent to what the visitors did. Visitors would repeat this form of salutation when leaving. If he were not engaged in conversation with someone, Maharaj would himself sit quietly with his palms folded in a Namaste until the last of the visitors had left. He did not care for formalities, he never assumed the pose of a Jnani. He lived entirely in the present moment, sincerely and spontaneously.

It is well nigh impossible for the common man to judge or evaluate a Jnani. The image which he has of the Jnani is one that is conceived by a split-mind in terms of the polaric opposites or interdependent contraries. How could it be possible for a man who is enslaved by his mind and intellect to understand — let alone judge — a free man, a man who has totally abandoned his identification with a separate entity and therefore acts in utter spontaneity? If the Jnani gets angry or does something which according to an individual's own concept (of the Jnani) is not correct, he will at once decide that the supposed Jnani continues to have an inflated ego, forgetting that his image of the Jnani has been formed by his own ego and that the action of the Jnani has wounded his own ego. The Jnani lives in the present moment, but whether in that moment there is joy or anger, it is forgotten the next moment; and this is not realized by the common man who has built his image of the Jnani on "perfection". The fact of the matter, however, is that *the Jnani is not "perfect" but "total"* — of a totality which includes all the polaric opposites like anger and love, and which, in any case, is not conditioned by any affectivity as such.

A visitor once asked Maharaj whether he did not find it difficult to carry on his business (of bidi manufacturing) after he had found self-realization. Maharaj explained that life is nothing more than a dream-play, that the apperception of this simple fact is enlightenment or awakening; that the Jnani thereafter continues to perform the daily routine diligently and astutely but with detachment, and therefore without anxiety regarding the results of his actions; and that the Jnani is like a good actor who acts the role that he is playing but deep down is never unaware that he is only playing a role and that his identity in "real" life is something totally different. When the visitor persisted in his enquiry and asked whether people in the trade did not take advantage of his detached state of mind and try to cheat him. Maharaj laughed and said that he was an excellent actor and therefore a shrewd businessman* he himself would not cheat others but would be alert that he himself was not cheated either, but if according to the script of the universal play, he was to suffer a loss, so be it. In a more serious vein, he explained that the seeker has a totally misconceived image of his own about the Jnani which he expects the Jnani to live upto, and when he finds the Jnani doing something which is contrary to his own notion of what is right or wrong, he feels let down and in his frustration sometimes goes to the extent of vilifying him; he forgets that it is his concept that has crumbled while the Jnani goes about his normal work without any sense of volition, quite unconcerned with what others may think of him.

Each person has his own concept about the Jnani whereas the Jnani has no image about himself and does not maintain any kind of pose. Indeed, with the dawn of Jnana what has happened is that all identification with an individual entity has been annihilated, and the psychosomatic apparatus carries on for the rest of its alloted span of life, within the totality of the functioning of all that is manifested, according to its own inherent, natural make-up with absolute spontaneity. This is the reason why Jnanis are found to be behaving in diverse ways; some are known for the mildness of their manner and behaviour while others seem to be extremely excitable and even irritable; some eat flesh, others are vegetarians; some smoke others do not; some are Sanyasins others are householders; some work for social uplift, others dispense spiritual knowledge, while some others do nothing at all and appear to be lazy

---

* for a detailed discussion on this point, see Chapter 11 — "The Play Goes On" - in *Pointers from Nisargadatta Maharaj*, Chetana, 1982.

parasites; some are internationally known, others have not moved out of their village or town. The important point is that whatever be the outward appearance and behaviour of the Jnani, he is firmly established in the universal consciousness, desirous of nothing, not even liberation. He lives on contentedly, accepting with equanimity whatever comes along, without any eagerness or anxiety in activity or inactivity because there is no volition. Being free of interrelated contraries, he is indifferent to religious merits, worldly prosperity, sensual enjoyment or even that something called "liberation". He neither abhors the sense objects nor does he crave for them. With a detached mind he accepts all experiences as they come in the natural course. He merely witnesses, without judging, all actions of the psychosomatic apparatus whether his own or those of others. Praise or blame mean nothing to him and he is indifferent to both.

In other words, the Jnani, by the very fact of the occurrence of Jnana, has no pose that he must maintain. Therefore, the very seeking of an image of the Jnani — what he looks like, the way he talks and the way he walks, the way he acts, or reacts to an event — is misconceived. Any such image would necessarily be based on the frustrations, hopes and aspirations, beliefs and whims — the general conditioning — of the individual creating that image. The image of a Jnani which a sincere but misguided seeker has, is generally an amalgam of a Yogi capable of mind-boggling feats of physical strength and stamina and exercising superb control over body and mind, a magician producing almost anything out of thin air, a seer capable not only of predicting the future events but even of controlling them, a super-physician who diagnoses and successfully treats incurable diseases, and finally a Guru who is capable of awarding instant enlightenment by a mere look or touch! The conceiver of such an image of the Jnani is therefore likely to be rather disappointed when he sets eyes on a Jnani like Nisargadatta Maharaj and finds him to be a most ordinary person with a most ordinary presence, living an almost ordinary life in a humble residence. Maharaj totally shattered the image of the Jnani that the seeker had created in his mind.

It is an interesting fact that among the many images that are created of the Jnani, a fairly common one is that of a sort of vegetable, totally impervious to whatever might happen in the world, and is expected to be a "sucker" taking advantage of whom would be as easy as taking a lollypop out of an infant's hand. Anybody may kick him around without any fear of reprisal or retribution — that is the image. And when there is a sharp, sudden and businesslike reaction from the Jnani, the perpetrator of the original deed feels that the Jnani has been living under false pretenses, that the Jnani is not a Jnani at all but an idol with clay feet, a God that has come crashing down from his pedestal. Actually, what might seem as a retaliation from the Jnani could well have been an object lesson to the conceiver of the concept to mend his ways and not the act of the Jnani's wounded ego. Indeed, the very basis of conceiving is the ego, and when the expected benefit from the Jnani is not forthcoming there is resentment and frustration. There is a very beautiful verse in the Ashtavakra Gita, the purport of which is : "The spontaneous unrestrained outburst from a Jnani is a glorious thing free as it is from motivation and preference, but not the unnatural and assumed quietude of the hypocrite who is still attached to his individual identity."

Maharaj repeatedly used to point out the futility of trying to see — and judge — a Jnani by relative norms and through the viewpoint of a split-mind which the common man usually does. He used to say that the perceived is a mirror in which the perceiver sees his own image. There is an interesting anecdote which illustrates this point:

At one end of the main road of the town, a Jnani was lying by the roadside, apparently doing nothing but acutally totally absorbed in the self, quite unmindful of the pranks being played by the children passing along the way. A thief passing that way saw the half-naked man lying apparently very exhausted, and came to the conclusion that he was a thief who got caught and was soundly beaten because he did not have the necessary expertise to ensure that he was not caught. A drunkard returning home saw him, sympathized with a fellow-addict and philosophized that a man should know his own capacity if he is to avoid trouble. A hardworking householder grumbled about lazy parasites sponging upon the earnings of those who worked hard and honestly paid their taxes. Then came a spiritual seeker who at once recognised the man for the Jnani that he was, suitably adjusted the man's clothing on the body and went his way after offering him a silent salutation.

There is another interesting anecdote about Kiechu, the great Zen teacher of the Meiji era:

One day the newly-appointed governor of Kyoto called upon him and sent in his card which read "KITAGAKI, GOVERNOR OF KYOTO". Kiechu read the card and said to the attendant "I have no business with the Governor of Kyoto. Tell him to go away and not disturb me." The attendant took the card back to the Governor and apologetically conveyed the Master's message. The Governor said "the fault is mine", promptly scratched out the words "Governor of Kyoto" on the card, and asked the attendant to present the card again to the Master. This time Kiechu explained, "Oh, it is Kitagaki, I would like to see him."

The anecdote is very significant inasmuch as it illustrates an important point that Maharaj often stressed. He used to ask the person who was curious about the personality of the Jnani whether he himself was capable of recognising the Jnani, whether his own ego was sufficiently subdued so that he could recognize Jnana (knowledge) as such without the individual. In the anecdote the Governor could have easily thought that the Master's "ego" had been exposed when he had returned the Governors' card. But when, instead, the Governor quickly acknowledged his error and at once corrected himself, he displayed his own maturity as a seeker by accepting the admonition as a valuable piece of guidance from the Master. As Nisargadatta Maharaj used to say, "The Grace is always there for the asking, always in abundance, but is the seeker capable of receiving it?"

That appearances can deceive even someone renowned for his perspicacity is very cleverly shown in a Taoist parable. Confucious once saw a man roaming about on the moors in shabby clothes, singing happily as he strummed a lute. Confucious at once decided that the happy man must be man of Tao — a Jnani — because what he was doing tallied with the image which he had created in his own mind about a Jnani. He asked the happy man, "Master, what is the reason for your joy?" And the happy man explained his reasons for the many joys which had contributed to his happiness, and Confucious, greatly impressed by the man's philosophy, exclaimed, "here is a man who knows how to console himself." The man had explained among his reasons that, firstly, he belonged to the noblest creation that is the human being; secondly, many die when they are young but he himself was nearly ninety years of age; thirdly, poverty is the usual condition in life at the end of which awaits death, but he had no dependents and was not worried about anything. This parable, though apparently in praise of Confucious has actually ridiculed him with great subtlety — (1) the very question is misconceived: genuine joy, which has no interrelated counterpart of sorrow, can have no reason at all; all reason belongs to phenomenal relativity whereas pure joy is of the entirely different dimension of noumenality; (2) Confucious displays his ignorance by immediately addressing the man as "Master"; (3) the happy man's pride in the human race as the noblest creation shows his separateness whereas the Jnani, always seeing the manifestation in its entirety, remains "whole"; (4) comparison with others who have died young clearly shows a lack of perception regarding the concept of time and duration, birth and death, in connection with the true nature of the human being; (5) Confucious exposes his own ignorance by his acceptance of satisfaction and consolation as the ultimate goal in life. Consolation is one of the negative virtues — what Gurdjieff called "buffers" — which would certainly make life more tolerable but do not make for postive contentment which has a vitally different aspect of opening itself out to the true knowledge of That-Which-Is. Buffers can only obstruct the apperceiving of What-is.

The Jnani himself is not in the least concerned with being recognized or acknowledged as such by others, but most people fail to understand this because their conditioning prevents them. As a Taoist Master has put it :

Superior character appears hollow,
Sheer white appears tarnished;
Great character appears insufficient;
Solid character appears infirm;
Pure worth appears contaminated.

Nisargadatta Maharaj used to say : You cannot talk to a well-frog about the magnificence of the ocean, or about the winter snow to the summer insect that is the creature of one lone season. How can I expect a pedagogue with his strictly limited range to understand what I say? I can speak of the profound knowledge only to someone with the keeness of mind that has enabled him to emerge from his narrow cacoon out into the open areas beyond the limitation of intellect and dialectics, and is thus ready to receive true knowledge.

Closely allied to this matter of the image which people form in their minds about the Jnani is the question whether there are different levels for the Jnanis. This question is dealt with at some length in Tripura Rahasya, an ancient work in Sanskrit, which was considered by Ramana Maharshi to be one of the great works on Advaita philosophy. The matter is reproduced in some detail because of the persistent curiosity of the average seeker. In chapter XV (9-18) the question is framed as under:

If one can be liberated during one's lifetime, in what way is the rest of the enlightened life regulated? What is the relation between the actions of the sages and their pure consciousness? If they are supposed to be immersed in the universal consciousness, how can they continue to engage in activity since consciousness can only be of one kind, and so also emancipation. What is more, such activity among the sages varies considerably: some engage themselves in ordinary activity, some teach, some worship personal gods, some keep themselves constantly in Samadhi; some go in for physical austerities; some conduct Ashrams for disciples; some are rulers of kingdoms; some engage in discussions on religious matters; some write books on their teachings and experiences while some feign total ignorance; some are even seen doing scandalous and obscene actions —and yet all are known as Jnanis. How can there be such wide differences in the way they lead their lives when surely the state of enlightenment could not differ from case to case? Or is it that there are different levels in knowledge and emancipation?

The question refers specifically to *the activities of the Jnanis* and the answer is provided in chapter XVII (162-166) as follows:

Jnanis may be classified as (1) the best, (2) the middle level, and (3) the lowest level. Those on the lowest level know their real nature and yet are influenced by the pleasures and pains accruing to them according to their prarabdha (past Karma). Those of the higher order remain in the universal consciousness even while reaping the fruits of their past karma, and their actions are like those of men intoxicated with liquor. The Jnanis of the highest order are firmly established in their real being; inspite of all the prarabdha they accept the most unusual happenings with equanimity, neither elated by pleasures nor depressed by painful experiences; they cannot be distinguished from ordinary people and are always calm and contented. These differences are due to the differences in their psychosomatic make-up and the degree of intensity of the understanding of their real nature; their activities depend on their natural tendencies, but their actions are like those of an inebriated person.

Later in the work, chapter XIX (79-112), a distinction is made according to vasanas (dispositions) which are stated to be of three kinds - (a) Aparadha i.e. skepticism in the teachings of the Guru, (b) Karma i.e. predisposition towards actions which prevents the capacity of contemplation and thus of grasping the subtle truths, (c) Kama i.e volition, the desire to obtain something and to work for it. Of these three types of Vasanas, the one of action provides the biggest obstruction and is said to be the personification of ignorance.

Those are the best type of Jnanis who are free from all the three Vasanas, and particularly from the least trace of that of volition. The Vasana of desire is not a serious obstruction to self-realization and dispassion is not a necessity. Such Jnanis continue to live as Jivanmuktas (emancipated when alive).

Sages with a subtle and clear intellect do not consider it necessary to eradicate their desires deliberately by replacing thoughts of desire by other thoughts because desires by themselves do not obstruct enlightenment. Their desires continue to manifest themselves (but are not pursued) even after enlightenment. They are the highest class of Jnanis.

He who cannot give up the will to make an effort cannot hope for enlightenment even if Shiva offers to be his Guru. Similar is the case of the one who cannot give up his skepticism towards the Guru's guidance. On the other hand, the one who is disturbed only by desires as such will reach the goal even though with some difficulty, and after some time and effort will be able to remain absorbed in the consciousness. He belongs to the middle class, in the classification of sages, as a sage without mind.

The lowest among the sages are those whose psychic predispositions have not been destroyed. They are still concerned with their thoughts and are on the borderline of being Jnanis. They appear to share pleasures and pains of life like an ordinary individual and will be emancipated only after death.

Chapter XX (116-133) of Tripura Rahasya makes another distinction among the sages — Some sages abide in consciousnes even while they are engaged in their normal duties; others can do so only when they are not otherwise engaged; still others can do so only at specific times by constant practice. These are the respective levels in a descending order.

He is the perfect sage who, though engaged in work, does not consider any one or anything as other than the self; who while doing his work efficiently remains as if he is asleep; who, whether he is working or not, is for all purposes never out of Samadhi; who, from his own experience, is capable of recognizing the state of other Jnanis; who realizes pleasure, pain and all other phenomena to be mere movements in consciousness, and feels himself pervading the entire manifestation. He is the perfect sage who, knowing the trammels of bondage (to be merely a concept), *does not care to seek emancipation and remains perfectly contented* (in the totality of the functioning of manifestation).

Chapter XXI says something more on the subject. Thus it is said (25-29)-

What comes to others as accomplishments through dispassion meditation, prayers etc. seem an integral part of his psyche, and come naturally to the perfect sage, whom neither praise nor insult, neither loss nor gain has any effect. He can give spontaneous answers (which have the stamp of truth) in matters pertaining to the highest truth and enlightenment and is never tired of talking about such matters (to the sincere seeker). He is totally relaxed without effort and perfectly contended in any situation.

Thus again (34-56) - The traits of a Jnani admit of many variations according to circumstances. Thus a Jnani (like Nisargadatta
Maharaj) who has been emancipated with the least effort may be
seen to continue in his old routine and may appear to be a man of
the world; it would therefore be very difficult to judge him as a
Jnani for any one other than a Jnani himself. The Jnanis of the
lowest order behave like ignorant men in regard to their attachment for their bodies. They enjoy physical pleasures with the zest
of an animal when they are not engaged in the search for truth. All
the same they are enlightened because the physical lust is only an
aberration during intervals of imperfection, and does not leave a
mark on them; the period of self-absorption, on the other hand,
greatly reduces the attraction of the material world of senses. The
Jnanis of the higher classes do not identify themselves with their
bodies. While the Jnanis of the middle order continue to be engaged in their activities and are aware of them, they remain detached from their action and are not concerned whether the activities continue or not, or whether they result in any benefits or not
because their activities are not motivated by volition. The Jnani of
the highest order remains completely detached from the body just
as the charioteer is detached from the chariot; he is pure consciousness, neither the body nor the doer, he acts in the world like
an actor in a play, and enjoys the world as a parent enjoys the
child. Total spontaneity of action is what distinguishes the Jnani
of the highest order from that in the middle order.

It is necessary to point out that this gradation of the Jnanis is an
analytical exercise in conceptuality undertaken to satisfy the persistent curiosity of the seeker. It is necessary also to bear in mind
that the demarcation in this analysis cannot be hard and clear-cut
not only because it is conceptual but because the various traits on
which the distinction is made would necessarily overlap one
another and make the distinction rather hazy. The essential significance of the analysis would seem to be to bring out the fact that
it would be futile to try to form a distinct image of the Jnani, and
that it is only a Jnani who would recognize another Jnani; and,
more importantly, the tests are useful only for the seeker to judge
himself and not the others.

Underneath all the apparent differences between Jnanis, there
is, however, a broad base of the apperception of the true nature of
man which makes them necessarily think, feel and act not from the
viewpoint of the individual (identity with which they have
already lost) but from the viewpoint of the manifestation in its
totality and its functioning. This is because such apperception
comports the understanding that sentient beings are *a part* of the

totality of manifestation and not in any way *the cause* of it, and therefore they cannot have any autonomous existence with independent volition. Such an understanding inevitably leads to the conviction that the core of our being can only be an extension of the core of the entire universe, that spontaneous action according to our essential nature is tantamount to being in harmony with the totality. Such harmony is based on the understanding that we must be ready to accept both the beauty and the cruelty of nature (including man and beast) without aiming for the security that the ordinary man always hankers for and which the Jnani *knows* to be merely an illusion.

How does this apperception of the Jnani work out in ordinary life? The simplest answer to this question was given by Nisargadatta Maharaj when he was once asked what he would do in a given set of circumstances. His childlike answer was : I do not know. Such an answer would at once   startle some, annoy some others, and frustrate a lot of people. But the answer is sincere and astonishingly accurate because the Jnani's action, being utterly spontaneous, just cannot be anticipated even by him; indeed, on two occasions, the action may be totally different even if the circumstances were apparently identical, and in each case the Jnani would see it not as *his* action but *an* action appropriate within the totality of the functioning of the universe. And, what is more, while the Jnani would be prepared stoically to bear the consequences of that action — or, rather, witness the consequences being borne by the physical apparatus — his sincerity would almost certainly be so obvious, his attitude of compassion coupled with genuine humility so transparent that it would naturally command and receive acceptance, respect and cooperation from others. In other words, even if the activities of different Jnanis may seem contradictory in the split-mind of the average person, the highest common denominator in all such actions is their intimate and inherent sense of "actionless activity", spontaneous activity entirely free of the element of personal volition.

This is also the reason why it might appear that the Jnani never overtly tries to do any good. Any overt act of trying to do "good" necessarily involves the interrelated concept of "bad" (and the Jnani is beyond all duality including the polaric opposites of good and bad); also, human affairs being extremely complex, some good done to one man could at the same time mean evil done to another, and rewarding one man would mean planting envy in the minds of others; and, finally, the criterion of good and evil may differ from time to time, from person to person. These very considerations would instinctively prevent a Jnani from condemning or blaming anyone for his actions or praising another for his, because he *knows* that the individual as such is merely an appearance, an illusion. All that the Jnani does is to witness all that happens without in the least trying to judge anything. Everything is a dream-play, an appearance in consciousness, perceived and cognized by consciousness through the medium of millions of psychosomatic apparatuses known as sentient beings.

As Nisargadatta Maharaj used to say, the average person cannot even comprehend the actions of a Jnani, let alone judge them, for the simple reason that they are not the actions of any individual but those of Prajna —the totality of functioning of the universe. The norms of the average person are based on the duality of interrelated, complementary opposites and not on the universal Truth. You can judge a Jnani only by being a Jnani, and then you will not be concerned with any judging because all comparisons are meaningless.

6

Nisargadatta Maharaj: No Compromise

The most important point to remember in Maharaj's teaching is that it contained no compromise with the social conventions or diplomacy or any other needs and requirements of what we call life. Life for him meant only "living", as part of the total functioning of *nisarga* or Nature or the totality of the phenomenal manifestation. His teaching transcended time and circumstance on which, he used to say, were based the main religions of the world. The result of this fact was at once the total acceptance of his teaching by the few who sought Truth with an open mind and the rejection of it as unacceptably hard and rigid by the many others who preferred the kind of soft diplomacy of Lord Krishna in his Bhagavadgita.

In the Bhagavadgita, everyone can find satisfaction: the Bhakta, the Karmayogi, the Hathayogi and the Jnani, all find support in Krishna's Gita because He has not only dealt with all these aspects of the spiritual search, but somewhere or the other He has said that each of the aspects is the "best"! Krishna befriended every kind of seeker whilst Nisargadatta Maharaj's teaching was essentially based on his insistence that the individual has no separate existence as such because he is a mere appearance in consciousness.

Lord Krishna's advice is addressed to the individual: "Come to me and I shall save you". Maharaj repeatedly said: "Please understand that I am not talking to you as one individual to another — I am consciousness talking to consciousness". Indeed, he was very clear that so long as one listened to him as one individual seeking guidance from another individual one would be wasting one's time. "All I do", he used to say, "is to show you your true nature as though in a mirror. This seeing of the true nature precludes the triad of the see-er, the seen, and the seeing. It is only when the phenomenal 'me' disappears that the noumenal "I" — the unicity — can shine."

Lord Krishna concedes the fact that it is extraordinarily difficult for an individual who has identified himself with a separate entity as the doer to see the phenomenal universe in the true perspective of the totality of the phenomenal functioning as an objective expression of the noumenal subject. Such a true perspective would bring in the apperception that the individual sentient human being has no individual identity but is merely an apparatus through which the perceiving of the manifestation takes place in the framework of space-time. But such a perception is beyond the intellectual comprehension of the average person who is perfectly satisfied to be concerned with his own individual role in this dream play which is what is called life. Lord Krishna, therefore, does very clearly mention the "nothingness" (prior to the arising of consciousness simultaneously with the concept of space-time and the concurrent phenomenal manifestation) as the true nature of man, though the "nothingness" is really the fullness of plenum in the noumenal state. But in His magnificent compassion for the individual who is vainly seeking to conceive the inconceivable, Lord Krishna is prepared to make the compromise of dealing with the individual within the framework of the conceptual phenomenality *AS IF the individual exists*. Such a compromise would necessarily include various concepts involving the many interrelated opposites like good and bad, heaven and hell, Karma and its fruits including the concept of rebirth. Such a conceptual compromise would afford a sort of crutch for the individual to lean on, until in the conceptual process of evolution some individual in due course would not be satisfied with this compromise and would seek out a Sadguru like Nisargadatta Maharaj who would put before him the mirror of stark truth, show him his inconceivable true nature, and tell him, "This is WHAT IS — take it or leave it; indeed, there is no question of taking anything or leaving anything because you *are* that WHAT IS — just BE, by letting the 'me' drop off."

There is one aspect of this matter of the individual entity — particularly the question of rebirth — that needs to be considered. Nisargadatta Maharaj, like Ramana Maharshi, in his talks sometimes mentioned rebirth in the context of self-realization from the point of view of the individual. And such references to rebirth are sometimes pointed out in support of the statement that both Nisargadatta Maharaj and Ramana Maharshi did believe in rebirth. This is like saying that they believed that the sun rose in the East and set in the West because they did mention sunrise and sunset in their talks! Similarly, both used the terms "I" and "You" and "He" in their conversation, but that does not mean that they believed in the separate indentity of individuals. Maharaj may well have used an expression like "By God's Grace", but that did not mean that he had abandoned his teaching that "God" is merely a concept in consciousness. Conversation would be well-nigh impossible if colloquial terms were totally eschewed. The use of the everyday phrases merely indicated a reference to what was generally and usually accepted by the average man, without necessarily accepting the veracity of such expression. Then, too, Maharaj had a keen sense of humour and satire which he employed quite effectively.

Maharaj, for instance, might well have said something like "efforts over a million lives would not bring about enlightenment", but it was surely a manner of speaking to indicate that any positive effort of a separate individual seeking separate liberation could only strengthen the ego and make it that much more difficult for enlightenment *to occur*. Then again, Maharaj could have said something like "It is only after thousands of lives that people come to me". He surely did not mean that the same individual soul (or whatever) had gone through thousands of lives any more than that an Einstein is born after thousands of lives as a scientist. The reference would obviously be to the process of evolution. Maharaj had repeatedly expressed that the individual is merely an appearance within the totality of the manifestation, that when death occurs, the physical apparatus is reduced to the physical elements, the breath mixes with the air in the space outside, and individual consciousness merges with the universal consciousness, leaving behind nothing of the individual as such which was in any case merely a phenomenon, an appearance. Ramana Maharshi did speak of rebirth, but almost in the same breath he also said that "life" is nothing but a series of moving pictures on the screen of consciousness. The reference to rebirth was the only base on which conversation with a thoroughly identified individual could go on, and so it was not dropped altogether; otherwise it would have meant a sort of intellectual blackmail: either you accept that the individual is merely a picture on the screen or we do not talk further! Both Ramana Maharshi and Nisargadatta Maharaj had far too much compassion to adopt this attitude,, and therefore they talked on a level on which the average person could hope to understand; but at every possible opportunity they would reiterate the final truth that nothing has *really* happened, that there is no creation and no destruction.

There is one final argument that must be dealt with. It may be questioned: If there is nothing like an individual entity, and all sentient beings are merely illusions or appearances in consciousness, where is the need for liberation or enlightenment? And yet it is a fact that there certainly are cases, few and comparatively rare though they may be, where something called enlightenment does occur. How is one to reconcile these two apparently contradictory facts? The simple answer is that there *really* is no contradiction. Whenever there *occurs* a case of such enlightenment, *no individual as such is concerned*. It is just an occurrence within the total functioning of the phenomenal manifestation, to fulfil some need within the functioning in order to maintain the equilibrium in the manifestation, until ultimately the manifestation itself disappeared and merged into the unmanifest Absolute, like a wave within the expanse of water.

It is only our deep-rooted conditioning—call it MAYA—which gives conviction to the concept that the illusory individual really exists. It is only this conditioning which raises the question "who" (or whom) whenever anything happens. *Who* is responsible for the accident? *Who* must get the credit or blame for a performance? *Who* painted the picture? *Who* wrote the book? etc., etc.. Whenever enlightenment happens, it is the other individuals who consider that an individual has become enlightened whereas the very basis of enlightenment is the total annihilation of the individual entity. Subsequent to the occurrence of the enlightenment, the body —

the psychosomatic apparatus — continues to live out its life span as an integral part of the total functioning "like a dry leaf in the breeze," and not as an individual entity with independent doership. That the physical apparatus continues to live out its life span according to its natural propensity without any individual identity is perhaps the reason why there is no prototype of a Jnani. Indeed, there strictly cannot be "a" Jnani; there can only be a noumenal living within the totality of the functioning, a mere witnessing of what we call "life".

Rebirth would thus seem to have relevance only in the dream play that this life is. Outside this limited framework the question obviously cannot have any meaning because "there is neither creation nor destruction." Even in this temporal dream play where sentient beings are created and destroyed in thousands every minute, evolution must form the basis for the play of *nisarga*. In the physicist's bubble chambers, infinitesimally small high energy "elementary" particles (many of whom have a lifetime much shorter than a millionth of a second) collide and annihilate each other or create new particles giving rise to a fresh chain of events. Similarly, every new child born is expected to play a particular role in the dream play so that the play may proceed to its inevitable conclusion. Therefore, the sentient being must be created in order to fulfil a particular function (whether as a Hitler or a Gandhi or an insignificant individual) and not the other way round: it is not that a new function is created just so that the individual soul (or whatever) be punished or rewarded for his Karma in a previous birth. The supposed individual carries out his destined function, and that function paves the way for the *destined* function of another supposed individual in the future according to the scenario of the phenomenal manifestation. The background screen of the movie is the consciousness. The consciousness within one individual apparatus merges with the universal consciousness when that apparatus "dies", and again infuses itself into another that is subsequently "born". It must be clearly understood that consciousness in one body does not differ in any way from the consciousness in another. It is the same consciousness providing sentience to all the sentient beings at all times. There must, of course, necessarily be a sort of "solution of continuity" between the new individual form and earlier form or forms, so that the story may continue and the show may go on. Evolution goes on. Nature does not start from scratch every time. This is no doubt the reason why a Mozart could compose music when he was only twelve, and a Jnaneshwar could produce the Jnaneshwari at the tender age of sixteen. But there is certainly no need for a concep-

tual individual (that cannot exist except as an appearance) to identify himself with a series of bodies in the temporal manifestation.
As the Buddha has put it: "As there is no Self, there is no trans-
migration of Self; but there are deeds and continued effects of
deeds. These are deeds being done but there is no doer. There is
no entity that migrates, no Self is transferred from one place to
another; but there is a voice uttered here and the echo of it comes
back." And then of course the problem remains: what about the
very first human being? On what Karma was his existence based?
The only answer to the maze of many such questions and problems is what the sages have said : the entire manifestation is a
concept, and nothing is created and nothing is destroyed. It is
rather interesting to note that a modern astronomer, as eminent as
Sir Fred Hoyle, says that the idea of time as an ever-rolling stream
from past to future is definitely wrong, that it is "a grotesque and
absurd illusion", and that "we are the victims of a confidence
trick." He might as well have said that we are under the illusory
influence of MAYA. Then there are the Feynman's diagrams
(which got him the Nobel Prize in 1965) in which particles are
made to move *backwards in time* though for a brief instant!

Everything becomes benignly clear in the true perspective of the
totality of manifestation as a conceptual creation by consciousness
in consciousness, perceived and cognized by consciousness
through the millions of apparatuses called sentient beings. The
malignity of problems arises only when there is a mistaken identification with the apparatus as a separate entity *that he thinks he is
in control of.* When one was born one had no choice, nor does one
have a choice when faced with imminent "death". In between
birth and death, however, man considers himself the master of his
destiny! If only one gave some quiet thought to the matter, one
would surely find that almost every significant event in one's life
has had an enormous element of "chance" or "coincidence" in it. If
the event was a happy and satisfying one, one would remember it
as one's achievement, a successful culmination of one's magnificent efforts. If, on the other hand, the event was an unhappy one,
it was due to sheer bad luck! How many times have we not expressed our mortification with words like "I really did not mean to
do it", or "I really cannot imagine how it happened" etc.. If we but
have the courage to admit it, we are merely a collection of characters — creatures of circumstance — playing our respective roles
without any autonomy or independence of action. Would it not
therefore be sensible to float along the stream of life, accepting
whatever comes, cheerfully with equanimity and forbearance?
And perhaps then in due course one would be overwhelmed with

an awesome sense of UNITY and a clear glimpse of the Universal Plan — of the Divine Play — in action.

Fatalistic attitude? Perhaps. But is it not the general experience that one naturally active and restless person and another naturally phlegmatic and indolent person would essentially behave according to their inherent nature and capacity, irrespective of any "attitude" or any other consideration? As Nisargadatta Maharaj used to ask: "How many hundreds and thousands of religious and social reformists have come and gone in this world since the dawn of recorded history ? Has there been any significant improvement either in human nature or in human behaviour or in the social conditions over this long period ?" When Ramana Maharshi was asked whether an individual had no free will at all, he is reported to have said that he certainly has the free will to enquire into his true nature by self-enquiry. And such self-enquiry would surely reveal that the individual is the ego, a mere concept which is itself the bondage and that liberation is nothing but the liberation from this concept of bondage. In other words the problem of rebirth concerns only the conceptual individual and therefore so long as the question continues to have any vexatious significance, there can obviously be no awakening from the life-dream!

And what exactly is this awakening? This awakening is the *concurrent* and sudden realization —

a) that all there is in phenomenal manifestation is a living-dream in consciousness in which the individuals figure as characters;

b) that the living-dream is the objective expression of the ONE subjective dreamer, a movement in consciousness which will in due course merge in the consciousness (like a series of waves arising and subsiding in an expanse of water);

c) that the individual as such has no separate existence other than as a character in this dream-play, through whose psychosomatic apparatus the ONE subjective dreamer witnesses the dream-play;

d) And, finally, that the subjective dreamer — the noumenal Absolute — simultaneously transcends, and is immanent in, the phenomenal manifestation, including the individual.

7

Understanding the Phenomenon of Fear

The basis of all fear is the entity, the identification with a particular body as a *separate* individual with autonomy and independence, with volition and choice. Fear, desire and all other
forms of affectivity are mere manifestations of the pseudo-entity
which constitutes pseudo-bondage, and what needs to be eliminated is this pseudo-entity rather than the manifestations of that
pseudo-entity.

Fear arises from the "other" because the "other" is always in
opposition to the "Self". It is therefore "dualism" which is the
basis of all fear. There cannot be the "other" concept unless there
is first the "me" concept. How does duality arise? It is the mechanism for the phenomenal manifestation of the universe. What we
are noumenally is consciousness-at-rest, the whole or the undi-
vided mind. When consciousness stirs into movement, the whole-
mind gets divided into two elements — a subject which perceives
and cognizes, and an object which is perceived and cognized. This
duality is the very basis of the objectivization of the subjective
noumenon. In this objectivization, all are objects and therefore
when one object perceives and cognizes another, the former
assumes subjectivity and considers his subjective function to be a
separate entity as a "self" and the perceived object as the "other",
although in reality both cognizer and the cognized exist only in
the mind in which the process of objectivization occurs and, as
such, can have existence only in relation to each other (as interdependent opposites) and never any independent and autonomous existence.

Nisargadatta Maharaj often brought out the important point in
this objectivization process of dichotomy, that the resultant entitification gives rise to discrimination and therefore to fear and unhappiness and bondage. Each object entitifies itself in relation to
all others and, in such capacity, compares them and judges them
and discriminates between them according to imagined opposites

such as good and bad, acceptable and unacceptable; such a comparison and judgment, of course, is based on personal standards and criteria which are susceptible to wide variations according to prevailing circumstances.

What we are, it must always be remembered, is the subjective noumenality but the identification with one separate entity *as opposed* to others gives rise to the unhappy concept of FEAR. As an Upanishad says, "Fear exists wherever an other exists." In other words fear is a manifestation of the relationship between "me" and the "other", and its basis is aggression. In fact, fear and aggression are interrelated and one is the cause of the other, and the basis of both is the need for satisfaction or gratification. It is understandable when the need is a basic need like food for the gratification of hunger, but we move on to an entirely different level when the gratification sought is based not on need but on greed, when the satisfaction sought is based on the need for power or status in society. Again if the fear is based on the possibility of imminent physical danger, such fear will disappear as soon as the danger disappears. One almost always sees the little infant clinging to a piece of the mother's dress in its tiny fist because there is the instinctive physical fear of being dropped, but as soon as the infant is placed on the floor or on a firm bed, it relaxes its fist because the danger is over. The primitive man's fear is similarly based on an instinctive feeling of danger and disappears along-with the danger, whereas man today is almost constantly under tension *as a matter of habit* because he is basically aggressive in opposition to the "other" who is regarded as a threat to whatever he is expecting and trying to achieve for "himself". Other than the fear of the physical injury, fear for the modern man — including the fear of death — is based on his entitification as a separate individual and his feelings of aggressiveness towards "others" as being dangers to his hopes and ambitions. Man today has in fact become so habituated to the state of constant anxiety and fear that he is indeed an addict to psychological fear: what is really a mere physical reaction to any imminent danger — almost every animal displays this reaction — has been turned into such a chronic state that man today thinks it strange if in some unguarded moments he finds himself relaxed and without the stifling sense of fear which has become his second nature. Our natural state — as an intrinsic part of the Totality — is one of relaxation. It is only the separation from this Totality which brings out aggressiveness, tension and fear; and it is only the surrender to this Totality, (a surrender not forced by a sense of frustration and bitterness but softly induced by a clear understanding of our true nature, of what we are in relation to the Totality) that can eliminate from our systems the unnatural tension and fear.

The simplest way to get rid of the phenomenon of fear is to understand what we are in relation to the manifestation of the universe as a whole. Indeed, as Maharaj said, understanding is all. Metaphysically, all there is is the apparent manifestation of what was unmanifest. Sentient beings are what the phenomenal manifestation is. What is unmanifest is purely subjective without any objective quality. The significant point one is inclined to forget is that the manifest universe is only an appearance that arises in consciousness, and that its arising is concurrent with the arising therein of the sentient beings (including the human beings). The arising of the apparent universe is not independent of the human beings, nor is it *because* of the human beings. Both the universe and the human beings therein appear together spontaneously and concurrently like in a dream. A human being is as much a phenomenon as any other phenomenal appearance in the universe, but the sentience in the human being — as in any other sentient being — which enables him to perceive and cognize and interpret what has appeared as the universe (and everything therein including all the other sentient beings) is the consciousness itself in which the universe has appeared. In other words, briefly, it is only consciousness (like the dreamer)which perceives and cognizes the universe which has appeared as the manifestation *within the con-sciousness.* There is nothing other than consciousness: The appearance of the manifested universe and everything therein is the static aspect of consciousness while sentience (by means of which phenomena are perceived and cognized through the senses provided in the physical bodies) is the dynamic aspect of consciousness which has nothing to do with the appearance of the manifestation. The dreamer dreams the dream while the characters living in the dream have nothing to do with the creation of the dream and all that exists in that dream. Similarly, human beings — like characters in a dream — provide only the functional factor in the phenomenal universe but have no independence or autonomy in living their lives; they are "being lived."

A clear understanding of the nature of the universe and the human beings therein should make it clear that the individual human being is essentially a mere phenomenal appearance that is "being lived" in this dream-manifestation; and the process of being lived totally excludes the idea of any individual volition whereby he could decide on what he wanted and thereafter make an effort to achieve that goal. Volition, choice, independence of decision and action — or whatever — can, in other words, never be an effective factor in phenomenal life. What in fact *every* human being is is the dreamer who is asleep, who can only witness the dream and everything that happens in it, and can take no active part in the dream by way of influencing the behaviour of any character in the dream, *including himself* —the dreamer is real, the dreamed character only an illusion like the entire dream. How can the dreamed character hope to play any role other than the one that has been assigned to it? When this is *clearly apprehended* by the human being, such apprehension tends to bridge the separation that has been created by his identification with a separate entity, and the sense of oppression and fear resulting from the earlier separative aggression gives way to a sense of freedom, oneness, LOVE. Such love can only be the result of the deep understanding and not the effect of a command to "love thy neighbour" (which would evoke an immediate query "why"). In other words, our life becomes an effortless, relaxed non-volitional living which actually results in a much more effective and meaningful living. It also means a far healthier living because of the lack of tension and fear which had earlier sapped our energy in wasteful pursuit of imaginary goals, with perverted values concerning status, prestige and power. A clear apprehension of our true nature indeed brings home to us the natural importance and inherent privilege of anonymity resulting from a dis-identification with a separate entity in the futile pursuit of an illusory status with an aggressive intent based on fear. Such natural living — apparently effortless because of the absence of the illusory ego which had assumed the role of the doer — actually results not in a lazy or wasted living but in an astonishingly effective living because the absence of ego leaves the mind open and receptive for the direct and intuitional promptings which must necessarily be far more effective than the working of the limited intellect. Every renowned scientist, artist, musician, writer has confessed that his best work has been the result of spontaneous and intuitional inspiration — the ego can only recoil and restrict, never expand. It must be noted, rather ironically, that such a confession is itself the confession of the ego! At the specific moment when the mind is open and receptive, the ego is absent and the identification is with the "non-being" because then the pseudo-subjectivity of the individual is eliminated together with his object; whatever is known in such moments is pure knowledge inasmuch as the triad of the knower, the known and the process of knowing is absent. It is only later when the ego is back that the individual realizes that what had happened was "extraordinary". The great Einstein has acknowledged that the essence of his theory of relativity came from beyond his intellect, suddenly and spontaneously from nowhere. Incidentally, therefore, it cannot but be accepted that in the scheme of the Totality, the theory of relativity and the whole mass of subsequent scientific discoveries of the sub-atomic physicist which is based on that theory *had to happen at the time it did.*

A study of the anatomy of fear would enable us to understand more clearly the phenomenon of fear itself. Both the interrelated manifestations of aggressiveness and fear have their base in desire; the need for the gratification of desire causes aggressiveness, and fear arises because of the possibility of not achieving such gratification. Remove desire, and there is neither the aggressiveness for achievement nor the fear of failure. The physical aspects of the phenomenon of fear are simple enough. It is an allied aspect of the instinct of self-preservation and is as useful as the reflex that keeps one from being scorched or prepares one to face the imminent danger of being attacked by some one. But this is totally different from the psychological fear or anxiety about not achieving something acceptable or something unacceptable being forced upon us. Such kind of fear soon becomes a habit which keeps infusing toxicity into the biological system and, over a period, ruins the very mechanism of the psychosomatic apparatus that constitutes our body; and this, of course, adversely affects the performance of that apparatus, which in turn further increases the fear and its effect on the body. Realization that such psychological fear is merely an aspect of affectivity (to which only the conceptual ego is susceptible) breaks this vicious circle. Such a realization brings about the dis-identification from the ego and creates a feeling of emptiness or hollowness and a sense of freedom from anxiety, which in turn releases an extraordinary amount of energy (that would otherwise have been wasted) which cannot but improve our day-to-day performance beyond recognition: it is so much easier to float with the tide than swim against the current.

Dis-identification from the ego — from a separate entity that was erroneously supposed to have an independent existence — automatically means identification with the totality of manifestation and its functioning. It is this that brings about what Lao-Tzu called his three treasures: the first is "Love" because of which fear disappears - love and fear cannot exist together; the second is "Never too much" so that by not expecting too much and therefore not straining too much one builds up a reserve of energy; the third is "Never the first in the world", so that by avoiding competition and ambition you avoid separation and envy from others and remain without fear and therefore tranquil and always in equilibrium, immune to affectivity. Competition, contention, greed all are based on desire and its gratification. And the joke is that such gratification is not the final satisfaction or satiation. Gratification of one desire or one set of desires merely gives rise to another. In Maharaj's words, to possess is to be in want (created by other desires). Desires must of course, be distinguished from needs or wants. The satisfaction of a jaded appetite by the most sophisticated food cannot compare with the satisfaction of real hunger by the simplest of foods. To this extent being in want is really to possess the key to genuine satisfaction and contentment!

In the ultimate analysis, therefore, it is clear that fear, desire, affectivity are mere manifestations of the pseudo-entity, and it is the entity rather than its manifestations — the disease itself rather than its superficial symptoms — that has to be annihilated. We can understand the anatomy of fear if we closely examine how our brain functions. It is important to realize that we normally use only a very small part of the brain, never the whole of it, with the result that the brain has remained conditioned by the knowledge stored in it, conditioned by the desire for security. If the brain were to function with all senses in full operation, one would be in complete tune with the universal consciousness because, then there would be no ego, no desire. But as our senses are never in total operation at the same time, the brain, operating only partially, severely restricts our consciousness from its timeless universality to a personal or individual consciousness, thus bringing about the ego which is caught between desire and fear operating in conceptual time — desire, fear, time, forming one movement in consciousness. Our existence is therefore trapped between desire and fear *in the context of time.*

One part of the structure of fear is that one is afraid that any acceptable relationship might come to an end and one would not want that; the other is that today is certainty and security while tomorrow is always uncertain and one is afraid of the uncertainty and insecurity. The core of the problem lies in time inasmuch as the knowledge of thousands of todays (which have passed into yesterdays) has given the brain a certain feeling of security; such knowledge implies experience - remembrance - memory, a sense of security for the brain which the tomorrow puts in jeopardy because anything could happen to the "me" tomorrow. In other words, knowledge has been accumulated in the brain by "myself" as the experiencer and it is the experiencer "me" who is afraid because he has no knowledge of tomorrow. The lack of knowledge about tomorrow causes fear because the "me" has previous knowledge of the pleasure that has been ephemeral and the hurt that the "others" have inflicted upon the "me". The knowledge of the past

hurt brings the fear of the future hurt. So, the problem really is :
Can one wipe out the knowledge - the scars - of previous hurts
which is in fact a protection against future hurts? Therefore, one
must ask onself : Why does one feel hurt? What exactly is it that
feels the hurt? Is it not the image one has of onself that is hurt?
Then, why does one have to have an image about onself, or about
anything, if it means being hurt by someone or something? The
core of the problem would thus seem to be : How does the image,
which really feels the hurt, get created? The answer clearly is that it
is thought or conceptualization which has created the image because thought seeks security in that image. In other words, *if hurt
is to be avoided and fear overcome, the creation of images is to be
avoided.* And yet the image about oneself has been built over a
period. The image is indeed past knowledge, through various
media like the home, the school, the culture, the tradition etc.,
which has been imprinted on the brain (in its restricted working)
through the process of comparing one's image with that of another
whether the other be a neighbour or a conceptual ideal.

And now that one understands that it is thought, the conceptualizing, the objectifying, which is the root cause of the fear of
being hurt, one can ask onself: Is it possible for the mind — the
brain — to be free of images, and thus be free from the fear of
being hurt? This fear of being hurt prevents a true relationship
between people. *Time, the fear of the unknown and thought which
projects what it wants for tomorrow, are all bound together in a package
that spells conflict, separation and misery.* So, can thought be restricted only to the technology of today and not be allowed to project itself into the conceptual tomorrow? In other words, would it
be possible to live in the NOW and HERE wholly and completely?
This can be done — this can happen — only when there is a true
understanding of WHAT IS, of the whole mechanism of thought that
has produced the ego which has temporarily eclipsed our true
nature. Such an understanding of the reality and the significance
of thought verily means SILENCE, in which there is no "becoming"
as a change from the "being". And then there is no hurt because
the mind has become completely still without compulsion or discipline or suppression into conformity. It does not, of course, mean
that the mind has become dead or that all knowledge or information has to be excluded; knowledge (fact and information) regarding the outside world can obviously not be excluded but it can be
used in an impersonal manner without any concepts being built
around it concerning the "me" and the "mine". When the fictitious "me" is absent, the mind becomes quiet, sensitive, intelligent and alert, — mind becomes no-mind — as when you are

listening to some great music or you are totally absorbed in some work (and it is in this sense that work is said to be worship.); and thought which is restrictive in measurement gives way to the apperception of the immeasurable. This can happen only when the body, the mind and the heart are in total harmony in the absence of the "me-concept" and the relevant thought based therein.

Most of us have enjoyed moments — or even brief periods — when there was a sense of total lightness and freedom, in tune with the silent pulse of the entire universe which betokens an innate wholeness and synchrony. There is no specific "reason" for this feeling and, indeed, the feeling itself disappears when one seeks the reason for it. Thought encroaches upon this natural rhythm and breaks its operation; thought distorts this natural rhythm of wholeness through desire and fear because it — thought-mind-consciousness — wants to enter into wholeness and the beauty and freedom of this rhythm, and it cannot do so because it is itself based on the dualism of the "me" and the "other". At this stage it must be clearly understood that there is a basic difference between enjoyment as such and the desire or demand for enjoyment. It is not enjoyment as such which causes any conflict in the mind but the thought that the desire or demand for such enjoyment *in the future* may not be available. In other words, thought pursues pleasure, sustains its memory, demands its continuance and produces the fear that it may not succeed. The only way to get rid of this fear is to *enjoy the pleasure or the experience of the moment in that moment and finish with it* so that there is no image or scar left on the mind. This is what the Jnani does, and that is why he is sometimes described (to the surprise and confusion of many) as Mahabhogi i.e. the supreme enjoyer, one who gets the maximum enjoyment.

The great moments of ecstatic harmony arise when there is no conflict, when there is no division between the thinker and the thought, between the observer and the observed, when thought does not bring about a dichotomy between the "me" and the "other". A deep understanding of this fact is all the "action" that is necessary because then the body relaxes, the mind expands beyond the dualism of the "me" and the "other", the heart is free from the fear of failure. Harmony prevails. Then, thought ceases to demand and seek experience and merges in the experience-ING; detached from the rigid and immovable centre of the "me" and its demands and desires, the experiencing is a beautiful free movement without any limiting boundaries. Harmony then prevails because, without preventing thoughts concerning the necessary technical knowledge and daily work, the mind, freed of "me" and its desires, is free to move in boundless space. Harmony means absence of conflict; it means stillness and silence, peace and tranquillity. Such silence is the silent pulse of the universe, the immeasurable vital energy of the universe which exists without any cause, without any reason (a fact which science accepts unconditionally). Such stillness and silence is the absence of the "me" (and therefore of the dualism), of the illusory ego and its imagined fears. And such stillness and silence comports the realization that all that exists is the *totality* of the manifested universe and its functioning, that the individual is an intrinsic part of that totality, merely an appearance in consciousness but endowed with the sentience that enables it to perceive and cognize other appearances in consciousness, and that therefore such a mere appearance cannot possibly have any independence or autonomy, nor any volition or choice of decision and action.

Whenever a visitor raised the question of fear and insecurity, Nisargadatta Maharaj would almost invariably deal with it by asking "Who is afraid ? Who feels insecure ? Go deeply into these questions and arrive at the answer." Those who expected a "satisfactory" answer, as if from a slot-machine, were disappointed by Maharaj's answer. And there were quite a few others who covertly felt that Maharaj was avoiding the issue. The foregoing analysis would clearly show that Maharaj was not only not avoiding the issue but that he had unerringly put his finger on the very core of the problem by asking a question that is so direct that it points to the answer that is buried in the problem itself —a Nisargadatta *Mahavakya*.

8

The Present Moment

"I" am the eternal present moment, the "me" is the conceptual flow of time from the future to the past, a flow that makes the relative present impossible to exist. By the time an event is perceived, cognized and interpreted in consciousness by the mind in duality — the split-mind — the event has already become the past. The duration of the process of perceiving, cognizing and interpreting an event makes it impossible for an event to exist in the present vis-a-vis the past and the future.

Scientists today have undoubtedly gone a long way in calculating, with the aid of mathematical instruments of incredible precision, the time-lag between the two elements of the perceiving of an apparent object in consciousness, and the conceiving and cognizing of it in memory as a specific object. The timing of participants in an olympic athletic meet is precisely noted to the hundredth of a second. Such precision could certainly be conceived even finer, but the significant point is that such a duration EXISTS. However incredibly quick the process might be, the fact remains that in any sensory perception — whether it be sight, smell, hearing, taste, or touch — the completion of the process is complicated and elaborate and involves chemical changes in several sets of cells together with the transmitting of nerve-impulses, leading to the conclusion of an interpretation which cannot be anything other than a mnemonic element in the psyche. In other words, the elaborate chemico-physiological process involved in any sensorial perception, inspite of its incredible speed, does require an apparent passage of time. This one fact must lead us to the ineluctable conclusion that the "present" becomes the past by the time we can know it as such, that therefore, there can not exist any "present", and indeed that we are in fact living not in the present but in a future which we cannot in fact know until it has become the past! Should not this undeniable conclusion lead us to the consequential understanding that "life" can begin to have any meaning or purpose only when it is realized that life is not taking us anywhere at any time — that *we ARE the conceptual present moment, totally unaffected by space-time living.* Nisargadatta Maharaj used to say, "you create unnecessary unhappiness for yourself by choosing to remain in duration. I am always in intemporality. I AM intemporality. Therefore, I am never unhappy."

Whether we like it or not, this analysis of the past-present-future cannot but lead to the understanding that life is actually nothing but a series of events like any kind of dream, and must therefore be only illusory and imaginary, however "real" our conditioning may make it seem. Our life is in fact nothing more real or substantial than the interval between the "once upon a time" and the "they lived happily ever after" with which a child is entertained at bed time. The past has no independent existence whatever because it is only a mnemonic impression of something that was extended in duration, and is thus only an instrument, a psychic device, to indicate "replaced elements" in the horizontal extension in apparent duration so that objects in the event may be perceived and cognized as a consecutive incident. There is really no reason to give a sense of actuality to such a device or continuance as duration in space-time; the past is already gone and the future which rushed into the past (without the present) is only a conjecture. This fact is sometimes brought into sharp focus when a series of events takes place with astonishing turns and twists over a certain duration— *the length of the duration is not of the essence* — which leaves one with a sense of *not having moved at all* in space-time.

I vividly recall one such incident in my life, where a series of events happened in quick succession over a period of just twelve hours. I have a cousin, Dattu (short for Dattatreya), who left India fifty years ago in order to study medicine, and thereafter settled in England, working for Government in later years as a consultant. During this period, he visited India only three or four times. He married a lovely and charming English girl, Kay, comparatively late in life, and they have a son, Anand, who was seventeen at the time of this incident that I am narrating. Dattu is almost exactly my age; we were both born in 1917. After a long interval of almost thirty years, Dattu visited us in India in 1981. He confessed that he had a strong urge to visit India and meet all his relatives; he had retired and was keeping very indifferent health then. He stayed with us for exactly a fortnight; he had no desire to visit places or meet people and stayed home most of the time. I really do not know what he expected from us by way of a reception when he visited us after such a long interval — we corresponded very infre-

quently and even then it was the wives who wrote to each other —
but it did seem that he was quite overwhelmed by the spontaneous love and affection with which he was showered by all of
us. When he left, he promised to visit us again but became
seriously ill the following year and by the time he came back home
from the hospital — he was unconscious for seven weeks after a
cerebral haemorrhage — he was a skeleton, having lost almost
forty pounds in weight. Thereafter, as he said, it became an obsession with him that he must visit India at least once again as soon
as possible. His family naturally were greatly apprehensive about
this desire of his and tried their best to dissuade him. When,
however, he found that he had regained his health by the end of
1983, he set about trying to persuade the family that he was strong
enough for a visit to India for about a fortnight, and that Bombay
was not "backwoods country" but a very modern city with first-
class medical facilities. The clincher was the fact that we had a
doctor in the family, my young nephew Mahesh who had qual
ified himself brilliantly as an M.D. So, Dattu finally arrived in
Bombay at the end of July 1984 and it was arranged that his son
Anand would arrive a week later and they would both fly back to
London together, on 21st August.

Both Dattu and Anand enjoyed their stay in Bombay, and it
warmed the father's heart to see the great fuss being made by all
family members about his young, strapping, handsome, six footer
son. And so, the day of their departure arrived and then, exactly
one hour before they were to leave for the Airport — just about
midnight — it happened! Dattu began to feel some uneasiness in
his abdomen as he was resting for a while before leaving for the
airport. Then followed in rapid succession a number of events:
(i) Mahesh, the doctor in the family, was sent for, he examined
Dattu, found that his blood pressure was very high and promptly
declared that Dattu could not possibly fly that night;
(ii) Dattu suggested that Anand might fly to London according to
schedule and he himself would follow by a subsequent flight
soon; this suggestion the young man threw out at once because in
the absence of a thorough investigation nobody really knew how
ill Dattu really was, and also because his mother would at once get
into a panic when she found that Anand had arrived alone;
(iii) Mahesh telephoned for the heart specialist to come at once;
the specialist arrived soon thereafter with his portable ECG
Machine but when he set it up, the Machine would not work!
Then, it did start working after it had received a few thumps with
the fist, but stopped again midway through the operation; however, there was enough on the graph for the specialist to be sure that

there was no cardial infarction, only high blood pressure which could soon be put right; so he prescribed medicines and pronounced that Dattu could fly after a rest of 48 hours;

(iv) Then came the question of informing Kay in England that her husband and son would be arriving a couple of days later and not the next day as planned; she could be given a cock-and-bull story about some confusion in the air-booking and confirmation;

(v) When Anand telephoned and spoke to his mother, he found her in hysterics wanting to know what was wrong; and she began to speak incoherently about a burglary that had just taken place and the police being there at that time, and kept repeating that she could not possibly live in the place alone, and insisting that they come home at once;

(vi) Young Anand then very quickly decided that he would leave at once and Mahesh promptly agreed to take him to the Airport in his car; by this time it was well past the reporting time at the Airport;

(vii) As expected, Anand was told at the airport that their seats were given away to others because they were not claimed in time. Mahesh was not allowed inside the checking-in area because only ticket-holders could go in, and he could see, through the transparent glass, poor Anand being sent from pillar to post, from one counter to another. It didn't help either that Anand knew no Indian language and that his English was not easily comprehensible to the clerks on the counter and vice versa! Fortunately, Mahesh then managed to see the Chief Airport Officer and convinced him that it was really necessary for him to go inside and explain to the airline officials the emergent circumstances that had prevented Anand from arriving in time and which prevented his father altogether from flying that night. Finally, after considerable effort, Anand managed to catch the plane — he was the last passenger to get in.

(viii) The next morning it was necessary to rebook Dattu on an early flight. Preliminary enquiries gave the information (a) that the return ticket which was booked in England through an agency for a particular airline could not be used for any other airline, (b) that, therefore, a fresh ticket would be necessary on payment of the fare in foreign exchange, which would be substantial especially if no ticket was available in the economy class. Once again, the indomitable Mahesh was the hero of the hour: he went to an airline where tickets for an early flight would be available, saw the Chief Manager, explained to him the circumstances in which Dattu could not fly on the original ticket, and persuaded him to transfer the ticket on compassionate grounds. And he returned home with the incredible news that Dattu could fly on the existing ticket, without any extra payment, on a non-stop flight, bearely 48 hours later — which Dattu did.

(ix) The entire incident almost predictably culminated with the news from Anand (from England) that the burglary had turned out to be only an attempted one — the burglar was frightened by the screams from the two ladies (Kay and her sister who happened to be with her) and the heavy barking by the dogs!

These rapid-fire developments, all within 12 hours, seemed to give an impression of unreality to the whole episode: a series of swiftly-passing dark clouds below, and the bright and sunny constant above. They seemed to emphasize the fact that the "present" must surely be nothing but conceptual as a presence, only a notion in mind, an appearance in consciousness having no factual existence whatever: We ARE here and now in the present moment, and can know no present in duration. In other words, the flow of the future into the past can only be witnessed in the present moment. Whatever we think we *are doing* in the "present" has already *been done* in the past that has been irretrievably lost. In these circumstances, can our volitional actions have any meaning in regard to their affecting the future? If not, then can what we recognize and believe as our "living" have any meaning either? Living, as such, can only be in a duration which must have a present and future, but when we realize that the flow of the future into the past is merely a fantasy witnessed by the "I" which is the only constant, here and now, it should be clear that there cannot be any objective "time", any duration, independently of this "I" which is conceiving it as such, here and now. In other words, the ineluctable fact emerges that space-time duration is only a device by which the objective manifestation of the supreme unicity of the subjective "I" could be extended and measured.

The question that would logically seem to arise at this stage is: Does it mean then that the most commendable efforts that Mahesh made, first to get Anand on the plane, and then to get Dattu's ticket transferred to another flight without any extra payment, were without any value at all, that they were quite useless inspite of the results that they achieved? This question is really misconceived inasmuch as the efforts and their consequences are not only treated in the question as a cause-effect relationship but, more importantly, the efforts are treated as those of an individual with an autonomous identity independent of the rest of the phenomenal manifestation, whereas in actuality every sentient being is as much a part of the spontaneous totality of manifestation as any other

object, each with its separate make-up; each tree has its own individual characteristics but it is only a part of the total phenomenal
manifestation; a sentient being is like any other phenomenal object except that it is additionally endowed with sentience, but such
sentience does not constitute autonomy and independence. Would it
not be more sensible to assume that in the totality of the functioning of the manifestation — the Lila — certain events must happen,
and for such events to occur certain circumstances and certain
phenomenal objects as individuals would naturally be featured
therein? If Anand was destined to go by that particular plane and
Dattu by another specific airline without any additional cost —
according to the script of the dream-play of the totality of the
functioning — obviously a Mahesh, endowed with certain physical and mental characteristics had to be there to play his role at that
time and place. Instead of assuming, for instance, that one had lost
money because one had placed certain bets, could it not as well be
viewed that one placed certain bets only because one had to lose a
certain amount of money? Nisargadatta Maharaj would ask: Why
do you involve yourself with events? Why not merely witness
them in the present moment?

There is considerable confusion regarding the cause-effect relationship and the "Karmic" idea of action and consequence. Every
phenomenon, being objective, would be dependent on temporal
causation because the cause-effect process, being dependent on
duration (time), is necessarily phenomenal. The claim of cause-
effect relationship would necessarily preclude the intrusion of any
volitional activity because there cannot possibly be any entity to
exercise freedom of will to interfere with the inexorable process of
causation. Clearly, therefore, there cannot be any specific intervention that can create any Karma. The cause of the confusion
lies wholly in a "psychic impulsion" conceived as a purpose for
intention or volition on the part of an imaginary independent
entity who finds either satisfaction or frustration, depending upon
the result of the cause-effect process. In other words, the cause-
effect relationship is an integral part of the functioning of manifestation, dependent on space-time and therefore obviously conceptual. There can be no action (or non-action) that any sentient
being can be said to perform in its volition because its own existence is only phenomenal and apparent as part of the manifestation, and therefore, there is no entity as such to perform any action. *Only events constituting the functioning of manifestation can be
subject to the cause-effect process, never a sentient being.* Only events
can be effects of causes and can thereby become causes of further
effects; they can never be interefered with by any apparent sen-

tient object, nor can they have any effect on that-which-we-are as the subjective unicity. That-which-we-are cannot be sensorially experienced except as an apparent extension in space, measured in terms of duration — as sentient beings — and therefore "time" is not some objective thing to which "we" are subjected, but merely a means of measuring our phenomenal extension in space. And it is because we objectify our spatio-temporal measurements and regard them as something not only independent of ourselves but something to which we are subjected, that we experience suffering; this objectivization of what is really subjective obfuscates and obscures that-which-we-are viz. our noumenality; it is the "Samsara" which keeps away the *nirvana,* though of course fundamentally they cannot be either different or separate, like the object and its shadow.

Enlightenment occurs only when "space" and "time" are recognized for what they are, that is to say, an inseparable aspect of the *mechanism* of phenomenal manifestation of what-we-are, and are no longer regarded as objective to what is itself conceiving them, not as something congnizable but as an aspect of that-which-is-cognizing, of that-which-we-are. In other words, *space-time is what-we-are,* we who are conceiving the space-time framework in order to experience phenomenally what we are noumenally. As Nisargadatta Maharaj used to say, I AM Time. Such apprehension of space-time as the phenomenal expression or functioning of our noumenal unicity annihilates objectivization together with our identification with an individual entity because any object and its subject are interrelated and one cannot subsist independently of the other . Indeed, release from the subjection to the concept of "time" or duration in relation to extension in space, is itself the liberation that is sought from the bondage of Samsara because the apperception of phenomenal (temporal) experience as an objective expression of what-we-are (subjectively) must mean the instant annihilation of all objective Samsaric experience in temporality. When "I" remain in the subjective intemporality of the presence here and now, of each *kshana* (the conceptual split-second), there is no objective duration in which to experience any objective experience of pain or pleasure and therefore, *nirvana* or equanimity prevails. When, however, the *Kshanas* are *horizontally* strung together into duration the subjective whole mind gets split into objective temporality, and experience happens to a "me" in this horizontal duality, the time-sequence that is the basis of all objectivization as the Samsara.

What all this boils down to is the basic fact that *in the Kshana - the present moment - the "me" cannot be present.* What captures the

illusive "present moment" is that PRESENCE which represents
total phenomenal absence, *the perceiving as such* in which are inherent both "space" and "time", the eye that can see everything
except that which is seeing, the "I" that is spaceless and timeless and which is therefore the noumenal intemporality. Nisargadatta Maharaj repeatedly stressed the necessity of understanding
this position very clearly.

The essential understanding then would seem to be that before
we can know ourselves as the noumenal "I", we must get rid of
the illusion of the "me" with which we have identified ourselves.
The real difficulty in this conceived operation of the destruction of
the   "me"   as   a   positive   effort   is   that
*the "me" cannot be destroyed so long as its duration is also not des-
troyed.* The very basis of a positive effort is duration. Perhaps we
could remove the notion of the "me" and we can indeed do so
during a period of meditation, but as long as the sense of duration
remains, so long will the "me" continue to reappear. The problem
really is quite simple inasmuch as we have only to apperceive that
"time" cannot possibly be anything objective to what we are, that
it is an intrinsic aspect of what we *appear* to be in consciousness as
phenomenal objects. What-we-are is neither temporal nor finite
for the simple reason that "time" and "space" are merely conceptual adjuncts by means of which what-we-are (whatever it be) is
objectivized in the "split-mind" as phenomenal objects or individuals through whom the objective universe becomes sensorially
perceptible. Never mind the fuss that is made about "bondage"
and "liberation"; this is the simple basic fact: *Whatever is experienced cannot be anything other than what we are.* However, such
experience can only happen in phenomenality, as contrast between interrelated opposites — basically positive and negative but
affectively as pleasure and pain, acceptable and unacceptable — in
the duality that is the very basis on which "we" are created as
phenomenal objects in the divided mind. The problem centres
around the conditioning that has taken place which acts as a
screen to cloud our true nature; and the solution clearly lies in
understanding the nature of relativity (the inherent adjunct of
duality) and thereby apperceiving that the space-time-framework
is not something independent of appearances but only a device to
enable the various individual phenomenal objects (the human
beings and other sentient objects) to perceive one another. Such
apperception is itself our natural state of perfect equanimity, or
nirvana, or satori.

An analysis of the inner processes of the split-mind which create our existing conditioning would help to speed up the process

of de-conditioning which is necessary to bring out the required apperception. The direct and immediate result of the integral combination of the two concepts of a "me" and the space-time structure is conceptualizing which can be translated as fabricating objects in the split-mind. The great sage of this century, Ramana Maharshi, declared boldly that "Thinking (conceptualizing) is not man's real nature." Maharaj was wholly in accord with this statement. It can be readily seen that the teaching of almost all great Masters — whatever the approach or the words used — is clearly to impress upon us the basic fact that it is objectivization which prevents us from seeing our real nature: objectivizing takes our attention to "this" which is unreal and thus prevents us from seeing — and establishing ourselves in — "that". That "what-is", not being anything objective, cannot be objectivized. "What-is", being subjectivity itself, cannot be any kind of object; *being the eye — the "I" — that sees, it cannot itself be seen:* IT is itself the seeing, the hearing, the tasting, and any kind of functioning.

It is of the utmost importance to realize that there cannot be any prescriptive method to bring about a cessation of "thinking" for the simple reason that any such effort would emanate from a "me" that is itself nothing but a concept, a phenomenal presence which must necessarily be absent so that the noumenal presence may be felt. The very best that any prescriptive method can do is to help the apprehension that it is space-time which is the basis of conceptualization; that, therefore, it is space-time that is the primary hindrance to apperception of our true nature; and that it is only by apprehending the non-objectivity of space-time, and thus eschewing both the positive and negative aspects of conceptuality, that noumenality can enter. In other words, so long as there is a phenomenal "me" making an effort — or making an effort for not making an effort — the noumenal "I" cannot enter because the situation is not vacant!

The only benefit of any prescriptive method — by whatever name it is called — is to the extent that it can bring about an understanding of WHAT IS; no method can "bring about" any transformation or reorientation. It is interesting to consider, from this viewpoint, what a psychologist calls an "inner gesture" which is embodied in his method which is expected to bring about the realization that the state of satori is our eternal state irrespective of the phenomenon of birth and death. This "inner gesture" primarily concerns the analyzing of the inner processes that at present prevent our living in our normal eternal state, which he calls our "imaginative-emotive-processes". These imaginative-emotive-processes, which are in fact the tendencies to conceptualize and objectivize, result in the dissipation of our energy. How do these dissipative tendencies arise? They arise because of duality, because of our being dichotomized from the totality of manifestation as various "me"s as opposed to all the other "you"s and "he"s. What is the solution? — Obviously to "regain" our cosmic identity which we have never really lost. Any positive action in trying to locate something that has never been lost would be stupid. All that is needed is the understanding that the seeker cannot find what he is seeking because the seeker is himself what he is seeking — the seeker is the sought.

An analysis, on the suggested lines, of the process which brings about the phenomenon of conceptualizing is helpful in going to the root of the problem. It tackles the matter from the viewpoint of "Energy mobilization" and its disintegration. It considers Energy as constantly arising from "below" the level of the mind (from consciousness), such energy being of the noumenal nature that is, pure and non-objective, and therefore, timeless and spaceless, and operating in totality "in the moment without duration". This Energy loses its noumenal nature as it passes the "Existential-Biosocial level" and assumes form and direction, — form, by way of thoughts and direction, by way of emotions; and the pure Energy thus gets disintegrated through conceptualization and objectivization, through the "imaginative-emotive-processes". The pure energy gets dissipated by our usual attention which is passive in an infructuous manner through conceptualization in the dualism of temporality, in which the phenomenal "me" reigns supreme to the exclusion of the noumenal "I" — *the phenomenal "me" dissipates the pure energy generated by the noumenal "I".* Once conceptualization begins, any suppression of thought obviously makes the matter worse. The remedy for the problem — the "inner gesture" — is not to let our normal attention operate in its passive mode but to be actively attentive, with intense yet relaxed alertness, to "the very birth of energy." The point would seem to be that instead of being involved with one's emotions one should be interested in their very birth. This is, of course, similar to what the modern sage J. Krishnamurti calls "choiceless awareness", whereby conceptualization is prevented because there is nothing objective to be perceived by a "me" — there is only witnessing of whatever takes place spontaneously: *there is suspension of thought without any suppression.* The inner gesture is realized when the totality of one's tendencies is accepted before they take an actual form, and then they do not appear; and this means that one is already "grounded in pure non-dual organic consciousness."

Ramana Maharshi has a different viewpoint on what is essen-

tially the same problem : preventing objectivization. He starts
from the fact that the first and foremost of all thoughts on which all
other thoughts are based is the primal "me-concept". He was, of
course, fully aware that the "me-concept" itself is the mind and he
insisted that the mind must be demolished. But the mind which is
itself the "me-concept" cannot be expected to demolish itself. The
Maharshi therefore recommended what he called "self-enquiry"
— the constant and *intensely active* enquiry "who am I? " Such an
enquiry stills the mind because the "me-thought", which is the
basis of all conceptualization, suspends all other thoughts and in
the process finally itself gets destroyed "just as the stick used for
stirring the burning funeral pyre finally itself gets consumed". It is
an essential part of this self-enquiry that, whatever thoughts
emerge during such enquiry are not only not to be pursued but are
to be subjected to the same basic enquiry "to whom has this
thought occurred? The answer, of course, each time must necessarily be "the thought has occurred to me", and when this "me" is
subjected to the enquiry "who is this 'me' , persistently and constantly, the mind turns back, the rising thought subsides, and the
phenomenal world ceases to be perceived as an objective reality.
   Nisargadatta Maharaj used to asseverate that "understanding is
all". By "understanding" he obviously meant something very
much deeper than a mere intellectual comprehension. A query
would often arise in response to such an incredibly simple statement that all that is necessary is "understanding": but what is to
be "done"? Maharaj would have a hearty laugh and say that all
anyone had to "do" was to "sit quietly". The words in Marathi that
Maharaj used were "Swastha Basa", the colloquial and apparent
translation of which would be "sit quietly", but there is a deeper
meaning to the pregnant words —"Swastha" has the deeper
meaning "anchored in your true nature (consciousness)" when the
word is split into "Swa" (One's self) and "Stha" (established in or
anchored in). Those who accepted the literal or superficial meaning would then again ask Maharaj how they could carry on their
normal life if they were to sit quietly. Maharaj never lacked a sense
of humour and his reply was that his answer "sit quietly (or the
deeper meaning "remain anchored in consciousness)" referred to
the original query as to what the visitor should do in addition to
the "understanding" of man's real nature. It obviously did not
mean that the person should sit idle without doing anything, and
that the answer did not refer to the "me" of the normal working
life. In a more serious vein he would explain that it is possible to
live one's life fully and yet remain anchored in consciousness,
exactly as the play actor acts the role of a prince on the stage while

he is firmly anchored in the knowledge that he is actually a pauper. In the ultimate analysis, he would ask, who is asking the question?

Any "who" - or "whom" - can arise only in the mechanism of
relativity, only in a conceptual space-time context, and therefore
only as an appearance in consciousness, as a character in a dream.
From the very beginning of time there could not possibly have
been any "who" (and therefore any "me"). Utterly and totally absent noumenally, the "who" is phenomenally ubiquitous, present
everywhere all the time in the form and name of the millions of
"me"s. He is the seeker who seeks, and he is the seeker who ceases
the seeking when he finds that the seeker himself is the sought.
The "who" can appear only in the mechanism of relativity, a
psychological process whereby are created psychically various objects as *images in consciousness* so that they can be compared with
one another in their respective qualities. This phenomenality
occurs because that is the only way —duality or relativity in which
there is a perceiver and the object perceived —whereby noumenality can objectify its subjectivity. In phenomenality all are objects, but in its functioning as manifestation, such conceived objects require a subject, the *process of conceiving becomes the conceiver* and each object becomes the subject of all other objects. This is
how the "me-concept" or the ego arises, but it can be nothing but
an empty concept.

Let us tarry a while to ask : "if then there is no "who" (and
therefore no "me") and only phenomenality as the manifested objectivity of the noumenal subject, why should anyone be interested
either in bondage or in liberation? Why should any one be interested in anything? Ah, THERE WE HAVE IT. Why should "anyone" be *interested* in "anything" ? The circle is now complete, and
we have returned to the innocence —but not the ignorance —of
our infancy. Again, do we not ask "who" has returned to whose
infancy? We do indeed, and when it is apperceived that there
really is no "who" at all - apperceiving being the functioning itself
- the "who" (and therefore the "me") merges in the apperception
and all the phenomenal "me"s of the split-mind merge in the
wholeness and holiness of the present moment of intemporality
that is the noumenal unicity. It is on this basis that Ramana
Maharshi pronounced the ultimate and basic truth (which Nisargadatta Maharaj also asseverated in his own words very often) as
under:-
    There is neither Creation nor Destruction,
    Neither Destiny nor Free-will,
    Neither Path nor Achievement;

This is the final Truth.
It is on this basis too that Bodhidharma is said to have told the then Emperor of China that there is no doctrine, and nothing at all holy about it. There can be no doctrine because there is only the understanding that there really is no entity either bound or to be liberated. This understanding is the beginning and the end of all Truth — beginning, because in the absence of the entity all teaching, method and practice become irrelevant, and end, because beyond this understanding there is no other "enlightenment."

If the understanding is clear enough and deep enough to amount to apperception, it anticipates and provides the answer to the query : what happens to the "me" during its life-span through the duration of its phenomenal appearance? True apperception restores the much-maligned "me" —and all the "me"s to the rightful place because apperception naturally comports the understanding that noumenality and phenomenality while totally separate conceptually, are noumenally inseparable because phenomenality is the objective expression of the subjective noumenality. Obviously, therefore, all the phenomenal "me"s *together in their totality* cannot be separate from the noumenal "I" —the noumenal "I" cannot but be immanent in the "me"s: The shadow may be a shadow but there cannot be a shadow without the substance. In other words, noumenon is at once transcendent and immanent in the phenomena. This clear apperception demolishes the conceptual separation in duality between the "me" and the "other (me's)" and brings about the understanding that the "me"s do not "live" their life-spans as independent and autonomous entities, but "are lived" in the totality of functioning. In other words *the "me" becomes the understanding itself and auto-matically precludes the existence of a "me"* who could ask the question how "he" should live his life. The individual life becomes the totality of living in the absence of any individual volition or non-volition, positive or negative.

Can we not now understand what the Chinese sage meant by his answer when a disciple complained of not having received any spiritual instruction from the sage inspite of his long stay with him. The sage looked at the disciple in genuine astonishment and said "what do you mean by saying that you have not received any spiritual instruction? All this time, have you not seen me eating when I am hungry and sleeping when I am sleepy ?" He obviously wanted to convey to the disciple that spiritual enlightenment meant the understanding that no individual with autonomy and independence of choice and action can really exist, that this understanding has led to the total annihilation of his identity with a separate entity, with the result that life then on meant only "being lived" as an intrinsic part of the totality of functioning — a natural, spontaneous, free living, with total acceptance of whatever life may bring not in the horizontal duration of space-time but in the vertical noumenal intemporality of the HERE-AND-NOW. In other words, the sage conveyed by his extraordinarily simple words that Truth consists in being aware of WHAT IS without thinking about it, relying on spontaneity for such action as may be necessary in the circumstances of the present moment.

9

Return to Infancy

The infant is regarded in many religions as an example of the way in which man should view the world and what happens in it. The basis of this view is that the child does not think, and therefore does not have any concepts about life - it lives in the *kshana*, the present moment. Sometimes, when Nisargadatta Maharaj mentioned this fact, the query would arise whether the child could therefore be considered as a self-realized human being. Maharaj's answer would be that the query itself should be carefully examined as the answer lay in the problem itself.The query was: Can the child be considered to be self-realized.? The child is not capable of any realization at all, let alone self-realization, because to realize anything there has to be intellect, and the child in its earlier stages does not have intellect except in its most elementary state. Almost every spiritual teacher has condemned conceptualization as the barrier to self-realization . When Ramana Maharshi used to say "Kill the mind" he was not unaware that the mind (and intellect) is the very instrument which has to be used for self-realization

Development of intellect is a gradual progressive process. If this were not so, and if intellect had appeared at birth with all its possibilities and potential, the child (without the subsequent conditioning) would certainly realize the immanence of the Absolute in all phenomenal objects, the one abiding principle in all phenomena, and could then indeed be considered as being self-realized. But then if every child were thus to be self-realized, the play of Maya would be over; indeed, it could never have started! The fact of the matter is that there is gradual mental transformation in human beings from the state of being a baby without any intellect as such to that of an infant or a child and then on to the level of the adult with verbal thinking.

Intellect appears in a child at the age of about two years, or perhaps a little later in some cases, but until then the baby has only the animal level of thinking which is neither verbal nor logical. At this level the baby, like the animal, superficially resembles the Jnani inasmuch as the thinking of the baby at the pre-verbal level is completely fluid without the conditioning of the intellect. In such thinking mental images of the moment as well as the background of mnemonic impressions both contain the duality of nature through the simultaneous and concurrent existence of convergence and divergence, harmony and disharmony. The big difference between the two states - the baby and the Jnani - is that in the case of the baby the two dual states exist together in the primordial state of apparent confusion and chaos of which the baby is not aware, whereas in the case of the Jnani the convergence and divergence exist in perfect balance and conciliation because of self-realization which has happened through the instrumentation of the intellect. It is thus intellect which is the basis of the difference in the state of infant and that of the Jnani.

The thinking of the baby, as of the animal, is restricted to its reactions to the extraneous world, its physiological sensations concerning the extraneous circumstances. Both the image of the moment in the baby's consciousness and its mnemonic background, i.e. the memory, are limited to the physical aspect of existence. The baby cannot conceptualize fanciful concepts of any kind and is therefore totally free of any mental conditioning like guilt and bondage and the interrelated concept of freedom and enlightenment. It is only when consciousness identifies itself with the individual child and the child begins to think in terms of a separate individual entity, that the child reaches the level of general intellectual ideas but loses its original "innocence" of non-conceptualization. The child begins to "think" and express such thinking in words, gradually establishes a connection between words and general ideas, and at the same time becomes aware of its own individual activity in the subject/object relationship. This state, starting with wilfulness, culminates in the firm establishment of the ego as an autonomous independent entity as the "me" in opposition to "the other". Child psychologists have discovered that while the baby's (and the animal's) thinking needs objects in the extraneous world to grasp, the advent of the intellect demands, in addition to actual objects, symbols to represent objects in the world and to establish a relationship between objects and symbols so that such symbolization — thought-words — gives a sense of coherency and congruity, a sense of meaning and *apparent* permanence to "life" and the outside world on a psychosomatic level. While the baby is only concerned with its physical needs and is not really concerned with the concept of preserving its life, the growing child with intellect wants life (integration, existence) and rejects death (dis-integration, non-existence). On the gross level — the somatic level — the child then perceives its body as a real object of manifest integration and thereby gets the sense of security against non-existence; on the subtle level — psychic level — such reassurance of his existence is provided by the symbolic integration manifested by his thought-words. The child is so fascinated by this acquired power of creating its own world of thought-words-forms that it will spend an astonishing amount of time creating an imaginary world of its own with its events restricted only to convergence and integration which is wanted, to the exclusion of all divergence and disintegration which is not wanted. Such a subjective world which the child fabricates in which to play makes for a continuous source of assurance about the security of its existence. The events in this fabricated world appear so real to the child that he is often punished by his unimaginative parents for "telling lies".

The development of the intellect is gradual and progressive, from associating particular words for particular objects to forming verbal concepts about abstract matters and then on to metaphysical questions like "what exactly am I". During this evolution the child, when it is about three or four years old, comes across the phenomenon of death and the concept of dis-integration which until then was unknown; indeed, *the child at this stage discovers the idea of "life" only through the interdependent concept of "death"*. This discovery of "death-life" coincides with the discovery of other interrelated opposites like happiness/unhappiness, success/ failure etc. Then the child recognizes its identity as a separate

individual with volition, and decides   that he wants   life and
does not want death. In other words, the child accepts the integration function of nature and rejects that of disintegration. When my
son explained to his girl, four years old, in answer to a query, what
death is, the girl very firmly told the father "I don't want to die"
and closed the subject so far as she was concerned! From then on
the idea is firmly established in the mind that integration means
"being" or existence and non-integration means disintegration,
death and the annihilation of beingness. Therefore, man does not
realize that non-integration truly means not disintegration into
nothingness but being merged into the unmanifest fullness of the
plenum, the totality of the potential unmanifest from which has
appeared the totality of the actual manifest. The conditioning gradually becomes so powerful that it becomes almost impossible for
man to accept the suggestion that death means going back to the
source from which the total phenomenal universe appears. The
identification with a phenomenal object as a separate entity is so
consummate that though he may be prepared to accept death as
denoting the destruction of only the body he cannot give up his
separate identity, and conceptualizes that the entity (called by
various names such as the "spirit" or the "soul" or whatever)
moves into another world in another form at some other time, still
retaining the identity. *He does not realize that by his refusal to accept
death as a finality he prevents himself from being the Reality.* It is the
power of the Maya that man accepts the illusory phenomenal
world as real and rejects Reality as illusory nothingness.

From the time this partiality for integration ("Life", existence,
happiness) gets firmly established in the psyche of the child along
with its opposite, the aversion for disintegration, he starts pursuing happiness which is in fact a purely subjective state which is
conceived as being totally satisfying. The "me-entity" thereafter
pursues this concept of happiness with determination and this
pursuit of hapiness is inextricably involved with the "not-me" or
the "other" which is seen as the enemy. (The "friend" is encom-
passed in the extension of the "me" entity until he should later
happen to turn into a "foe"). The animal organism certainly realizes its vulnerability to certain things or foes which can do it
physical harm, but what the intellect does is to create a fictitious
"me" and a fictitious "not-me" entities and thereby *generalizes into
fiction* a problem which for an animal organism is only a particular
problem at a particular time. While the animal organism deals
with its specific problems only when they arise, the human organism keeps on accumulating tension because there cannot be any

manifest conflict and decision regarding a problem which is basically illusory. When the mind deals with this problem (which it has created itself) and sanguinely believes it has demolished the problem, out of its ashes arises another similar problem for the simple reason that the problem has really no body and is illusory. In fact, each conflict with the illusory problem makes it doubly strong. The pursuit of happiness by the "me" very soon turns into the concept of happiness pursuing the "me-entity" instead, and the hunter becomes the hunted! This chase of the will-o-the wisp would necessarily continue because *the me concept chases the happiness as an object whereas happiness is merely a concept.* This illusory chase cannot cease until there is a clear apprehension that duration itself is a concept, that what truly exists is only the kshana, and that anything based on time and duration is purely illusory.

Volition and desire leading to the pursuit of the illusory happiness inevitably mean fear of not succeeding in this pursuit. And this fear of failure is, again, inevitably allied to the hope of one day being freed of this fear. So it is a sort of double-bind, chasing the illusory happiness and at the same time seeking freedom from this compulsive chase after happiness! The crux of this problem lies in the concept of time — while chasing the mythical happiness, man has no time to enjoy the present moment. Actually there is no such thing as the present because by the time one thinks of the present it has already become the past. Therefore, what is vital is not thinking about the present but actually *being the present moment* — and that is nothing other than the freedom which man has been chasing, nothing other than the liberation or enlightenment or self-realization which man has been seeking. But what actually happens is that man wants both happiness and the freedom from the pursuit of happiness *as object,* and he wants them at the same time. In other words, man seeks intemporality within the framework of temporality, and permanence of unicity in the duality of impermanent phenomenality. It is this terrible problem which makes man suffer the horrors of hell. Until he realizes that reality, the supreme subjectivity, cannot be grasped as an object by another phenomenal object that man is, this hell must continue.

Nisargadatta Maharaj used to say that among the people who came to see him, a few might have come out of curiosity or in order to accompany some one who wanted to visit him, but most of them were there because they had experienced the horrors of the conditioning of duality, had vaguely glimpsed the nature of the problem, and had been directed to him by some "supernatu-

ral" force through various incidents which were generally interpreted as "coincidences". Everything in the functioning of manifestation is a matter of evolution, and when the intellect arrives at
a certain level of understanding and beyond that finds itself at a
sort of dead end, the "individual" finds himself directed by a
combination of coincidences to the proper Master. But, as Maharaj used to point out, before this happens the problem should have
received full consideration from the intellect and the helplessness
of the intellect should have caused a certain intensity of frustration
and agony. Idle curiosity aroused by mere reading of books is not
enough to produce results.

To return to the basics, the infant has no such problems of life
because it is only concerned with living from moment to moment,
not with "life" as such. It is only when consciousness identifies
itself with the individual form that the "me-concept" is born, intellect arises and the thought-concept-words operation comes into
being and creates the problem. In other words, as the infant was
not aware of its individual identity — the "me-concept"—there was
no intellect to conceptualize the problem. Intellect creates the
problem based on the "me" and "not me" duality. At a certain
stage, the intellect recognizes that a problem has been created,
tries to deal with it and finds the problem getting worse because it
is only in the framework of relative duality that intellect can function. The problem will be solved only with the realization that the
source of the problem is the intellect itself and its conceptualization, only when intellect goes to its own source and naturally finds
that it cannot know its own source. It is at this stage that the
Master — or the Guru — points to the truth, the Reality which is
immanent in all manifestion including the human being. And it
is only the human being who can realize Reality; man is the only
sentient creature who can have this realization because it needs
intellect to bring a sentient being to the point of the take-off into
realization, and the human being is the only one who has intellect.
And when this realization takes place, the Jnani is once again like
the infant without the "me-concept" but with the significant difference that the infant without intellect is ignorant whereas the
Jnani with his intellect has realized his true nature. In the infant
innocence is coupled with ignorance, while in the case of the Jnani
innocence and knowledge go hand in hand.

In order to understand the problem in its full significance, it is
necessary to examine the mechanics by which intellect creates the
problem and then attempts to tackle it to the limit upto which it
can operate. It can be seen that the baby, being without any intellect, is not different from the animal organism inasmuch as it lives

from moment to moment. When it is hungry, it cries; it does not "know" what hunger is. All it understands is the physical discomfort which it expresses by crying, whatever the kind of discomfort and the degree of such discomfort may be. The baby is not different from its thinking and feeling — it IS such thinking and feeling — whereas with the appearance of intellect, there is a definite feeling of duality inasmuch as the child *knows* that "he" is hungry or that he is happy. While the baby can only howl with pain or gurgle with satisfaction, the child with intelligence is able to distinguish between himself (as the apparent subject) and the object of the discomfort or satisfaction. From then on, the child understands which object or circumstance gives him discomfort or pain, and which object or circumstance gives him satisfaction. The child thereafter thinks in terms of the acceptance of integration and the refusal of disintegration or non-integration. Such thinking really belongs to the world of speech which itself is based on the duality of preference and rejection. The sage Jnaneshwar, in his Amritanubhav devotes a chaper to "The Word" — the thought-word — in which he gives a remarkably perceptive analysis of the structure of the world of thought-word or conceptualization.*

It must be remembered that conceptualization, apart from the most elementary thinking, depends almost wholly on the acquisition of language which itself depends on words; words are symbolic gestures in which are inherent certain autonomous ideas. And, when the growing child associates the autonomous ideas with the words which are used by those around him, language becomes the platform from which his conceptualization takes off. The arousal of intellect in the child, coupled with the association of certain ideas with certain words, gives rise to the extraordinary fertility of the child's imagination. It is easily noticeable that the child generally prefers bedtime stories with happy, integrative themes and avoids those with disintegrative themes containing words like "ghost", "witch" or "death". In other words, it is a very clear indication of the manner in which the human child, through the use of the language transmitted to him by the older generation, creates a personal world of his own. Although such a world may be based on the hard facts of the "real" world (or it could sometimes be entirely imaginary) the fact remains that it is his personal world, a representation of the world which is entirely personal and is different from the outer objective world. It is, in fact, not an objective world but purely subjective world, a world of thought, a world of the word. This subjective world of thought-word need not be based or structured on the actual articulation of specific

*The Author's *Experience of Immortality* — Chapter 6. (Chetana, 1984).

words. It is, as a matter of fact, structured on a verbal monologue in most cases, though in some cases it is a not uncommon sight to see a child (or even a grown-up person) talking to himself and thus creating his own subjective world based on actual verbal articulation.

Just as the totality of manifestation (the macrocosm) represents a balance between two divergent interdependent tendencies, one of life-integration-covergence and the other of death-disintegration-divergence, the structure of our conceptualized verbal world (the microcosm) shows the same kind of balance of syntax or reason balancing the two interrelated opposites — one is an egocentric, converging, integrating structure of subjective meaning and the other a non-egocentric, divergent, disintegrating structure without a subjective meaning. Thus, for instance, if one's verbal thought can create the idea "the teacher teaches children", there is nothing to prevent verbal thought from creating the idea "the teacher frightens elephants". Both manifest a movement in consciousness (which is the essence of the mind), but while both reflect a syntactical structure, each is totally opposed to the other inasmuch as one is converging and has meaning, the other is diverging and apparently meaningless. The first sentence is associated with the "me-entity" and conveys a meaning which one associates with the outer world whereas the other one is not. There is no doubt that the divergent verbal structure is part of the general nature of things and truly comes into its own in the dream state (whether it be a proper dream or the drowsy day-dream) when different objects and different times and different scenes flit about in a sort of free-wheeling manner, totally indifferent both to the conventional confines of space-time and to the rules of logic or reason, establishing inconsistent connections and anomalous analogies between cabbages and kings, which not only disappear when the person wakes up but which he cannot really explain in specific verbal terms on a rational basis.

The important fact in this analysis is that man is generally not aware of the fact that while he understands that one sentence has meaning for him and another is meaningless, *both are an intrinsic part of his thought-process.* The Master — the Jnani — is certainly fully aware of this fact and therefore attaches so much importance to spontaneity : he has given up his partiality towards the convergent language *as against* the divergent language. The Zen Master would give an answer to a question, which the disciples might consider as containing deep metaphysical import, in terms which apparently not only do not have any relevance to the question but seem utterly childish. Thus for instance, to a query concerning the effort to be made for enlightenment, the Master may look outside and say "How lovely the garden looks" or something similar, the intention being to break the disciple's attention from the habitual restriction of convergent thinking and take it to the absolute functioning of the mind.

It is important to realize that one's normal convergent way of thinking — and speaking — is not the result of an unconscious habit but that of a definite partiality for the convergent way as the right way because of its apparent meaningfulness which one accepts as against the *"undesirable"* meaninglessness of the divergent way. Such an attachment is distinctly allied to that part of one's psychosomatic structure which is the animal functioning which refuses any disintegration of its organic structure. It must be remembered that the human being is an amalgam of three essenses — inanimate, animate and intellectual — which are interdependent in their manifestations and act concurrently at each point of the organism. The animal "wish to live" (the integration) thus projects itself by identifying the intellectual convergence with what it considers as "real" and acceptable, and rejecting the intellectual divergence as the not real and therefore not acceptable. The result of this partiality for convergence is a world of dualism, of contradictions, which prevents the seeing of Reality. In other words, what we see is not the in-seeing or true seeing. If we see two objects made of clay, almost invariably we choose the one which has a pleasing, proportionate appearance and reject the other as ugly and unwanted, instead of seeing the identity of both in the same substance (clay) of which they are made. The distinction between beauty and ugliness is not only subjective but quite arbitrary. Because of our partiality for convergence and our rejection of divergence, we fail to see that both objects — rather, all objects — are mere appearances in consciousness, and *all* verbal structures are movements in consciousness. In other words, this *volitional* creation of dualism results in the feeling of bondage from which man seeks freedom. In the words of Nisargadatta Maharaj, we make a choice, and instinctively feel the guilt for such foolishness.

In regard to true seeing, there is a story in the Mahabharata concerning the great sage Ashtavakra. When Ashtavakra was in his mother's womb, his father used to sit beside his wife and recite the Vedas. To the great surprise of both of them, the unborn baby once cried out in anguish, "father, I have listened to your recitations of the Vedas, and I regret to have to bring to your notice that you often make mistakes in your recitations". Ashtavakra's father, a renowned scholar, was so enraged at this remark which he took as a grave personal insult that he cursed his unborn son that he would be born with eight deformities in his body — hence the name Ashtavakra which means "with-eight-distortions." It so happened that soon thereafter Ashtavakra's father accepted a challenge to debate with the Pandit at the Court of King Janaka but was defeated, and in terms of the challenge, was banished from the kingdom. When Ashtavakra was a lad of twelve, King Janaka held a debating contest and the most renowned scholars were invited. When he heard of this great event, Ashtavakra went to the city and could get admittance into the court only with the greatest difficulty. As he entered the court, waddling in his ungainly manner, there was a burst of laughter from all and even the pious king could not altogether restrain a smile. Ashtavakra, when he heard this laughter, joined in it in an uninhibited manner. King Janaka was greatly astonished at this spectacle and said to Ashtavakra, "I can understand, young man, why these other people are laughing, but I wonder what makes you laugh?" Ashtavakra, still smiling, replied, "I was laughing, O King, because it seemed to me a huge joke that this assembly is supposed to be an assembly of great scholars, but I see that it is only an assembly of cobblers (Chamars) who are familiar only with skins and leathers; they see only the outward appearance and have no idea of Reality." The King was so stunned by this answer that he let Ashtavakra have a debate with the most renowned of the assembled scholars. Ashtavakra defeated them all and King Janaka himself became Ashtavakra's disciple. The knowledge which Ashtavakra gave to King Janaka is contained in the small but exquisite volume known as Ashtavakra Gita or Ashtavakra Samhita.

To get back to the mechanics of intellect, conceptualization is a process where only one part of the intellectual operation is favoured not by just ignoring the other part but by specifically rejecting it. One might choose the subject on which to conceptualize (although quite often even that is not of one's own choosing) but the thought-words that come thereafter are mostly spontaneous and all that one can do is to receive them. What happens then is that we are so conditioned to accept the convergent ideas and reject the divergent ones that we feel ourselves enslaved by nature, whereas it is not nature that enslaves us but our attachment to one particular part of what nature offers. We forget that divergence is also very much a part of nature. We forget that nature is not different from us—we ARE nature. Indeed, it is this separation from the rest of nature (that we ourselves create) which is the cause of the conflict both within and without. This separation is inherent in the misconception that the meaningful part of our thinking is our very own whereas that part which is divergent and meaningless is what is forced upon us. Thus we are divided against ourselves and it is this dichotomy — created by ourselves — that is the conceptual bondage in which we find ourselves. In other words, it is our attachment to the convergent part of our thought-language structure that is the root attachment, which branches out into a host of other subsidiary attachments.

It is this root attachment that must disappear, based as it is on the "me-concept" and the illusory happiness which this "me" seeks for itself.

It is thus the functional dualism of the mind, that is expressed in the structural division in the language, that we create in our personal conceptualized world which is the cause of our bondage. It is not that we cannot accept the divergent thought, or that intellect is incapable of fabricating divergent language. The fact is that we are not normally willing to accept it. But it certainly can be done and when that is done, when both the convergent and the divergent planes are allowed free operation, they get superimposed on each other resulting in what is known as the "fasting mind" or the vacant mind or the no-mind state, the most alert state in which the mind can find itself because of the total freedom in which it can then operate. Indeed, it is in such a state of mind that creativity finds its best outlet. It is in such a state of mind that the artist, the scientist and the martial arts expert produces his finest performance. Such a radical "re-shuffling operation" would perforce necessitate the intervention of — or, rather, the inviting of — mental processes normally kept away from the usual deliberate reasoning, i.e. thoughts arising in the unfamiliar area of divergence. Such an invited intervention is effective only when the rational controls are relaxed and we lay ourselves open and vulnerable to the less specialized, more fluid mentation, marking a retreat from articulate verbal thinking to vague, visual imagery which to the logical mind would seem meaningless.

Nowhere perhaps can the practical application of this principle of balance in the operation of the intellect be seen as in Japan. Some of the foremost scientists in the field of sub-atomic science are Japanese and it has been freely suggested that it is perhaps their inherent affinity with Zen that is responsible for their revolutionary *divergent thinking* which is the basis of sub-atomic physics. As regards the arts, the Zen artists—both poets and painters—have as their favourite subjects what might be called natural, specific and secular things. Not only are the subjects natural but the techniques themselves are natural, involving what is known as the art of artlessness or what Sabro Hasegawa has called the "controlled accident" — neither the purely convergent nor the wholly divergent elements but a natural balance between the two. The essential point is that there is no dichotomy, and the total opera- tion of the intellect is considered as natural as the formative be- haviour of plants or birds. In other words, there is a beautiful natural blending of discipline and spontaneity — discipline being not constructive and spontaneity being not licentious. It is in this insight that opposites are interrelated and necessary for the exist- ence of each other in a vivacious balance which avoids conflict. This insight also makes it clear that where a conflict does arise, it is superficial and easily rectified when it is seen in its true colours. Thus for instance, a most striking feature of the Sung landscape — as in most of sumi-e type of painting — is the relative emptiness of the picture which is not just the unpainted part of the material; indeed it is the apparent emptiness which gives the picture its very life and soul. The secret of this type of painting — that is in fact painting by restraining oneself from painting, or "playing the stringless lute" — is of course, balancing form and emptiness, balancing the manifested actual and the unmanifested potential, balancing the natural silence with the spoken word, and thus suggesting the limitless potentital of the void from which suddenly arises the phenomenal manifestation. A stranger to this type of painting at once notices an absence of the regularity and symmetry that characterizes convergent thinking and which is almost predictable; instead he sees something apparently eccen- tric and shapeless, and yet uncommonly well balanced, throbbing with vitality.

The principle of the balanced intellect — or the no-mind state which Nisargadatta Maharaj demanded from his listeners — is the one which the best masters in Japanese swordmanship have not only recommended but insisted upon. The no-mind is the most alert mind. It must be stressed that the principle of balanced thought does not exclude the concentrated attention that must necessarily be given to the routine or the technique. Indeed *con- centrated attention, to the exclusion of distractive thinking, is the very essence of Zen* philosophy. What is insisted upon is that the par- tiality towards convergent thought, to the deliberate exclusion of divergent thought, be avoided. At a certain juncture in one's work there are occasions when the thought-language must be given free rein and this can be done only by avoiding one's partiality to- wards convergent thinking. The Master Swordsman knows that the unknown has no ego-consciousness (which conscious thought has) because it does not move at the level of duality. Therefore, when conscious thought is left behind and there is no thought of winning the contest, the sword then moves *by itself* where it should move. As Sun-Tzu, a great warrior and an authority on warfare is said to have put it, "To win every battle is not the best aim; the perfect victory is to win without planning to win". The no- mind state means great alertness, and in this state the mind is free of all conflicting thoughts of life and death, victory and defeat, and, therefore, functions at its most natural and effective level. The Zen master-swordsman is more than a mere wielder of the sword. Like the master-archer in the Hindu mythology, he is beyond all duality.

It needs to be understood that we are not so much under bondage as under lopsided development. When the infant gets endowed with intellect, both sides are well balanced — the convergent and the divergent — the divergent side being, if at all, the more favoured one. But persistent conditioning from those around slowly swings the pendulum towards the convergent side as if it were a magnet, and prevents the pendulum from returning to the other side. This imbalance can get corrected only by a clear apprehension of the cause of the imbalance. And in this apprehension the Guru's word is invaluable because it comes from one who is already realized and is living his life in perfect balance without volition, and accepting the unknown alongwith the known in perfect equanimity. As this understanding gets stronger, the earlier conditioning loses its hold and the automatism of divergent thought is allowed freer movement towards the inherent balance between convergent and divergent thought. It would thus be seen that the earlier development of convergent thought is not really the villain as such because it is the first part of realization through the use of the intellect. It is the *attachment* to convergent thought that is the villain; and when the divergent side is also adequately developed and the happy balance restored, the realization comports the knowledge that there really is no villain at all! This normal balance needs no development; it is only this realization that is the liberation which is sought; realization which is the return to the source, to the WHAT IS, a return to the innocence and freedom of infancy.

The infant lives in the bliss of ignorance, while the self-realized Jnani lives in the bliss which is beyond both ignorance and knowledge. In fact, the Jnani is no longer an individual inspite of the presence of intellect. Both the infant and the Jnani are an intrinsic part of the totality of the functioning of phenomenal manifestation, one in the absence of knowledge and the other in the fullness of the knowledge of reality. When the psyche of the infant gets endowed with intellect during the course of its natural development, it is balanced between the integration/convergence element and the disintegration/divergence element; it is only as a result of the conditioning from extraneous sources that it begins to veer definitely towards integration and keeps out non-integration, until finally it considers the latter to be foreign to its nature and something to be shunned. The Jnani, after apperception of the true nature of reality, realizes that duality is the very warp and woof of the phenomenal manifestation. He realizes that the volitional acceptance of one aspect to the exclusion of the other is precisely what causes conflict since the psyche is intuitively aware of its inherent natural balance between the two interrelated ends of duality. This apperception brings the Jnani back to the natural balance. This is how the infant proceeds from blissful ignorance to phenomenal ignorance and finally returns to *the Knowledge of* its original bliss, and the circle is completed.

After the circle is completed, the Jnani continues his phenomenal existence till the end of his allotted span in perfect adaptation to whatever might happen, without losing his inherent sense of equanimity. His living then is non-volitional living. He lives in the conceptual present moment; he neither thinks of the past (whether painful or pleasurable) nor of the future (with hope or fear). Thus while the past and the future are based on volition and wish-fulfilment, presence in the HERE-AND-NOW is eternal because there is no individual who can know it phenomenally. The Jnani's "being present in the present" is *phenomenally* non-volitional living; *noumenally* it is being in the intemporality of the awakened state. Therefore, the life of a Jnani appears to others to be purposeless. In the words of a Zenrin poem:

The wild geese do not intend to cast their reflection;
The water has no mind to receive their image.

10

No Independent Observer Exists

Nisargadatta Maharaj often used to say that from both points of view — the physical worldly viewpoint and the metaphysical un-worldly viewpoint — the sense of an independent, autonomous entity as an observer, *as opposed to* that which is observed, is what causes a distorted view. There is a basic unity in the millions of manifested phenomena, and a mutual understanding in all objects and happenings, the ignoring of which leads to a gross miscon-ception — the misconception of the independent observer.

Maharaj used to say also that the infant has the intuitive sense of omnipotent oneness in the totality of phenomenal manifestation; he loses this sense of oneness when consciousness subsequently identifies itself with the individual body, and the operating centre in the sentient human being assumes a pseudo-subjectivity as an autonomous observer *vis-a-vis* all other objects; and the subse-quent conditioning by the parents and others completes this pro-cess of identification. Is it not curious, asks Traherne in his Cen-turies of Meditations, that the infant should inherit the whole world and delight in those mysteries which the learned books never care to unfold? The first light of dawn made eternity man-ifest. All the world was his, the skies, the stars, the sun and the moon, and he was the only spectator and enjoyer of all of it, with-out any proprieties or fragmentations, until he was corrupted and made to learn the dirty devices of this world. The infant accepts all experience in its entirety and, unlike the mature adult, does not dissect, disintegrate and analyze it into divisions and oppositions which create problems of their own. It is perhaps for this reason too that the infant and the child are more inclined to favour a story or a myth or a visual image rather than a verbal description.

It is only through the strengthening of the conditioning both at home and in school that the child proceeds gradually to accept the factual description rather than the visual image. Could it not be that this preference of the younger child for the visual image evoked by the story is an instinctive understanding that factual description almost necessarily depends upon an interpretation by a *separate* observer whereas the imagery has a freshness and wholeness of its own? The fact of the matter is that *there really is no independent observer*. There is only observe-ING. The observer is very much a part of what he is observing in the sense that the observing subject and the observed object together form the relationship of observing like the two poles in a magnetic field. A human being cannot be apart from the world as an observer observing the world; the observer himself is very much a part of the world. As Nisargadatta Maharaj used to say repeatedly, the observer and observed, as sentient human beings, are both objects in the totality of the phenomenal manifestation, and the assuming of subjectivity by one object in relation to other objects is a pure misconception. The Newtonian scientist was perfectly content to regard metaphysics with smug condescension, if not with positive contempt, from his superior stand as the purveyor of truth and reality. The twentieth century scientist, however, has been discovering that most things are not what they seem to be, that the Newtonian framework is not the entire reality, that space is not fixed nor time steady, that the cause-and-effect notions that had been accepted by science till the nineteenth century as common-sense were no longer valid, and that it now seemed that objects must be seen not by an exclusive nature of their own but in their mutual relationship. Indeed, the sub-atomic scientist has been confronted with facts that take him unbelievably close to the metaphysical truths which the Eastern mystic has intuitively experienced for many centuries.

Nisargadatta Maharaj used to say that what the mystic sees is really very simple to understand but it needs a special kind of intelligence and a special perspective, not an intensified intellect but a kind of transmuted intellect which can offer a totally different perspective, not by merely changing the direction from the same standpoint but by transferring the standpoint itself. Curiously enough this is almost exactly what the sub-atomic scientist says about the kind of intellect necessary to understand modern physics. It is a truism that what is perceived cannot be that which is perceiving. Every thing, every event is perceivable only because it is extended in the three directions of measurement called "volume". We can perceive many parts of our bodies that are objects to that which is perceiving. But the "perceiver" as subject of the perceived object cannot perceive himself. The perceiver, in other words, as the subject can see the volume — the three directions of measurement — as an object; and, therefore, the perceiver as the subject must necessarily be in a direction of measurement other than the three directions of measurement constituting volume. And, furthermore, just as volume includes the two measurements of length and breadth, the centre from which the perceiver operates as subject — the centre from which the perceive-ING as a faculty operates — must be apart from (or beyond) volume but must also *include* volume. This perceiving centre is obviously operating everywhere, all the time; and, therefore, must be THIS-HERE-NOW.

What we have then come to is the inescapable conclusion that the perceiving "we" — the subject as different from the physical body that is only the perceived object — must be a dimensional element not perceptible to our sensorial apparatus. And this is SPACE-TIME, obviously not tangible because whatever is tangible must be within the tri-dimensional element of volume that is included in this new dimension, just as the two-dimensional plane surface is perceivable and is included in the three-dimensional volume of a tangible form. What-we-are is, therefore, "formless", and space-time is the conceptual framework of measurement for the three-dimensional forms, and is merely a label given to what-we-are in the process of conceptualizing and objectifying the forms. And what-we-are being the cognizing subject, it would be absurd to imagine a three-dimensional form — an object — as an independent observer, a separate entity. All forms, all objects, all sentient beings including human beings, form interrelated parts of the totality of phenomenal manifestation which are held together by the same elemental energy; and, no part of that manifestation (the human being) can hold himself apart as an autonomous, independent observer.

The modern scientist, through his imaginative researches based on a thoroughly open mind, prepared to accept and consider anything that the researchers might reveal — however unbelievable or incredible — seems to be arriving at a frame of mind whereby the phenomenal universe becomes more and more intelligible only through the questioning of the very concepts, notions and scientific beliefs which were earlier most taken for granted. The modern scientist seems to be arriving at the conclusion which the mystic had arrived many centuries ago, that the phenomenal manifestation is a game — Lila — of hide and seek, that a new discovery would have been much more easily located if the scientists had but known where to seek, and that the best places to hide are those where no one would think of looking! Indeed, the modern scientist seems on the threshold of arriving at, or going back to ("REVERSING" as Nisargadatta Maharaj was fond of saying) the ancient Advaita aphorism: TAT TWAM ASI: That Thou Art. He is about to jump off the highest cliff of scientific intellect into the intuitive void of the mystic to find out for himself whether, as the mystic avers, the seeker and the sought are one, and to experience for himself whether the universe is indeed a dynamic, inseparable whole in which the observer is essentially included.

That the constituents of matter and the basic manifested phenomena involving them are not only interdependent and interconnected, but that it is possible to understand them only as integrated parts of a whole and not in isolation, is the conclusion arrived at by various models of sub-atomic physics in diverse ways. The mystic has always included the human observer and his consciousness (strictly speaking, "his" consciousness would not be correct because it is universal consciousness which pervades all sentient beings) in the universal interwoveness. The sub-atomic physicist too now finds that he cannot talk about the properties of an object because such properties become meaningful only in the context of an interaction between the object and the observer. Indeed, the new physicist finds that he becomes so involved in the world that is being observed that he actually "influences" the properties of the objects that are being observed. Many modern physicists consider that this intimate involvement between the observer and the observed thing is perhaps the most important feature of the quantum theory, and have therefore adopted the word "participator" instead of "observer". The mystic has always said that his "knowledge" is not observation by any means but that it is an intuitive experience which obviously comports the idea of the fullest possible participation to the extent that both the observer and the observed disappear in the noumenal function of observe-ING. As an Upanishad has put it, when everything has become only one's own self, then whom and whereby would one see, or smell, or taste? The modern physicist cannot, of course, experience this unity of all things as does the mystic because he must necessarily at present work in the context of a specified, limited framework. He must content himself with the intellectual conviction which is supported by his sub-atomic models that things and events in the whole world are woven into an inseparable "net of endless, mutually conditioned relations".

Pythagoras, some twenty five hundred years ago, is supposed to have described a stone as "frozen music", an intuitive perception which seems to be justified by modern science inasmuch as every particle in the manifested universe is supposed to adopt its characteristics from the pitch, the pattern and the overtones of its particular frequencies — its music. It would seem that the interrelated oneness of the universe has been exhibited in its diverse aspects perhaps the most important of which — though not generally so appreciated — is SOUND. The Hindu concept of *pranava* (aum) is obviously based on the idea of the sound, and it would not be so difficult to conceive rhythm, resource and harmony as being a most important factor in the universal web, the dynamism of the manifested universe and the music of the spheres representing the THIS-HERE-NOW, the immanence of the unmanifest absolute. Also it is hearing, more than seeing (reading), to which the Eastern Master has always given prominence, e.g. listening to the Guru's words.

The rhythm of relationship is a very interesting factor while considering the relationship between an apparent observer and the observed object, such as a speaker and a listener, or between one thing and another. There is a phenomenon which is known as entrainment — "mutual phase-locking of two oscillators" — according to which two or more oscillators pulsing at nearly the same time in the same field tend to "lock in" with the result that they are found to be pulsing at exactly the same time, the apparent reason being that it takes more energy to pulse in opposition, and nature generally seeks the most efficient energy base. Thus two pendulum clocks fixed side by side on a wall would tend to swing in one precise rhythm. Entrainment is a far more frequent occurrence than is generally realized; and it is believed to be a clear indication of the tendency in objects to move towards the universal pulse that is at the base of all existence. The movie "The Incredible Machine" contains a microscopic view of two individual muscle cells from the heart shifting closer together and then suddenly adjusting their rhythm so that they are pulsing together in perfect synchronization. Our internal rhythms are apparently not only in synchronization with one another, but are also entrained with the world in general. It is well known that our physical and mental states shift in rhythm with the changes of the tides, the daily cycles and the seasonal swing of the earth and the sun.

The pioneering work of Dr. William Condon of Boston University School of Medicine shows the interesting phenomenon that there is distinct entrainment not only between the speaker's words and movements but between the speaker's movements and the listener's movements, although of course a listener does not move as much as a speaker. Dr. Condon's studies even showed that a new born infant moves synchronously with the pitch and pattern of the mother's voice, and would seem to indicate that babies are born attuned to the universal pulse in addition to the heartbeats of the mother.

The quantum theory clearly suggests a connection between every particle in the universe, and the formulation of the physicist
J.S. Bell, known as Bell's Theorem, particularly brings out the fact
that spatially separated events cannot be considered as independent happenings, and that their significance lies in the interconnectedness of events *apparently removed in distance* in a manner
that cannot be either understood or explained by man's ordinary
experience. This suggestion brings the working of the universe
startlingly close to the Eastern mystic's intuitive view of the universe as a net of jewels — Indra's net — in which each of the
millions of jewels reflects all other jewels.

The mystic's intuitive view of the interconnectedness of the
millions of phenomena and events in the manifested universe has
received strong practical support from an exercise in General Systems Theory, a relatively recent inter-disciplinary school founded
by Von Bertalanffy, the purpose being the construction of theoretical models in order to discover general principles "universally
applicable to biological, social and symbolic systems of any kind"
— a search for unity in multiplicity, a search for common de-
nominations in the continuous flow of phenomena. Bertalanffy
found that all complex structures and processes of a relatively
stable nature display a form of hiararchic or holarchic organization
whether they happen to be living organisms or social organiza-
tions or galactic systems. Having got rid of the firmly-entrenched
Newtonian mechanistic preconceptions, now that it has really
opened out its arms to welcome the mysteries of the universe,
science has discovered among many other things that the hierarchic organization is a basic principle of living nature and the
universe in operation.

Contrary to the deeply ingrained thinking, "parts" and
"wholes" (parts being considered incomplete fragments as against
the complete wholes) cannot exist anywhere in their absolute
sense, not even in the universe itself as an operating organization.
The organism, like a living organism or a social organization, or
even the entire universe consists of a "whole" and "sub-wholes"
(not parts) in the sense that it is "a multi-levelled, stratified hierarchy of sub-wholes". Each member of the hierarchy — the sub-
whole — is a relatively stable integrated structure with considerable *apparent* autonomy, but at the same time subordinated to the
"whole". Thus, for instance, in a living organism, the circulatory
system, the digestive system etc., are sub-wholes which have
other sub-wholes like organs and tissues which in their turn have
their own sub-wholes, right down to individual cells and the
organelles within the cells. Each of these sub-wholes has a stable,

integrated structure with its own self-regulatory devices. The structure of the hierarchy can be represented with remarkable aptness by the diagram of an inverted tree with the sub-wholes forming the nodes and the branches forming the channels of control and communication. Such a diagram has been used, with suitable changes, to represent the "tree of life"; the simili has also been used in the Bhagwadgita and elsewhere for a similar purpose. It has indeed been used in various other areas to demonstrate the hierarchic organization in that relevant area.

Needless to say, this idea of the holarchy or hierarchy has been stressed here merely to point out that no individual — as observer or otherwise — can remain outside the universe as a separate point of observation or action with total autonomy. His existence, such as it is, can be only in relevance to the entire universe and all the interrelated phenomena therein. Moreover, the orderliness in which the universe operates is quite beyond the capacity of the intellect to understand, and this now seems to be appreciated by the modern physicist with the virtual disappearance of the sharp separation between subject and object, observer and observed; and the observer, like the mystic, is now accepted as an active "participant" in the *experience* (rather than an experiment), forming one whole with whatever is being observed. In other words, all there is, is the *experience,* without the necessity of any material substratum as the object of which the event is an experience. What this means, therefore, is that nature itself exhibits a holistic tendency to form wholes that are greater than the sum of its parts inasmuch as, in the physicist's terms, the proton and the electron do not pre-exist within the neutron but *something new is created.* If the universe is imagined as a vast quantum object, it divides itself into the multitude of living beings, planets and stars only if it is viewed in the divisive objectifying perspective, and not otherwise. As Nisargadatta Maharaj repeatedly pointed out, any divisive separation was only notional.

This is a startling conclusion to which the modern physicist has arrived at, and the layman today could well wonder if he is listening to a western modern physicist or to an eastern mystic. But the physicist has not arrived at the ultimate conclusion because he has to labour under the limitations of the intellect. Mind obviously cannot find its own source. On the contrary, it is only when the mind is at the end of its tether and gives up the struggle and becomes a void — the void of fullness — that the physicist will KNOW the whole mystery and get all the answers. However, the joke of it all is that *then* — in that state — the physicist will no longer remain the physicist wanting to know the answer to questions, but will have merged and become the absolute subject, beyond all experience, beyond all questions and answers. Thus there can be questions about the state of deep sleep for the observer only till the last split-second *before* he falls into deep sleep; thereafter there can be no observer, no questions, no answers, until he is awake again.

11

The Perfect Perception

The perfect perception is apperception : the immediate perceiving of the totality of phenomenal manifestation, and the inherent identity between the duality and non-duality. And yet the fact remains that such immediate or direct perception is so unusual that any expression of it by those who have had it would seem to most people to be sheer nonsense, to some people a kind of mystery, and to an extremely small minority as a very faint echo, the haziest reflection, of something deep within themselves that has nothing to do with what they appear to be to themselves. This is because we are so used to depend on sensorial perception for the existence of objects that we consider objective existence as the norm, and anything not sensorially perceptible as a "nothing". We have been used to ignoring altogether the perceptive faculty as such.

Why do we perceive an object, an event? Only because it is extended in space in its three measurements constituting volume viz length, breadth and height; also, we perceive the object because we are not within the volume of that object — the perceiver must necessarily be beyond the directions of measurement of the perceived object in order to perceive it. This may seem like giving undue importance to what is obvious, but it is basic to the problem: "why is our 'normal' perception not perfect perception?"The fact that we can perceive not only other objects but parts of our own bodies must clearly show that what is perceiving surely cannot be within the volume constituting either the other objects or *our own body*. In other words, the perceiver being the subject of the perceived object, can never perceive himself as the subject within the measurements constituting volume — the perceiving element must necessarily be in a measurement that is outside or beyond the three constituting volume. Where then could "what is perceiving" be, if it cannot be within the three measurements constituting volume? It is clear that there must be a "centre" from which perceiving could operate as a faculty, from which it could function as the subject of the perceived objects; it is also clear that centre must "exist" not within but beyond the three dimensions constituting the volume of phenomenal objects, and beyond the concept of space in which the objective dimensions are extended. This leads us to the inevitable conclusion that this "position" that is beyond space (and therefore beyond the allied concept of "time") must be such as to include the other three dimensions just as the two dimensions of "area" include the single dimension of length, and "volume" includes area. So, what could be the dimension beyond space and time and "including" space-time ? It could only be *the source* of the space-time from which the concept of space-time-phenomenality emanated — the eternal That which perceives everything we *think* we perceive, That from which the three directions of measurement (at right angles to each other) of volume must emanate, That which is the true perception, That which is always here and now, the eternal HERE-AND-NOW. We have always had sudden, flashing glimpses of this HERE-AND-NOW, but this-which-we-*think*-we-are has always ignored them because it is frightened of them. It is frightened of them because they represent the nothingness, the void, which is a negation of the objective appearance that we think we are. That nothingness is not really a void but the fullness of plenum which is *what we really are*, not as individuals but as the TOTALITY. The implications of this statement may frighten us for the moment, but let us at least understand.

The cause of all human misery is the one single fact that man disidentifies himself from the subjective perceiving centre which is the subjective functioning aspect of the noumenon, and identifies himself with the objective psychosomatic apparatus through which the perceiving takes place. Man forgets that he is in fact sentience which is the functional aspect of the consciousness that is our real nature, and mistakenly believes that he is a separate

entity represented by a particular psychosomatic mechanism. It is
necessary to find out how this comes about, first in a general
theoretical way and then in the practical details of everyday life.

The subjective centre must be clearly distinguished from the
objective centre because it is the confusion between the two which
suddenly makes one stop in one's tracks and ask: What am I doing
here in this world? What exactly am "I", other   than   this
physical frame that is born and after a time must die? We may
ignore these questions and brush them aside whenever they arise,
but they persist and cannot be denied. There is a clear
distinction between the subjective centre which is intuitively referred to when each one of us says "I" — the ultimate
symbol of what we are — and the tri-dimensional phenomenal
object that we identify ourselves with when we say "I" but
actually mean "ME". A deep apperception of this distinction
— between the subjective perceiving centre that we are and the
objective operating centre that we *think* we are — provides not
only the answer to those persistent, nagging questions about our
real nature, but, more importantly perhaps, saves us from considerable misery and unhappiness that man has unnecessarily
made himself heir to. The mistake that occurs is that we identify
ourselves with the objective operational centre — the mechanism
— and forget that we are the subjective functional centre which is
beyond phenomenality and which provides the original energy
(as consciousness and sentience) to the millions of mechanisms
known as sentient beings which, without that energy are only
"dead matter". This "mistake" is understandable and indeed not
illogical because all operations of the psychosomatic apparatus are
indeed directed from this objective centre; and this objective centre is thus mistaken for the subjective centre (sentience), the
switchboard is mistaken for the power-station. In actual fact,
however, the objective operational centre is only psychic just as
the heart or the liver is somatic, purely phenomenal and entirely
devoid of any subjective noumenal aspect — and therefore
obviously without any volition or autonomy or independence in
regard to any choice or decision.

This distinction between the subjective functional centre and
the objective operational centre shows us clearly how the identification with a supposed autonomous entity arises. The mistaken
identification of what we noumenally are with the operating organ
in the psychosomatic apparatus (that is our body) thereby
assumes a pseudo-subjectivity, a supposed "self" or "ego" with
supposed independence and choice of action. The condition
which brings about this situation is known as *"dualism"*, *a conse-*

quential aspect of the process of duality, which latter is a necessary condition in order that noumenon may objectify itself as phenomena. In the classic instance of the rope being mistaken for the snake, the perceiving of the rope is the primary delusion, that of the snake the secondary delusion. It is this aspect of the phenomenal world that Nisargadatta Maharaj used to emphasize repeatedly. Every time an object is seen, it is really the perceiving of its pseudo-subject i.e. the subject in its objective manifestation, because every object (sentient or otherwise) is really a mirror reflecting that which is seeing. Objects can have no existence other than as appearances, sensorially perceived and interpreted, which means that what is perceived can only be a reflection of what is perceiving i.e. perceiver-object is only an object and what is perceiving is truly the subject. The difficulty in understanding this obvious fact arises because the perceiver is regarded as an entity with independent existence whereas he is in fact only a phenomenal apparatus or object with certain characteristic reactions — the real perceiver is the perceiving itself, the subjective functional centre. In short, *perceiving as from the subjective functional centre (sentience) is perfect or true perception whereas perceiving as from the objective operational centre (the entity) is imperfect or split-mind perception.*

An aspect of perfect perception is to perceive that any object or event perceived has its existence only because we have perceived the object or experienced the event, only because one of our senses has cognized the object or event, and has interpreted it in the subject-object duality. *The object or event, therefore, cannot have any existence independently of our perceiving of it* as an appearance in our consciousness. In other words, an object exists only because it is perceived. And this perceiving of ours being only the phenomenal functioning of That-which-we-are (the noumenon), the entire universe and all that happens therein is only the expression of the subjective noumenon in its objective aspect. Objective existence cannot be other than sensorial perception — *remove sensorial perception and there is no objective universe;* and, of course conversely, if there were no objective universe, there cannot be any question of sensorial perception. Sensorial perception is the subjective aspect of all phenomenality or physical objectivity. In the same way, the apperceptive faculty is also the subjective aspect of all psychic activity because in the absence of the perceptive faculty, no image could be formed in consciousness. In other words, objective existence (whether physical or psychic) and the subjective perceptive faculty are naturally dependent in an object-subject relationship. It is only in the total negation of both these aspects that totality occurs. All thought and all phenomena are based on the concept of space-time, and since space-time is not some perceptible or cognizable "thing", it must follow that the perceive-ING and cognize-ING — and indeed all functioning in general — must be noumenal. As the sage Jnaneshwar puts it, subjectivity and functioning are like "sky and space, or wind and movement. or flame and light." *

The essential element in perfect perception is the fact that there is really no perceiver/perceived relationship in the manifestation of the phenomenal universe. What exists is the *function-ING* of the whole mind, and this objective functioning is conceptualized by the split-mind as subject perceiving the object; there is really neither any objectivizer nor any thing objectivized. The sentient human being makes the cardinal mistake of viewing the phenomenal world as something separate from himself whereas he himself is an intrinsic part and parcel of the *totality* of manifestation which is the objective aspect of the unmanifest Absolute subject. Sentience certainly enables sentient beings to perceive (and cognize) phenomena, but it is not responsible for the arising of the phenomenal universe. Phenomenal manifestation has not taken place *separately* in order that the human beings may perceive and cognize it. Sentient beings come into existence along with the totality of manifestation as part of the universe, simultaneously and concurrently with the entire universe. The capacity to perceive the universe through the psychosomatic apparatus (the sense organs, the cognitive faculties), which the human beings — and all sentient beings — have, is a subsequent indirect arousal. Thus there is a clear-cut, though of course notional, difference between the creative aspect and the cognitive aspect, between the creation of the totality of manifestation *including the human beings* and the congnition of manifested universe by the human beings. A clear understanding of this position makes it obvious that *the perceiver and the perceived object* are both objects in the phenomenal manifestation, that each of the two sentient objects (the two human beings) becomes the perceiver when the other is the perceived object, that the subject and object are thus interchangeable and interrelated concepts. In other words, the perceiver cannot perceive the perceiver and the perceiver-cognizer is in effect only the act of perceive-ING-cognize-ING, the thing cognized being its counterpart. What is more, the *perceiving by human beings* is necessarily false because in such perceiving both the supposed subject and object are merely appearances in consciousness. Thus

*Author's *Experience of Immortality* - Verse 158, Chapper - 7, Chetana, 1984.

in the absence of consciousness as in deep sleep or under sedation, there cannot be any perceiving even though the pseudo perceiver exists. True perceiving, perfect perceiving, is the non-
perceiving, the perceiving that is beyond body and thought. A
pseudo-subject perceiving an object itself becomes an object when
he is perceived by some other pseudo-subject. But when there is
true perceiving — consciousness perceiving consciousness and
the appearances therein — what can there be to perceive? There is
no object, only the one true subject, the entire manifestation
being its objective expression. This is the transcendence of the
subject/object dualism, the total phenomenal absence which is the
potential presence, the turning back of the mind from outward
objectifying (which is what perceiving in dualism means), back
inward to its wholeness or the non-objectivity from which objectivity arises.

Perceiving as such is a noumenal function of the manifestation
of the phenomenal universe, and such perceiving is pure perceiving because there is no thing seen and there is nothing (object
assuming pseudo-subjectivity) that perceives. Although our long
and persistent conditioning will not easily let us accept it, the fact
remains that as sentient beings we are objectively nothing but
illusory dream-figures. All phenomenal existence itself is merely
an appearance in consciousness, and all the characteristics of sentient beings — the form, the perceiving, the knowing, the feeling
etc — are also nothing but movements in consciousness as in the
dream. All actions and movements and events are extensions in
the conceived structure of space and time in order that they may
be sensorially perceived and measured in duration, but they all
happen in consciousness, exactly as in the dream. The significant
point to be understood and remembered is that consciousness, in
which everything happens like a dream, is also the dreamer; this
is the subjective and dynamic perceiving aspect of the static consciousness, while the objective aspect is the perceived dreamed
and discriminated element. In other words, the dream that is the
phenomenal manifestation occurs in consciousness, is perceived
and cognized in consciousness and is interpreted by consciousness through the duality that is the basis for all phenomenal manifestation. This duality, it must be constantly remembered, is
merely the mechanism or the instrumentation through which the
manifestation occurs (and is of course a concept) with the result
that the perceived can be nothing other than the perceiver; the
subject (not the pseudo-subject which is also an object) and the
object, inseparably united when unconceived and unmanifest,
only *appear* as dual and separate when conceived in the phe-

nomenal manifestation.

This would be clear and more convincing if we analyzed the dream state. What appear to us in the dream as living, factual characters with feelings and reactions — *including ourselves* — are seen on awakening to be mere illusory figures, wholly devoid of any choice or volition. This life, in which we think we are the subjects in relation to other human beings as our objects, is really a living-dream which is not in essence different in any way from the personal dream. We are totally mistaken when we think we are autonomous and independent entities who can think and choose and make decisions. If we would but calmly review any period in our lives, we would surely find that while we thought we were making the decisions, actually events have happened according to a master plan on a vastly magnificent scale in which we were mere pawns. The point is that in this living-dream that life is, all characters are merely objects in the dreaming mind (which is the content of consciousness) through a process of duality that is given the name of "causation". There is no subject as such with the inevitable result that the object is the subject, that the perceived is the perceiver. There is an interesting anecdote about the Chinese Sage Chuang-Tza. One morning he told his disciples that he had dreamt that he had become a butterfly flitting about in the garden from flower to flower, and now he was worried. The disciples laughed and said, "it was only a dream, Master". Said Chuang-Tza, "Wait. If you think there is no reason to worry, you are wrong. Now, when I am awake, I am puzzled. I have a very serious doubt: If Chuang-Tza can dream that he has become a butterfly, why cannot the butterfly dream that she has become a Chuang-Tza? Now, who is really who?. Am I a butterfly that is dreaming that she has become a Chuang-Tza.?"

The living-dream, viewed phenomenally, is merely an appearance in consciousness, perceived and cognized by consciousness, and to that extent is indeed an appearance as illusory as the appearance of a mirage. But, viewed noumenally, the phenomenal manifestation is not only not nothing but is everything inasmuch as *the essential elements in the dream cannot be anything other than the dreamer himself*. This-that-dreams, the subjective aspect of consciousness, is indeed the dream and everything in the dream. In other words, the sentient beings which are phenomenally mere objects in the manifestation are truly the pure subject, the potential plenum, although phenomenally it may appear as the void of nothingness that results when the interrelated opposites of duality are superimposed into total negation. *In this living-dream what awakens is not the object: The awakening happens in the dis-*

identification of the dreamer from his object, in the diappearance of the illusion, in the dissolution of the entity in the discovery that what seemed as an object is indeed the subject. When true perceiving is recognised as the objective functioning of the the subject, the pseudo-subject disappears and the ego-entity gets annihilated. *True perceiving, perfect perceiving, is thus not seeing phenomena as our objects.* As soon as we perceive phenomena as our objects, we establish an objective relationship with things, and create a dichotomy between subject and object, self and other. It is this apparent separation which is the cause of human misery and what is known as bondage. Perceiving noumenally is perceiving not objectively but subjectively, seeing phenomena as our selves. Such noumenal perceiving or true perceiving is no-seeing, or rather, neither seeing nor non-seeing because neither the object nor its subject exists otherwise than as an appearance. True perceiving is ceasing to perceive objectively, is ceasing to conceptualize, and therefore means seeing the phenomenal universe without choosing, without judging, without getting into a subject-object relationship. What happens when perceiving thus becomes noumenal or perfect perceiving? Nisargadatta Maharaj's answer to this question was : "nothing — and everything". "Nothing" because all that happens phenomenally is nothing but an appearance, a movement in consciousness; it is nothing but conceptualizing, and when this stops, nothing happens except that you (as the subjective "I") remain what you were "before you were born". And "everything" because the nothingness of the phenomenal void is really the fullness of the phenomenal potential plenum; when conceptualizing stops, the false seeing, the out-seeing stops, and what remains is *the in-seeing, the source of all seeing — not the seeing inside by the entity but, the seeing from within — seeing from the source,* which is noumenal seeing without any entity.

Perfect perceiving establishes a direct relationship between the noumenal unmanifest and the phenomenal manifestation: the manifestation may adopt any number of forms, but substratum of all of them is the consciousness which is immanent in each and every phenomenon like gold is immanent in all gold ornaments whatever their shapes and names. Whatever is perceived is then seen to have no existence independently of the noumenal consciousness; *consciousness is the only subject* and all phenomena, including all human beings, are objects that appear in the consciousness. In other words, perfect perceiving means the understanding that the universe is not different from us, that there is no difference between the manifested and the unmanifest, the temporal and the intemporal. The difference is only in appearance, and while this difference seems irreconcilable like all opposites phenomenally, it disappears altogether in the absence of conceptualizing because "difference" itself is only a concept. In deep sleep, when conceptualizing ceases, there is no question of difference or differentiation. In such total conceptual absence, there is neither the conceived, perceived object nor the conceiving, perceiving subject — all there is, is noumenal functioning in whole mind without the dualism of the split-mind. In its static state, when consciousness is in repose, there is nothing for consciousness to perceive or cognize because there is no manifestation; and even when movement gives rise to the phenomenal manifestation and the conceptual perceiver therein, there is nothing other than consciousness. In brief, *whether there is any phenomenal manifestation (and the conceptual perceiver) or no manifestation, what is constant and changeless is the substratum of consciousness.*

It is therefore clear that when an individual perceives an object as the subject of that object, he does not see it in its totality as objective manifestation of the subjective unmanifest, but as a mental representation in response to the out-seeing, as the reaction to the sense organs, the cognitive faculties. It is instructive to go into the mechanics of how perception, and attention in general, work in practice. Several thinkers including J. Krishnamurti have made a penetrating study of this aspect of perception. One aspect of the matter is that one may not in reality perceive an object "as it is in itself, in its totality", but what is perceived is not totally unconnected with the reality of the outer object because the mental representation is based upon certain particular aspects of this reality and is therefore *partially in agreement with the outer object.* The result is that the cognition, while not being wholly untrue, is only partially and *inadequately* true. However, the agreement of the mental image to the reality of the object, inspite of its being partial and inadequate, does indicate an identity of structure between the object and the perceiver, an identity between the two objects in the phenomenal manifestation (the perceiver and the perceived both being objects). If, for instance, the note 'A' is produced near a violin, the violin string producing the relevant note will start vibrating on its own by resonance. That something in a perceived-object to which the sense organs in the perceiver-object respond, *awakens* in the perceiver-object a complex mental vibration *that had already existed there;*the perceived object did not create the mental vibration, it only awakened or triggered it. This is significant inasmuch as the division between the perceiver-object (posing as the subject) and the perceived-object as the object of the pseudo-subject makes the interaction between the two objects partial and inadequate. The perceiver as the pseudo-subject is not completely open to the emanation of the perceived object, the response to the resonance is not deep and complete but superficial and partial. If the response to the emanation from the perceived object were full and uninhibited, the image in the mind would have been wholly adequate and the perception would have been perfect. The perception then would have been one of the totality of the object, of the totality of the perceiver, and of the substratum which makes all objects identical beneath all apparent differences, like gold within all gold ornaments.

Man's ordinary perception lacks the hypostasis, the underlying essence of the whole mind which alone is able to realize the underlying identity under the superficial differences in the millions of phenomena in the manifestation. This is because man's ordinary perception is done in the divided mind in which the non-duality is substituted by the discrimination between subject and object, by an identification with one object as against the others; hence the inadequate mental representation of the outside object. This separation between subject and object-this conditioning-is so powerful that even an intellectual appreciation of the fact of the illusoriness of the universe as a phenomenal manifestation does not remove it : each individual, in this understanding, keeps himself separate from the illusory universe;*the illusoriness of the universe is accepted but not that of the individual; the objective universe may be illusory but the pseudo-subject still considers himself very much real.*

It is thus that while the outer world may offer to release in a particular psychosomatic apparatus total resonance, the pseudo-subject, identified with that apparatus or body is not prepared to accept that total resonance because he considers himself the self and the outer world a powerful not-self or other, a natural enemy who would destroy his individual entity and would annihilate his subjectivity (pseudo-subjectivity) into a nothingness, a void --for him a consummation devoutly to be resisted. There is thus the absence of a complete interpenetration between one sentient being and another which would have meant perfect perceptive attention; on the contrary the partial relationship means a constant conflict between one another among the different entities constituting the world. In other words, the imperfect perceiving means a hand extended to the outer world in order to grasp whatever could be grasped and not the open hand of friendship and co-operation that represents the full and total resonance with the outer world:*the outer world is seen not as the image in the mirror but the face of* *an enemy.*This is the principle behind Maharaj's words:"My grace is always there in plenty, but are you ready and prepared to accept it?"

A closer look at the mechanics of this interrelationship between the subject (the cognizer-object) and the object would show that, if the emanation that comes from the object to the subject through the sense organs is considered as a current of cosmic energy connecting the centre of the object and centre of the subject, the refusal of the subject to the total resonance of the object would consist in the fact that the current, instead of being allowed to exhaust itself at the centre, is diverted by the subject towards his periphery or the false and illusory centre. In other words, the cosmic current, instead of exhausting itself at the noumenal subjective functional centre, is passed on to the objective operational centre that is the periphery. The result is a lack of illumination at the subjective noumenal centre and strong illumination at the false, illusory, objective centre:perception becomes imperfect, resulting in false interpretation, MAYA. The periphery to which the current gets diverted is constituted of what we know as "feelings". There is nothing in the outer object-the outer world -that could possibly create the conflict in the subject because the cosmic current or energy is the same in both the objects in the manifestation. The disruptive dualism *that is the cause of the conflict exists not in the outer world but within the pseudo-subject;*the noumenal subjective centre does not receive adequate support while the objective operational centre takes over the function of perceiving. In other words, the subjective "I" is forgotten and the objective "me" (the pseudo-subject) takes over. It is not that anything is closed instead of opening or that anything is refused instead of accepting but that *the false perceiving is superimposed on to the centre of perfect perceiving.*The sub-structure of subjective reality cannot but remain unchanged but Maya gets superimposed thereon; the ocean remains unchanged except that there are waves on the surface.

The result of perceiving from the viewpoint of subject/object relationship is that the identification with a separate entity prevents extension of total response and interpretation with the outer world because it makes the outer world an enemy rather than the unified objective expression of the subjective noumenon. The identification with a separate entity prevents the perfect perception that there cannot really exist any opposition between "self" and "not-self", that the basic duality that is the necessary framework for the appearance of manifestation is only a concept along with space and time and that, therefore, the entire manifestation, including the individual who considers himself the pseudo-subject, is a mirror-image in consciousness of the subjective reality. The one single factor that prevents total interpenetration between the individual and the outer world is the fear and the horror of insecurity, of being gobbled up by the outer world, of being totally annihilated. It is this fear of total negation that makes positive phenomenal presence so protective and therefore essential, and affective life so very necessary. Inspite of the fact that life is in many ways full of conflict and misery, one clings to affectivity with desperation. While the individual thus desperately clings to his individual affectivity, he is also just as desperately seeking liberation from the misery and bondage. In other words, *he is seeking liberation for himself as an individual,* and is terribly frustrated when the Master — almost every Master from time immemorial — tells him that problems will never cease so long as he "desires" something from the viewpoint of the individual. This is indeed the core of the Nisargadatta teaching.

What amounts to a dilemma for the individual is that he wants to be sensitive to the world insofar as it could afford affirmation of his beingness, but is totally insensitive to the world to the extent that it could deny him that. He refuses to understand that this in effect means that he wants to preserve his separateness and at the same time refuse duality and thereby knock out the very basis of phenomenal manifestation. The only answer to this apparently insoluble problem is to have a clear apprehension of the problem so that the impasse itself becomes the way out. Nisargadatta Maharaj used to say that understanding is all, and that one should let this understanding take deep roots so that it would in due course bloom and blossom into intuitive, spontaneous action. Knowing the true nature of the individual in relation to the totality of phenomenal manifestation, one must take life as it comes along. We must be the spectator (witness) of the spectacle. To the extent that an individual uses his ordinary perception and attention in accordance with his wish to experience the outer world only in identification with a separate entity, he is a spectacle without a spectator; to the extent that he would prefer to be insensitive to the outer world, he is a spectator without a spectacle; when he accepts life as it comes along knowing it is nothing but a living-dream and yet acting intuitively *as if it is a real world,* he would be able to be the spectator of the spectacle.

This brings us to the mechanics of the difference between the perfect perceiving by the subjective functional centre and the imperfect perceiving by the objective operational centre — the former indicated by the subjective personal pronoun "I" and   the latter by "me", identified with a separate entity. The former kind of perceiving is a sort of non-dual outer perceiving that could be called "sensing" while the latter kind of dual, inner perceiving could be called "feeling". The outer or sensory perception is based on resonance that connects the outer world and the individual psychosomatic apparatus through an essential identity in the general structures, the classical example being the general structure of gold which is common to all gold ornaments whatever the shape or form. The inner perceptions, on the other hand, relate to a personal structure (and not a general structure) inasmuch as the resonance is divided between two separate poles within the pseudo-subject understood as an agreeable feeling or a disagreeable feeling. The two constructs — the general and the personal — present wide difference in their respective perceptions. The general human construct could be said to represent the cerebro-spinal system which creates mental images based on emanations received from the outer world; the personal construct would represent the vegetative nervous system, the autonomous or vago-sympathetic system which is not concerned with the outer world but reacts to the feelings that are generated through the mental images of the outer world because, unlike the unified cerebro-spinal system, this system that is diffused throughout the whole organism is intimately connected with each of the innumerable cells in the organism. While in the outer perception there is a resonance between two objects as two distinct microcosms (each a replica of the macrocosm of the totality of manifestaion), the resonance in the inner perception (which produces an emotion either of joy or of sorrow) is a resonance between "two structural modes of a single microcosm". *The outer perception of sensing means awareness of the outer world whereas the inner perception of feeling means awareness of "me" as a separate individual entity.* The individual discovers his personal construct by noticing first that the same sensory image seems to produce different opposing resonances in himself and others, and then that the inner resonances have a dualistic nature of being agreeable or disagreeable. A series of experiences and judgments is the base on which the personal construct is gradually built up. In fact there is a constant rearrangement as more and more experiences are collected, catalogued and classified in memory as agreeable or disagreeable, positive or negative, self or not-self. Indeed, in course of time there is a continuous interaction and rearrangement of judgments between the existing judgments and fresh experiences within the personal construct. It is an interesting fact that this gradual building up, as Nisargadatta Maharaj would say, goes as far back as the human organism in the womb. The fetus identifies itself with the organism only in its potentiality in the absence of any contact with the outer world. When the baby is born this potentiality is actualized but the contact with the outer world being through resonance in a structural identity, there is no exclusively separate identification with the organism. This identification appears subsequently as the *interpretation* of experience. The new-born infant is obviously not equipped to *formulate* any thought, but the timeless source of thought, viz. Consciousness, actualizes the non-formulated thought in the psyche of the new-born that he is one organism and there is something other than his own organism. A significant corollary of this fact is the interesting phenomenon that the more elementary and general a thought, the easier it is to actualize but more difficult to express consciously. Indeed, while consciously formulated thoughts proceed from the particular to the general, the unformulated thought in its actualization proceeds from the most general to the particular. The very first thought, as Nisargadatta Maharaj used to say, is the thought "I am", the sense of presence.

It is seen that apart from sensing and feeling, the judging and classifying of experiences in a dualistic capacity lies in certain implicit convictions or beliefs or false identifications which exist in the human organism not only as fetus in the womb but, as Maharaj used to say, as memory extending back to the life of all the forebears inasmuch as the sperm seed that created the fetus was the actualization of all those memories of earlier "lives". All beliefs flow from this storehouse of memories inherent in every human being, and form a chain the first link in which is the erroneous belief which leads to the identification with the organism as a separate entity, the subject *vis-a-vis* the rest of the outer world as the object. Such identification as a separate entity with supposed independence of choice regarding absolute opposites (primarily the good and the bad) is indeed the Biblical "original sin". Such exclusive identification leads to the belief that this "me" as the subject is entitled to have absolute happiness, a belief that presupposes that there has been something wanting which obstructs such absolute happiness and therefore establishes the need for an experience that will achieve the goal. This need leads to a search for such an experience *through a contact with the outer world* because, in the absence of the outer world, the individual fears the loss of his separate individual existence, a loss which would make his search senseless. While the material stimulus of some drug or the subtle, psychic stimulus of a Yogic exercise could bring about this satisfaction that is sought for, the lack of stability in such an experience makes it incomplete and therefore unacceptable as the end of the search. The search, however, can actually come to an end only when the very illusoriness of such a search is realized in the sense that the ultimate experience would necessarily involve the total annihilation of the very individual ego who started the search!

To come back to the mechanics of sensing-feeling-experiencing, the whole purpose of an experience is to judge its effect in relation to the constant search for happiness. Indeed, to experience is to judge whether the experience essentially is agreeable or disagreeable, whether or not the experience brings one closer to the essence of our beingness. In other words, all experiencing, all judging, is always a "partial interpretation" for the simple reason that it is in the dualism of the relative functioning. The only impartial judging would be according to the absolute criterion of Reality, and then there could be no judging at all. According to strict sequential order, the individual first senses, then feels, and finally experiences and judges; but the process in practice is more dynamic in the sense that the underlying factor in all the three processes is the need based on the constant search: the need starts the wish to experience which leads to the wish to feel and the wish to sense.

We are now in a position to observe the manner in which our psyche usually functions, the process in which our wish to experience directs our conscious thought. In doing so, we must go further back to the origin of thought. Why should a particular image form itself in one's consciousness from among the many memories stored in the mnemonic bank? Why shouuld a particular image force itself either by itself or as a reaction to an outside stimulus? In other words, assuming that one has a choice at the core of one's conscious perceptions, and on the basis of the fact that there can at any one time be only one conscious mental image, what is it that brings a particular image to the forefront to the exclusion of all others? The answer is that it is the wish-to-experience that conditions the nature of one's attention, based on the identification with a particular organism as a separate entity which treats the outer world not as a heterogenous objective manifestation of the subjective reality (that it is) but as one of irreparable multiplicity. It is one's wish-to-experience *as a separate entity* that turns the outer world as the multiple enemy. What, then, directs the choice of one's perceptions is the mnemonic storehouse, the associations appropriate to that particular personal construct, the specific affinity (either positive or negative) to a particular outside stimulus from among the many. The same complex spectacle affects the conscious attention of different people in different ways. While watching a usual scene along a road, different people will react in different ways because each one is more sensitive to certain images than others either positively or negatively. Indeed such reactions could well vary in different circumstances or at different times because in the meanwhile the personal construct has adjusted itself to the intervening experience.

It is necessary at this stage to distinguish between two kinds of thought — the unconscious intemporal thought (or spontaneous thought) and the conscious temporal thought which is really conceptualization. The unconscious thought represents the spontaneous perception instantaneously recorded and faithfully modelled on the homogenous but united outer world and has nothing to do really with the personal construct and the wish to experience; the conscious thought, on the other hand, is conceptual, illusory, and represents a temporal succession of images more or less removed from the immediate reality because it is based on a choice that is dependent on the respective personal construct and the wish-to-experience. The eye-witness accounts of an accident, for instance, will all be remarkably similar if recorded instantly but, when time is given for conscious thought to operate, concepts based on individual sensitivity and partiality (positive and negative) will have been at work, and the subsequent reports will vary to an alarming degree.

What are the characteristics of the unconscious thought, and how does it operate? Qualitatively, it does not differ from what is known as whole mind (as opposed to the mind that is split by the duality of subject/object), the potentiality of all thought, because the conscious perception of the present reality by the unconscious thought, although limited to those vibrations which reach the sense organs, is nonetheless a direct manifestation of the whole mind; it is not corrupted by the exercise of any choice or volition by any personal structure. Unconscious thought, or direct thought, is the process of objectivization of what-we-are, which constitutes the apparent universe and maintains it in the apparent seriality of temporality. This direct or unconscious thought, a multitude as differentiated from a multiplicity, evanescent as the *kshana* (split-instant), is a glimpse of eternity. On the other hand, conscious thought or conceptualization is characterized by the personal identification of a "me" with a particular organism as a separate entity together with the dependence on duration for its existence. Conscious thought or conceptualization cannot take place unless the central character of all such thinking is a personal entity and the thinking relates to the outer world only in so far as it concerns this "me" over a certain period.

What happens in the case of conceptualization is that the "me" in his search for happiness finds that the outer world is not prepared to fall in with his particular needs — the enemy resists — and so the "me" finds it more feasible and far easier to achieve the happiness he seeks in his fertile imagination through a world that is wholly centred on himself and one that he is able to control and condition. When a person in moments of leisure watches the usual scene on the road, the perception is at first an unconscious one, modelled on the immediate outer world; there is a "structural identity" between the outer world and the perceived image inasmuch as such an unconscious perception comports the perception, perhaps partially or even in its totality, of the entire scene as a heterogeneous, global picture and not of a multitude of aspects not only separate but opposed to one another. The conscious perception, on the other hand, is quite different because it is based on a choice made according to the constitution of the personal construct and is thus centred on a "me". First there is the immediate, instantaneous unconscious perception of the general structure, and then from among the multitude of aspects in that unconscious perception, attention gets centred on a particular aspect, like a particular face or a particular build in an individual on the street, or a particular vehicle, or whatever, and renders it conscious *by isolating it*. The significant point is that *the conscious mental grasping of a particular aspect in the unconscious perception takes place in duration* inasmuch as while the grasped image has already passed into the past, the phenomenon of conscious grasping projects the "me" into the future. Unconscious thought is without duration because it is instantaneous though, of course, it may appear continuous through incredibly rapid renewals; conscious thought on a particular aspect would stop the projector (and the rapid renewals) and remove the stationary "shot" from the apparent reality of the scene into an imaginary film of its own. Concrete proof of this would be found in one's everyday experience of watching a play being acted on the stage. To the extent that the mental images reproduce faithfully what is happening on the stage, there is no conscious thought as such, but off and on while watching the play, the mind wanders and certain images are fabricated either having some relevance to what is happening on the stage or even none at all. Such conscious thought is imaginary thought, a fabrication of images which is totally removed from the apparent reality.

It is this kind of thinking or conceptualizing that Nisargadatta Maharaj used to urge his visitors to eschew when he asked them to listen to him and not merely hear him, to go deeper into the meaning which he wanted his words to convey and not merely accept their superficial meaning. Some particular word or idea would, in the case of some visitors, stop the instantaneous, unconscious, direct perception of what Maharaj was saying and send them into conscious temporal reveries of what they had read or heard some time somewhere else that was in accordance or not in accordance with what Maharaj was saying. It is obviously such thinking, such conceptualizing, such fabricating of images in the split-mind that Ramana Maharshi had in mind when he declared, "thinking is not man's real nature." Perhaps it is failure to grasp the direct meaning immediately that brings about thought; when direct or unconscious thought leads to spontaneous action where is the need for conscious thought? Conscious thought finds an opening only when the "me" intrudes and grasps any residue that might have been left.

The conclusion that we finally seem to have arrived at is that it is the imperfect perception, the conscious thought, the habit of conceptualizing which leaves us with the impression that the outer world hurries by so quickly that we are left with the sensation of having so little time, of not being able to "stand and stare". But a perception of the false as false makes it clear that it is not the present which is fleeting past us with a sickening speed but that the present moment is indeed eternal and it is the conceptual past and future (in which there is no room for the present) that are the fleeting illusions. We have discovered that the horizontal succession of time, the sequential duration is a consequence of the single-track verbalization of our split-mind which does not grasp the outer world instantaneously but interprets it perversely by grasping bits and pieces of it and calling them things and events. And this split-mind, with its conscious thought and imperfect perceiving, does not realize its almost total irrelevance concerning the spontaneous working of the psychosomatic organism with its heartbeat, its breath, its complicated nervous system, glands, muscles and sense organs. The comforting thought is that, as Nisargadatta Maharaj said, *understanding is all*. The split-mind can heal itself into its original wholeness — and holiness — as soon as it stops grasping because they are not different, the former being only a specialized activity of the latter in order to carry out the working of every day life. The split-mind must keep its place and restrict its activities to its specialized or technical calling. Only understanding can accomplish this; any effort would only be an effort of the individual illusory entity operating through the split-mind.

The fitting conclusion to this subject would seem to have been provided by the Taoist poem:
> In this moment there is nothing which comes to be.
> In this moment there is nothing which ceases to be.
> Thus there is no birth-and-death to be brought to an end.
> Wherefore the absolute tranquility (of *nirvana*) is this present moment. Though it is at this moment there is no limit to this moment and herein is eternal delight.

12

Apperception Itself is Reality

When the warrior Kosunoki Masashige in the fourteenth century Japan went to his Zen Master at the most momentous point in his life and career and asked him how he should conduct himself, the master is reported to have told him, literally, "cut off two heads, and let one sword stand cold against the sky", which is to be interpreted as "abandon relative dualism and interconnected polaric opposites, and remain firmly in the absolute unicity which is the source of all dualities." The "one sword" symbolizes the force of intuitive spontaneity which in its directness does not dichotomize itself like the intellect with its pros and cons — the one sword of reality which, like Chuang-Tza's famous dissecting knife, never wears out inspite of long years of use in cutting up the joints of selfish duality. The spontaneous wielding of this one sword of reality goes straight ahead without the least lingering or irresoluteness of the intellect.

By the one sword is meant the direction to transcend the subject/object opposition. In the seeing of the object by the subject, the mind "stops" with the isolation of the object instead of following its own nature of "flowing" from one object to another. In the case of swordsmanship, for instance, when the opponent makes a move to strike you, the mind "stops" when the eyes catch sight of this threatening move; but, instead of having any thoughts whatever of counter-attack thereby allowing the mind to stop, if you proceed towards the opponent you are in a position to turn the opponent's move against himself. This is the principle of judo self-defence. The principle is that the mind-intellect in its inherent dichotomy divides itself into subject/object whereas intuitive spontaneity keeps the mind whole and functioning in its natural fluidity. The perfect action takes no cognizance of any self or opponent or the conflict, because the whole action, the whole event becomes part of the action of totality and destiny. This working of the "mind-flow" as against "mind-stopping" is seen more effectively when watching someone being attacked by a number of people — then, there is no interval for the mind to stop, and the victim meets one foe after another almost continuously, and, more often than not, he is astonished that he has done so well and thanks his gods or the stars. What has been working is the intuitive spontaneity unweakened by the intellect intervening with conscious thought concerning the pros and cons of the situation, or the subject/object relationship.

When J. Krishnamurti talks of seeing or listening "in totality" what he means — as I understand it — is to let the mind flow in its natural way and then the seeing or listening is total. The botanist's way of looking at a tree is different from the infant's way of looking at it; the music critic's way of listening to a performance is different from the way an ordinary person with a musical ear would listen to it. Preconceived ideas prevent the totality of seeing or listening, and it is preconceived ideas based on their technical knowledge and mnemonic hoarding that deprive the botanist and the music critic or the art critic from their seeing or listening in totality. It is true, of course, that each serves a particular purpose in the framework of his own functioning, and to that extent he performs his job. Whether he would have performed his function in a more superior or effective way if his seeing and/or listening had been in totality, is a moot point.

One of the inevitable difficulties which one faces is the basic contradiction between effort and relaxation, to learn the technique and yet not to apply it. This contradiction has to be faced by the student in almost every game or sport. And even the student of Advaita philosophy cannot escape it. It is the experience of almost every student of every active physical sport that his earliest efforts were much better than his proficiency after he had had some lessons, and this experience is so frustrating that it has led many to abandon the game or sport altogether. The reason is simple : in the first innocence and ignorance of the niceties of the game, the student relies entirely on his intuitional reflexes and does not do too badly; but when the training starts he is taught how to handle his implement (the golf club or the tennis raquet or whatever), how to maintain his stance, where to concentrate his mind and various other technical suggestions; the result of all these training tricks is that they stop the natural fluidity of the mind and make the mind stop and enquire if what he is doing is right or wrong. Then gradually, depending upon the sincerity and persistence of the student — and, of course, his natural aptitude — the technique gets to be a habit and to that extent moves into the background, the mind gradually recovers its natural fluidity until the student becomes an adept. At the level of the adept, success or failure depends almost entirely on the extent to which the mind is not allowed to "stop" by an extraneous thought of success or failure; and the tragedy of the matter is that once the mind is thus preoccupied, it is almost impossible to get it back to its smooth, fluid working because the only way to empty a mind of a particular thought is only by filling it with another! And in this confusion, the opposing adept will have taken full advantage and raced ahead. It is undoubtedly because of this situation that Lord Krishna advises Arjuna to give up all thoughts of winning or losing, and to fight in the no-mind state: "You are entitled only to do your best, to put in your best effort; you have no right to the fruits of your effort (which would depend upon your preordained destiny)". It should, however, be clearly understood that this no-mind state is not the vacant mind of an idiot but the most alert mind in the heat of the deadly battle, undisturbed by any extraneous thought.

The mind is the content of consciousness, which latter is the objective sense of presence of the pure subjectivity of the Absolute; as such the mind is the totality of the functioning of manifestation as a whole. But when the ego, the sense of "me" as against the "other" in the subject/object relationship intrudes on the original mind, it becomes tainted, corrupted by this intrusion; and, thus becoming interested in one isolated object, it abandons its original totality or fluidity and stops or lingers on that object. This stopping of the mind in duality brings rigidity in the free flow of the mind, and then the intuitive spontaneity of the resulting action gets lost: you can swim in water but not in solid ice. The original or whole mind does not discriminate within the totality and has no affective choice to seek like the affected split-mind. What the problem boils down to is the question : How is it possible to keep one's mind in its original no-thought state of total fluidity when the very function of the mind is to think? How is it possible to make the mind a no-mind ? This problem comes up all the time in all areas whether it is participating in competitive sport or seeking spiritual advice from a Guru.

Visitors to Nisargadatta Maharaj used to find themselves confronted by this same mysterious dilemma. Maharaj would ask them to pay full attention to his words and would also add that words themselves have no significance; if someone referred to something he had said only the previous evening he was quite capable of saying that what he had said the previous evening was dead and gone, and that the visitor should put his question afresh. Then again, Maharaj would suddenly ask someone if he had understood what was said. If then the visitor said, "yes, I think so" and then proceeded to explain what he had understood, he would be interrupted at once with the words, "No, you have *not* understood." Once, as soon as Maharaj had explained a point at length with great patience, one of the visitors made the spontaneous gesture of slapping the ground hard with his hand. He was at once terribly embarrassed when he realized what he had done, but found Maharaj pointing a finger at him, his face beaming with gratification: there was no doubt that the visitor had indeed understood the point, and, more importantly KNEW it without the slightest doubt. In that understanding of the visitor which needed no confirmation there did not exist the triad of the one who thought he had understood, that which was supposed to have been understood, and the process of *intellectual* understanding.

There were other instances of apparent contradictions confronting the visitor. Maharaj would say great effort is necessary in the spiritual quest; and, perhaps within seconds, he would say : "you are only an appearance in someone's consciousness — how can an appearance make any effort? This contradiction is perhaps resolved by the *Doka* — a poem of Tao — whereby a renowned Japanese Samurai warrior had advised his sons of the secret of successful swordsmanship. The purport of the *Doka* was that it is not the technique as such but the spirit behind it which is of the essence: "now, it is dawning; open the screen and let the brilliant moonlight in." Perhaps the most intriguing contradiction concerning spiritual practices in regard to Nisargadatta Maharaj was the one about meditaton. To several visitors he would unequivocally advise the practice of meditation, and yet he would often say that meditation is not only useless from the point of view of liberation but that it could well be a definite obstacle and hindrance. Some-times when an explanation was sought, he would only smile and say that there was in fact no contradiction and ask the visitor to work it out for himself. At other times, he would give an explana-tion: meditation in the early stages is useful to purify the psyche; it is like a crutch but if you came to depend on it too much for the support it gave, the crutch would indeed become an obstacle for all time. For the physical and mental beneficial effects that meditation very often provided, many aspirants were unduly attracted to it — meditation then was not unlike a drug. And the ultimate apparent contradiction arose when Maharaj sometimes said that the seeker was wasting his time in his seeking because there was nothing to be sought: the seeker and the sought are one. In regard to all these apparent contradictions Maharaj had one unchanging piece of advice: "Never forget that there is no individual entity with autonomy of existence and independence of choice and action; there is nothing that you as an individual can understand or apprehend; there can only be understanding or apprehension *as such;* therefore, let there be listening to what I say, without any individual listener; *such* listening will lead to the kind of apperception which is itself liberation — liberation from the very concept of bondage, and liberation from the illusory individual.

To get back to the question of how to keep the mind in the thought-free state whilst executing any action — whether it is a golf shot, or a tennis stroke, or running, or putting the shot or any person-to-person contest — the essential point is that when the mind recoils or constricts or lingers by the centering of attention on any object or aim or target, it cannot function in uninhibited freedom and spontaneous fluidity that is its normal working, and obviously therefore the result is not likely to be anywhere near perfection. What needs to be done is to keep the mind away from the persons involved in the contest, away from the instrument and the technique that is being used, and to go into the action itself smoothly with the body and mind relieved of all tension: *it is the thought which is the tension.*

I would give two instances in which I was personally concerned. When I was once playing golf there was such thick early morning mist that I could not see even ten yards ahead. I teed the ball on the first tee, and when I took my position to hit the ball there was no question of thinking where the ball should go because there was nothing to be seen in the distance. I felt utterly relaxed and I just concentrated my attention on a smooth, easy swing. The result was astonishing — I found the ball sitting right in the middle of the fairway a considerable distance farther away than usual. I had swung at the ball without the disadvantage of a split-mind full of what I should do and what I should not do. At another time, I found the ball in a most inconvenient position near the green; I could not see the flag on the green and I could only guess the distance roughly; also all I could do was to guess the line of direction; nor could I decide how hard to hit the ball. The only thing was to relax, concentrate on the swing itself and *let go*, forgetting everything else. After executing the shot when I approached the green, I found the ball sitting six inches from the hole! Obviously the intuitive, spontaneous action of a natural, relaxed swing had done the trick, any conscious thought of technique being never in attendance: the distance, the direction, the strength of the shot were all intuitively judged and executed.

The same principle would seem to hold good when the concerned activity is one of mentation. During the last two to three years in the life of Nisargadatta Maharaj I had the privilege of translating his talks along with my good friend Saumitra Mullarpattan and occasionally one or two others.In the early stages, I used to find the work of translating rather taxing. Then suddenly one particular day I found myself thoroughly enjoying the exercise and at the end of it Mullarpattan said to me that I seemed to have been "in good form" that morning. When I asked him why he had had that impression, he said that I was extremely relaxed and I was using gestures (to make my points clearer) far more than I usually did. Only then did I realize that Maharaj's words did seem to mean so much more that morning that there was hardly any "separation" between his words in Marathi and the translated words in English - there seemed to be a natural spontaneous flow from Marathi to English without the mediacy or intrusion of the translating intellect. What is more, since that day this spontaneity in the translations never wavered at all, and it was gratifying to note that the visitors too were responding with equally spontaneous enthusiasm. I would also mention that it was very soon thereafter that the inspirational writing started, which was in due course to form the contents of *Pointers From Nisargadatta Maharaj.* *

Almost everyone at some time or the other has had the personal experience of the working of the whole mind when action takes place of its own accord almost in the emptiness of perfection when there is no thinking, no reflecting: "Victory is for him even ere the combat, who with no thought of himself abides in the no-mindness of the Great Origin." It is necessary to remember that the state of mind referred to as the no-mind state is not the mental

* Published by CHETANA (1982).

state of a zombie; it is not supposed to be a mental state without thoughts or feelings when you are in readiness for a physical or mental action. It is the state of mind which is free from the *disturbing or distracting* ideas or reflections or affections of any kind, a consciousness free of "me-and-the-other" concept, so that one's natural genius and instinctive faculties are free to function at their best in unison with one's knowledge of the technique.

This should explain the mystery of how to keep the mind — the natural function of which is to think — in a thoughtless state, or, how to make the winning effort without any effort. The secret would seem to be *to put the desire to win out of one's mind* and let one's natural aptitude and the acquired technique work out their own combined destiny. A similar explanation is to be found in regard to the contradictions which a spiritual seeker is often faced with. Ta-Chu Hui Hai, one of the Tang masters, when asked "what is great *nirvana*.", is supposed to have answered "Great *nirvana* is not to commit oneself to the Karma of birth-and-death"; and when further asked, "what is the Karma of birth-and-death"? the answer was "to wish for great *nirvana* is the Karma of birth and death! This would apparently seem to be utterly illogical, and yet it is very similar to what Nisargadatta Maharaj said about the seeker wasting his time in his seeking because there was nothing to be sought. The first answer of the Chinese Master that in order to attain *nirvana*, it is essential to transcend *samsara*, the karma of birth-and-death, is understandable. It is the second answer which puts one in quandary: how could the wish for *nirvana* itself be the bondage of birth-and-death? The answer lies in the word "wish" or "desire". It is the desire which is the cause of bondage, irrespective of whether the desire is for any material benefit or for liberation. It is only the apperception of "what-is", the apprehending of the unicity between the manifest and the unmanifest, of the non-being of any individual as a separate entity, which makes us realize our true nature and removes the misapprehension regarding bondage and liberation which are both mere concepts and therefore incapable of creating either bondage or liberation. All logic and interpretation is limited to the framework of the relative intellect and cannot reach the level of the intuitive potential of the Absolute.

An analysis of the phenomenon of volition or desire would reveal that the basis of desire is the ego — or the "me-concept" — thinking in terms of the future, and it is intellect which binds these three factors together: the desire (and the choice), the "me-concept" and the temporality in which all of them function. It

would be rather interesting to see how this analysis actually operates in actual life when considered from the aspects of (a) a game
like golf — the technique and the practice of it on the one hand
and the game in the actual operation of a match on the other; and
(b) the spiritual instruction from the Guru and its theoretical practice on the one hand and its actual use in everyday life on the
other.

In the game of golf, as in any other game or sport, technique
must naturally have considerable importance. In learning the technique, the significant consideration should be the mastering of the
technique for the sake of the game itself — for the love of the
game. This is very different from wanting to learn the technique in
order to defeat a particular person or to defeat "all comers" ; in the
former case the mind that would work is the whole mind undisturbed by any encroachments from the "me-concept" and its
ambition; and the love of the game will provide all the necessary
persistence and determination unhampered by the corroding
acidity of rivalry and competition. Love makes for naturalness and
fluidity whereas hate and ambition undoubtedly cause upheaval
and interruption. Secondly, listening to the professional teacher's
advice regarding the technique of the game of golf needs the sort
of concentration which relies on utter relaxation of the mind, uninhibited by any doubts in regard to its efficacy against imagined
rivals. If the listening is interrupted by various thoughts concerning the use of the technique, such listening would obviously not
yield effective results. If the listening is done with the relaxed
fluidity of the whole mind, without being eclipsed by the "me-
concept" and the relative thoughts, it will translate itself into action equally smoothly during the practice sessions. During a practice session it will be the ego wanting to make a perfect shot, and,
in order to do that, trying to remember the theoretical advice that
was given by the teacher. The result would be disastrous because
of the absence of the natural fluidity that would have come about
if the listening had been total, unhampered by the "me-concept"
or the ego. In other words, the really effective learning as well as
the practice is synonymous with the absence of the ego and its
desire and ambitions.

From the amount of chaos that the ego can create during a mere
practice session, it is easy to imagine the amount of damage it can
cause during the combat of an actual match. When a golfer finds
his ball in a rather difficult position, his mind is assailed by all
kinds of doubts and alternatives, and the necessity of making a
choice. Each golf club is designed with a particular purpose, depending on the height and length which the ball is supposed to

achieve; and, therefore the alternatives begin from the decision concerning which club to use and how hard to hit. Obviously to decide between alternatives is the function of the intellect, and the intellect needs an ego to function; the ego itself, being a bundle of desires, obviously cannot make a truly objective judgment regarding the choice or selection either about the particular club or about the way it is to be used. The desire and, innately allied to it the fear of failure, must inevitably colour both the choice and the execution of that choice. What actually happens is that the fear of failure makes the mind lose its fluidity because of the inhibition and rigidity induced in it, and this rigidity gets translated into the faulty physical execution of the shot. In other words, the ego desires and demands a successful shot the result of the shot being in the future, so that the execution of the shot in the present moment does not receive the necessary concentrated attention. If the ego on the other hand does not intrude in the consciousness, the golf club, the hands that hold the club, the body to which the arms are attached all act together (without conscious deliberation according to the technique supplied by the teacher) with a natural grace, fluidity and spontaneity unhampered by the ego — *all in the present moment*, indeed in that timeless moment when in fact there is no awareness of the ball or the striker of the ball. The same instinctive and intuitive activity is seen in the natural functioning of many animals which is truly as much of a natural wonder as is the manifestation of the universe itself (and, of course, the arising of consciousness and sentience), e.g., the spinning of its web by the spider or the wasp constructing its castle under the eaves.

Most of the near perfect actions or performances, and almost all the works of creativity happen in this state of egolessness, when the tenet "Thy Will be Done" is actually put into practice. It is in the absence of the ego, in the absence of intellectual and psychic affects, that the whole mind takes over the individual action as part of the total functioning and reaches near perfection. Intellect can only work in duality, in split-mind, dividing and discriminating, preferring and rejecting, choosing and deciding; and therefore its working necessarily falls short of the fluid spontaneity of intuitive action. When the sword is used with the intention of killing, it is the ego that does the killing; on the other hand, when the sword gets lifted under compulsion, without any desire to kill and gain something, the enemy turns himself into a victim and it is the sword and not the man that does the killing — the performance of the sword is one of perfection because it is not hampered by any intellectual or psychic affects: let thy will be done. In other words, when the mind is devoid of all thoughts, all emotions, all desires to win, the instrument — whether it is a sword or a golf club — almost assumes an independent existence, becomes a sort of an extension of the arms, a part of the body, and the man and the instrument together work as a unit and what they do becomes a part of the functioning, not of the ego but of the totality. The pulse of the man gets synchronized with the universal pulsating, the mind and the body-instrument combine in perfect unison; and the astonishing part of the whole thing is that while the per-former himself is almost unconscious of the performance — in the effective annihilation of the subject/object relationship — the watchers are very keenly aware that something extraordinary is happening, that the performance they are seeing is almost super-natural. Similar superb performances are sometimes witnessed when the actor or the singer happens to be in such a no-mind state of consciousness and is not aware of the performance until he comes back to earth at the end of it; or when the horse and rider move as one inseparable entity and break the course record.

The same facts would seem to apply to the technique and its application in the realm of spiritual search for one's true identity. Nisargadatta Maharaj repeatedly advised visitors to keep the "me-concept" out of the room together with all the other "luggage" when listening to him. "Do not" he would say, "hear with your ear but let the consciousness listen; do not let the mind struggle with the words, let consciousness absorb the true meaning behind the words that I want to convey." He would also urge them to remem-ber constantly that learning and knowledge are not necessary to get the understanding, the apprehension, the apperception of "what is". All knowledge as such is as much of a burden as ignor-ance, and therefore, Maharaj would repeatedly ask visitors to throw the words away and retain only the knowingness: words have the dangerous power of either confusing you or clinging to you and, either way, remaining a burden. We are already the noumenal Absolute and we do not need any relative knowledge. All that is necessary is to remove the covering of ignorance that has come upon our knowingness in order to let it shine in its original brilliance. What we are is knowledge, pure and pristine; we need no other knowledge — is a lamp necessary to see the very source of light that the sun is.? This covering — the Maya — that has come upon our original state of unicity is nothing other than volition or desire, wanting something different from what is — or is likely to be in future —, the desire for prosperity and security which the ego demands. All that is necessary is to realize the illusoriness of the ego and, by inference, the illusoriness of the demands of that ego. Such realization means in effect the end of

conceptualization and leads to the perfect fluidity of consciousness in its functioning as the totality of manifestion. When conceptualizing ends, the "me-concept" vanishes because the very
basis of conceptualizing is the "me", and with the disappearance
of the "me" the fullness of emptiness or the plenum of nothingness is revealed, which in its functioning means the spontaneity
that makes for perfection.

The logical question now arises : if it is the desire to change
"what is" that is the culprit which causes a disturbance in the
smooth and spontaneous working of the inner harmony and the
universal pulse, how is this desire to be eradicated? Even this
desire to eradicate desire is a form of desire — perhaps a negative
sort of desire but nonetheless a desire. The dilemma becomes
worse confounded when the answer is provided by a Guru like
Nisargadatta Maharaj with a counter question : Who has this
problem? The point is subtle but extremely important. It is the
illusory ego who is concerned with the desire, and it is also the ego
who wants to know how desire is to be eradicated! The actual
answer is simple enough and is contained in the problem itself. If
we analyse the problem, the following aspects emerge : (a) the
"me" who has the desire cannot exist without its interrelated
opposite in duality which is the "other", (b) the desire is a change
from "what is" now to something better in the future — again
duality of "bad and good" or "good and better" or "acceptable and
not acceptable"; (c) the desire is for something which can only
happen in the "future", and time as such is not a thing but only a
concept. What this means is that the illusory or *conceptual "me"*
wants a conceptual change in the conceptual future — *and this is all*
that "desire" is. How can desire — a mere concept — be got rid of?
The realization that the entire problem is merely a concept without
any substance is itself the solution. A mere intellectual understanding of this fact is not enough because intellect always has
questions. It is only intuition which is directly connected with
consciousness that has no questions because it deals with totality
and in totality there is no duality of "me" and the "other". The
total phenomenal manifestation is merely the objective expression
of the noumenal unmanifest. When the noumenal unmanifest is
extended in conceptual space-time, it becomes the phenomenal
manifestation of which every sentient being is an integral part,
and in which the noumenal absolute is immanent. It is only when
the individual separates himself through conceptualizing, from
the totality as a "me" in opposition to the "other", that he himself
creates problems and himself seeks solutions. Maharaj would repeatedly asseverate that "what is" is truly simple and that there is

nothing difficult or mysterious about it. The apparent difficulty which is made into a mysterious confusion by organized religion is merely a clouding, an obnubilation, a psycho-intellectual darkening or eclipse brought about by the ego. Indeed this eclipse is the ego, a phantom created by a "conditioned reflex" — call it Maya, if you like — which perversely and persistently draws our attention, like a trickster, away from "what is". It is the same ego which , by creating the desire to "win" against the "other" (and through that the fear of failure), interrupts and vitiates the free and fluid movement of the mind expressed through the body in any normal activity.

There is no such object as an ego. It is merely thought which expresses itself through the word; word is merely vocalized thought. The ego is just the *imaginary* objectivization of "I" brought about by conceptualizing. That is precisely the reason Nisargadatta Maharaj would repeatedly try to impress on his visitors that no amount of thinking or doing could get rid of the identification with the imaginary "self" as apart from the "other". The simple fact is that I AM, *but not as* "me" — and every one of us sentient beings can and must say the same thing. What is more, apart from I AM, there is no I as such. "What is" is the totality of the potential, the I AM — the absolute Presence — which is not aware of itself until the consciousness of presence arises on this potential like a ripple or a wave on an expanse of water, and concurrently objectivizes itself as the *Totality* of manifestation. To repeat, there is certainly no "me", the ego, which is merely an illusion; there is no "I" as an object: All there is, is I am — absolute, formless presence, total potentiality, pure subjectivity.. Ramana Maharshi called it not "I" (or by any name) but the throbbing "I — I". Once this is clear — that there just cannot be any "me" or "you", but mere "I — I" or "I AM" — then it should be equally clear that *it is sheer stupidity for a "me" (or a "you") to seek Reality as some object other than myself (because whatever one "seeks" must be something "other").* The implication of this conclusion stares us in the face: what the seeker seeks can be nothing other than the seeker himself — I AM as the absolute, formless, infinite, intemporal PRESENCE, the potentiality of the plenum, the noumenal source of all phenomenality.

Can we leave the matter at that? If we did, would we not have missed the one basic — and ultimate — ineluctable fact of the matter.? Is it not this: the deep apperception of the fact that the seeker is the sought — the fact of the circle being complete — is itself the end of the search for Reality? Indeed, *the apperception is itself the Reality* because there is no one to apperceive anything. It is in this sense that Nisargadatta Maharaj, when pestered with the question of what one should "do" in one's daily life, would say "you may do whatever you like", — a statement that was hard for a visitor to accept. Before giving such an answer, Maharaj would have explained that understanding is all and everything; when one knows what fire is, there is nothing to "do" in order to further understand what fire is. But the hardgrained conditioning would prevent the visitor from accepting the statement because he had not earlier, as Maharaj had urged, listened to him with his mind (consciousness) instead of his ears. The visitor would not give up his identification with a separate entity and it is as this separate individual that he has asked Maharaj how he should act in his daily life. When Maharaj had pronounced that understanding is all, he did so on the basis that the understanding had brought about the dis-identification with a separate identity. Once this dis-identification had taken place — and metanoesis had occurred — all actions would be intuitive and spontaneous as part of the totality of functioning, and living would be a sort of noumenal living; living exactly as before, but now without affective attachment, cheerfully accepting whatever life had to offer. The humour in Maharaj's statement, of course, was that even if the questioner continued to live as a separate individual, he could still do "whatever he liked" because whatever had to happen would continue to happen although the individual would unnecessarily accept the responsibility for the actions. The course of events — the functioning of manifestation — would not change because of the imagined volition of the phenomenal objects called human beings.

13

Karma — The Process of Causality

Nisargadatta Maharaj often expressed how difficult it was to explain to his visitors what he KNEW intuitively. For instance the inexorable causality — cause-effect-relationship — the average intelligent man could understand from his dualistic and limited viewpoint, but the mystic saw things with the noumenal, universal, all-embracing vision which cannot admit any viewpoints at all in it. Nor could the mystic's vision bear any close analysis as such with the result that there was always an almost unbridgeable gulf between what the average person in all sincerity, tried to understand and what he got from the mystic. And, of course, even if the average person announced that he was prepared to accept his own ignorance and would therefore accept what the man of science said, that did not take the mystic any further because the scientist had no more inkling of what the mystic was talking about than the man in the street. That was the position until comparatively recent times.

Now, science has come to the aid of the mystic. The sub-atomic physicist has come to the conclusion, after probing the behaviour of sub-atomic particles, known as quantum mechanics which puts the matter of causation completely in the background. The quantumn theory of Planck — the new "law" of Indeterminacy — replaces causality, and is now more or less accepted where the microcosmos is concerned, and it seems that there is really no reason why it should not apply to the macrocosmos because size must be taken to be as relative as anything else.

Until the quantum theory came along, certain "realistic" assumptions were taken for granted by all scientists, and it is these arbitrary assumptions which created an almost insurmountable barrier to the understanding of what the mystic knew intuitively. These assumptions were :
(a) there is a "real" world whose existence is independent of any observer;
(b) in this "real" world, any phenomena that is sensorially per-

ceptible must have a physical cause, and therefore valid conclusions could be drawn about cause and effect from consistent observations;
(c) physically separate objects and well-separated events must be
regarded as truly distinct. Thus if a shell is exploded and certain fragments spin off and have parted company, they cannot
thereafter influence one another.
    The quantum theory, whilst passing the supreme test of any
scientific theory that it "worked", had three very peculiar features
which irked and irritated many scientists of the day. They were :
(a) the theory does not predict unique outcomes but only states *probabilities*.
(b) to add insult to injury, as it were, it accepts "uncertainty not
    merely as an irritating headache but as something one must live
    with: the uncertainty is accepted as an intrinsic feature of the
    sub-atomic world;"
(c) it comes to the fantastic conclusion that the observer and the
    object he observes cannot always be considered as separate and
    distinct (which is what the mystic has always been saying).
    Even Einstein, whose "equations of relativity" were the basis of
the quantum mechanics, could not wholeheartedly accept the
principle of uncertainty and the transcending of objective reality.
As Descartes had earlier exclaimed that "God cannot deceive us",
Einstein repeatedly asserted that he just could not accept that
"God plays dice with the universe." Both laboured under metaphysical dogmas and could not grasp the idea of the divine spirit as
being at once transcendental to and immanent in the manifested
universe. Werner Heisenberg, on the other hand, averred that the
quantum theory excludes a totally objective description of nature
based on the premise of a physical world existing independently
    the human observer.
    The new vision of the universe thus gives up the long-
prevailing view of it from a materialistic viewpoint, and now
seems to approximate the Eastern vision of not a physical reality
but a metaphysical reality. The new formulations of physics in
ordinary language, devoid of the mathematical jargon, are trans-
logical and therefore seem more like the paradoxical aphorisms of
the Upanishads or the riddle-like Koans of Zen Budhism. For instance, Sir James Jeans describes the phenomenal universe as a cosmic sphere the inside of which would seem to be made of "empty
space welded to empty time".
    The debate, whether the "realist assumptions" which seemed
self-evident and apparently worked in the macro-world were in
fact true, was for several years on a more or less academic level. But
in the nineteen seventies the instruments for actual experiments

began to become available, and in 1980-81 an experiment took place at the University of Paris which may radically change man's view of the "reality" of the physical world. In this Paris experiment — exceptionally well-designed and scrupulously executed — two sub-atomic particles,emitted by an atom, flew apart not unlike the fragments of an exploded shell. According to what the "realists" held to be the commonsense view, the two sub-atomic particles, now apparently distinct and separate, should have had no influence at all on each other, but they did! The interpretation of this fact clearly meant that either a signal had passed between the two sub-atomic particles which travelled faster than the speed of light (Einstein's postulate was that nothing can travel faster than light), or, that the two particles, although apparently separate were really never distinct separate entities but had remained integral parts of a greater whole.

This new vision of the universe is based mainly on two essential elements which take modern science very close to the Eastern mystical in-seeing:

(I)   What were mutually exclusive opposites have had to be accepted as a pair of polaric, interrelated complementaries. In nuclear physics continuity exists along with discontinuity. All at once, particles are destructible and indestructible; energy and matter interchange; probability pattern makes it impossible to state specifically whether in a given place a particle exists or does not exist. Nuclear physics basically deals in potentials and tendencies. Eastern mystical literature is full of such apparent paradoxes, usually expressed in negative statements (neti, neti — not this, not this) trying to transcend the pairs of opposites.

Contemporary physics would seem to have arrived at the definite conclusion that no "event" in the universe is exclusively separate but that it is involved with almost every other event. The Mach Principle (of the physicist Ernst Mach) states that the inertia of a celestial body or system depends upon its reaction with all the rest of the universe. This was the principle which perhaps prompted the postulate of Einstein that the presence of matter and energy actually "curved" space-time. Compare this with the mystic's view of the whole universe as his objective body, a conceptual rather than a material construct mirrored in consciousness within, and without any outside support: in other words, a mere reflection, mind-stuff.

(II)   A most important implication in the postulations of the new physics — and the one which takes science even closer to the very basis of Advaita (non-duality) — is the bridging of the gap between the subject and the object, between the observer and the object observed. The mystic has always held that all there is, is a sort of relationship in which *there is know*-ING— the knower and the known being like the poles in a magnetic field, and not two separate opposing things — the knowingness (sentience) provided by Consciousness, the eternal one subject.

What the quantum theory says is that any division of any object — particle, atom or whatever — is purely a mental construct: it is a whole whose "parts" are sub-wholes in themselves, and those parts can be discovered only when the wholeness of the object is destroyed. For instance, the neutron does not "consist" of proton and electron; the proton and electron are "created" when the neutron is destroyed. Similarly, the universe as such is not "constituted" of the millions of its "parts" or objects like human beings or stars or whatever. It is only in the eyes of the apparent observer that the division takes place — a fact that has always been apprehended intuitively by the mystic. As Einstein has put it, in the new physics *the field is the only reality* and there is no place in it for both the field and the matter. Every thing event or event-thing exists only in relation to all others. And what is the substructure behind this field and its physical existence, or more appropriately, appearance? It is nothing other than Eddington's "mind-stuff" or the mystic's "consciousness". It is the totality of the potential in which the totality of the actual appears, in which particles are spontaneously produced and destroyed or reabsorbed, in which matter appears and disappears. It is the "void" (actually, the "plenum" or fullness) of the Upanishads or the Tao of Chan, which cannot be sensorially perceived but only intuitively apperceived — and therefore constitutes the ultimate impenetrable barrier between science and metaphysics.

With this development of the nuclear physics and the ineluctable conclusions to which it has arrived, the mystic can now tell the layman: you may not accept what I have to say because it is based on intuition and experience and not on sensorial perception, but surely you will accept the conclusions to which your scientist has arrived intellectually — you may not accept my beliefs based on intuitive experience but you will surely accept the conclusions of the scientist based on scientific analysis and laboratory experiments.

To come back to the question of causality to which the layman attaches so much importance, and which seems now to have been replaced by the "law" of indeterminacy, the essential point is that both are a matter of conceptualization and therefore, it would make little difference whether the process of manifestation is explained by a "law" based on the concept of causality or by one based on the concept of statistical probability. While cause-and-effect has been accepted for centuries and seems more acceptable because it appears obvious and observable in operation, the concept of indeterminacy or statistical probability is equally obvious from the viewpoint of the modern scientist and is certainly more in accordance with the mystical insight. The point, however, is that both are conceptual constructs invented to explain the mechanism of phenomenal manifestation, and therefore, have no significance outside the framework of phenomenality. No form of objectivization could possibly have any distinct nature of its own and, therefore, the object that is the observer and the object that is the observed are both "that which is looking" — Consciousness. The neo-physicist may not apperceive this fact but that is the conclusion which he has arrived at when he postulates that the observer is a definite factor within whatever experiment that is undertaken, and that the observer is really a "participant".

Nonetheless, an understanding of the mechanism of phenomenal manifestation would appear to have some significance from the point of view of the practical aspect of metaphysics.

A comparative study of indeterminacy and causality would show that the incidence of indeterminacy lives far more happily with metaphysical understanding than the more obvious incidence of causality. Any one factor could be taken for an analysis because all are interdependent, but perhaps the most substantial one would be the factor of the individual and his volition. If it is accepted that causality must necessarily exclude volition, it is much more so in indeterminacy. The very basis of the teaching of Nisargadatta Maharaj and almost all Masters is that no entity, as such, of an autonomous nature can exist and that identification with such an illusory entity is bondage. If this is accepted, cause-and-effect would be at once deprived of its most essential element in regard to events. Indeterminacy basically precludes any compromise of accepting the "self" as being subject to causation, a compromise which leads many seekers to be tempted into accepting dogmas based on causation, Karma and rebirth. It takes not a little courage of conviction — which the Guru's word provides — to eliminate volition and causation, the basis of both of which is the illusory entity or the ego.

KARMA — THE PROCESS OF CAUSALITY

It is identification with an illusory, imagined autonomous entity supposed to be born, to suffer, to die, that is the basis of the process of causality — Karma — leading to the concept of bondage and rebirth. Such identification arises because of "looking out" as from an imagined phenomenal centre, the "me" instead of the all-pervading noumenal centre "I" in which there is no room at all for "me".

It is necessary to understand this matter of identification very clearly. The identification that causes bondage is not an identification of noumenality with phenomenality as such, but an identification with *separated and discriminated* phenomena which entails the taking over of subjectivity by what is purely objective. Phenomenality as such is merely the objective expression of noumenality and is therefore integral in noumenality — the question of identification in this sense does not really arise. What creates the illusory ego-self (with its bondage) is the identification caused by the attribution of subjective function to the *separated* phenomenon, to the objectivization of a functional centre in each such phenomenon. It is this illusory ego-self that considers itself subject to casuality-Karma-rebirth. Identification with the illusory entity is bondage, disidentification provides the liberation — *both are conceptual.*

Nisargadatta Maharaj often said that in several kinds of mystical experience of the cosmic consciousness or universal consciousness, the difference between what is volitional and what is not volitional seems to vanish altogether so that what you expect is exactly what does happen. This feeling then could be interpreted either that everything is voluntary or that everything is involuntary the very notion of a difference being a relative concept and quite irrelevant otherwise. This absence of difference is in fact the principle of polarity inseparably binding together what appear to be irreparable opposites. Everything happens by itself on the principle of what Lao-Tzu calls "mutual arising"; when everyone knows beauty as beautiful, there is already ugliness; when everyone knows good as goodness, there is already evil.

Based on the analogy that every point on a sphere could be considered as the centre of the surface, every sentient being in the world could be seen as its centre, and so could every organ in every organism. As Chuang-Tza has vividly put it:

If there is no other, how could there be any I? If there is no I, who could be there to make any distinctions? This may be true, but what causes these varieties? It might seem that there would be a real Lord, but there is no indication of His existence. If we do believe that He exists, we do not see His form. He may have Reality but no form. The hundred parts of the human body, with its nine openings, and six viscera, all are functioning in their places. Which should one prefer? or like them equally? -or some more than others? Are they all servants? Is it that these servants are unable to control each other but need another as ruler — or do they become rulers and servants in turn? Is there any true ruler other than themselves?

It would seem that such a view of the universe vitiates the basic law of cause and effect. But it could very well be that the notion of causality is merely one way of looking at an event by connecting the various stages in which the event could be broken up, not as mere stages but as a chain of cause and effect; the only single event is in fact the spontaneous manifestation of the phenomenal universe. For instance, when a train comes out of a tunnel, we could as well say that the engine is the cause and the guard's compartment the effect. Lack of rain in an isolated community would mean ipso facto starvation, but it could be broken up into a cause and effect chain like lack of rain causes drought, drought causes famine and famine causes death. Then again, I win (or lose) money because I place a bet. Could it not be that I am destined to win (or lose) money and that is why I placed the bet? So, causation or destiny are merely descriptions of an event broken up analytically into convenient parts. Nisargadatta Maharaj urged his listeners not to chase the shadow of causation because in this Lila all events-things are interconnected.

We can only conclude that what exists is a unified field and the "multitude of things" are not different entities but merely differentiations or forms. As Jnaneshwar has put it so poetically in his Anubhavamrita, when Prakriti (manifested energy) found that her lord Purusha (the unmanifest Absolute) was without any form, she felt so ashamed that she clothed him in millions of forms which keep on changing every instant. To quote Chuang-Tza again,

> The knowledge of the ancients was perfect — so perfect that at first they did not know that there were things. This is the most perfect knowledge — nothing can be added. Next, they knew that there were things, but did not yet make distinction between them. Next, they did not yet pass judgments upon them. *When they proceeded to pass judgments, Tao was destroyed.*

14

Where God Abides

Where God abides, let us hasten,
There let us seek our restful haven;
To Him our weal and woe we must surrender;
It is He who will remove our hunger.
On him we shall rest our cares and fears;
for He is the ocean of bliss and cheer;
Abiding at His feet let us ever be found,
for are we not, says TUKA, His offspring beloved?

This is one of the simplest and most moving Abhangas of saint
Tukaram, perhaps the most beloved saint of Maharashtra, who
wrote in the mid-seventeenth century nearly five thousand
Abhangas, being the outpouring — spontaneous and sincere — of
a tortured soul entrapped in the ephemeral joys of this world and
the searing miseries which are inseparably bound with the fleeting pleasures. Elsewhere he says, "How much I have suffered, O
God. If all my suffering could be dropped on a hard stone, it would
break into pieces." He is conscious of his vices and sins: "in
body , speech and mind many evil acts have been done by me...
hatred, betrayal, arrogance, adultery, thoughtlessness, crooked-
ness, and many more are my defects; I have done many unjust and
unrighteous things...". He prays to God not to abandon him.
"Thou art an ocean of compassion", he says, and prays to Him for
direct guidance and not to make him dependent on false Gurus
because, he wails, he finds only arrogance in the houses of the
learned. Those who are well versed in the Vedas only quarrel with
one another, those who call themselves Gurus are found to have
no control over their minds and keep growling with anger. Tukaram started with the sincere belief that it was possible for him as an
individual to have a vision of God. He made every possible effort
and tried various means towards that end, but all to no avail. He
became more and more despondent, and at one stage came to
belive that Godhood was a meaningless and empty word, and
even abused God: "People in days gone by have known that Thou

art a liar, and now I know the truth of the remark". He went on to rant and rave : "The name that thou hast obtained in the world is empty .... I do not now consider that any God exists .... my faith in thy existence has made me lose all within and without". Finally, he concludes, "for me, God is dead .... I shall no longer speak of God, I shall not meditate on His name...Vainly have I followed Him, and seeking for Him all this time has been in vain." He ultimately decides to commit suicide and at last Tukaram's extreme agony bears fruit, and as in the case of many other mystics, the deep darkness is suddenly relieved by great self-illumination, and in one particular Abhanga he expresses the state of self-realization: "when I look at God's face, I am blessed with infinite ecstacy. My mind is fixed on this vision and my hands firmly grasp His feet, as all the accumulated agony suddenly vanishes and gives way to great bliss." He, however, realizes that all visions are mere appearances in consciousness and describes his highest experience, when all separation between God and devotee disappears totally: "I gave birth to myself and came out of my own womb .... Tuka looks both ways and sees Himself by himself... God is the giver and God is Himself the one who enjoys." The essence of *Bhakti* is transformed into pure Jnana! Nisargadatta Maharaj often gave this instance of Bhakti being transformed into Jnana.

In this particular Abhanga, Tukaram, having himself gone through the experience, echoes the sentiments of man, tortured and stultified by the utter failure of his volition and intellect to grasp the ultimate reality, the transcendent and immanent ground of all phenomenal manifestation. At the same time he also provides surrender as the only solution that is possible. It is necessary, however, to understand the full significance of the word "surrender"

If one examined one's own life, what does one find? Does not one find that one's life is in fact a shabby, shoddy, sorry affair — full of conflict and struggle, ambition and competition, sorrow and grief? Man realizes this state of affairs at odd intervals in the mad rush of the daily life and asks himself — and has been doing so from time immemorial — whether this is all that life means. Man *knows*, deep down and instinctively that there must be something beyond what one goes through in life, beyond what one sees as "life" with all its suffering and chaos and disorder, beyond the daily battle and the recurring wars, — something beyond the very concept of time, something beyond conceptuality itself, something untouched by any experience pleasant or otherwise, unchangeable, immutable, pure and sacred. Indeed he knows deep down that *it is there* because in odd moments it has descended upon him unasked and spontaneously made him one with the universal pulsing with its frightening stillness and silence — frightening because of its unfamiliar immensity and intensity that totally absorbs one's sense of individuality. Man, however, seeks this absolute reality as an individual, employing his intellect in his search, and then he finds that thought cannnot take him to the source: it cannot because that source which thought seeks is its own source. The result of this frustration is that *the concept* of God as the creator gets created. But it is not the solution to the problem because thought has created the problem and thought has also created the concept of God. Therefore, much as thought might try to brush it aside, the persistent, nagging question remains: If God created the universe, who created God? The very question is pregnant with a sense of blasphemy and guilt for the adult but the innocent infant at a certain age is not satisfied with any superficial answer with which the adult might try to fob him off. What has in fact happened is that man has conceptualized God in the *image of himself* attributing to it the noblest sentiments and qualities that he himself wants but lacks. To reach *that-which-Is* beyond God, intellect is powerless. That which is timeless cannot have any path leading to it because a path can lead only to something fixed and immobile whereas that-which-Is, the source of all thought, can only be the potential plenum throbbing with energy that is present everywhere and not at a single point. Thought is the result of memory and the cause of action. The chain is : action (experience) - knowledge - memory - thought - modified action (experience) - knowledge... In other words the entire chain is based on partial or divided knowledge because the entire experience happens to a "me" as opposed to the "other", and thus based on experience of a single suppositional entity. Nisargadatta Maharaj often stressed this particular point.

The very possibility that there must exist the divine Ground, totally apart from the God that is merely a concept, merely an invention of human thought, is difficult to comprehend. The wonderful Sufi story that illustrates this point admirably has been related earlier but could well be repeated here with advantage. A banquet is being given in honour of the king, all assembled guests are seated according to rank, and only one chair remains vacant awaiting the arrival of the king. At this point a ragged Sufi fakir walks in and sits in the chair reserved for the king. The chief minister is very upset, angrily approaches the fakir - and the following dialogue takes place :

c.m.- How dare you sit in that chair? Are you an important minister, even senior to me?

FAKIR: No, I am more than that.

C.M. - Are you the king?

FAKIR: No, I am more than that.

C.M.:- Are you the prophet?

FAKIR: No, I am more than that

C.M.:- Then, are you God?

FAKIR: No, I am more than that.

C.M.:- (Horrified) - How can you say that? More than God, there is nothing.

FAKIR: Yes, and I am that NOTHING, which is everything.

That there is something perennial and eternal which is substantial to all phenomenal manifestation and conceptualization - the immanent and transcendent Ground of all being — is to be found in the basis of all organized religions, but, as Maharaj used to say, unfortunately the myths, legends and rituals, the purpose of which was merely to make the understanding of this Ground easier, have lost their original significance with the result that organized religion has become a mere ritual of the worship of a symbol, whether it be the Christian icon or Hindu idol or a particular scriptural book of some other religion. Whether moulded by hand or through conceptualization, organized religion today is represented by a God who is an invention of man's thought and is given a form based on the relevant concept. The result — a most unfortunate one — of this development is a dichotomy between "religion" (a few minutes of inattentive "prayers" based on fear and hope) and actual living. We say we believe in religion and act most unreligiously;we say we believe in peace and prepare for war with deadlier and deadlier weapons. The consequence is competition, struggle, conflict, sorrow and grief.

It is against this background that Tukaram says : Where God abides let us hasten; there let us seek our restful haven.

It may be useful to digress a little and see the astonishing extent to which "god" as a concept has developed through the ages, the successive steps by which man came to frame the conception of a deity. It would appear that man first came to believe in many gods (polytheism) through primeval ancestorship — it would be more correct to say corpse-worship — and later came to believe in one single supreme omnipotent God (monotheism). The earliest method of disposing of the bodies of the dead was without doubt by burial. From the very earliest time of the neolithic age man buried his dead and continued to do so right up to the end of the neolithic culture, perhaps for the reason that he considered it necessary to preserve the dead because to him a dead man must have seemed one whose essential being had left him temporarily and might well return to the body at any time. The original love for the dead man which induced the relatives to keep the corpse at home, well-tended and cared-for, gradually turned into fear that the return of the dead — if not in the body that went into decay then in a less tangible double or spirit — would mean (for the surviving relatives) being harassed and plagued by the dead. It is to protect themselves against the vagrant tendencies of the dead that the surviving relatives started the practice of ancestor-worship, and as additional protection later invented the practice of cremating the dead. The conception of dead relatives or ancestors as the main known objects of worship is to be seen throughout the earlier phases of human evolution and survives undiluted or otherwise, to this day. For instance, ancestor worship continues to be the principal religion of the Chinese (overtly or covertly) and several other peoples even though there might have been the subsequent superimposition of other elements of a later religion. In fact, in the beginning it is seen that an exceptionally powerful and friendly ghost is regarded as a God because certain prosperity that has come to the family and the community is associated with the death of a particular individual. Indeed, the growth of a higher concept of Godhead is found to be closely related to the rise of chieftainship and kingship. A powerful king would certainly be regarded after his death as a god in course of time.

A god must have a temple and the origin of temples can be traced to the shed or hut erected over the grave ostensibly for the protection of the dead but more likely for the convenience of those who brought offerings for the dead. The temple however assumed gradually increasing architectural proportions and more intricately beautiful decorations commensurate with the growth in the size of the kingdoms and the spread of art in various forms, so as to impress upon the people the power and magnificence of the god who inhabited the temple. It is not surprising therefore that people soon forgot that the deities worshipped in such noble edificies were once humans like themselves with the same physical wants and mental passions. The earliest idols, representing the deities within the temples, were not images representing the dead persons but actual bodies, preserved according to the available technical knowledge. The actual bodies were soon to give way to various types of representative figures or idols. Indeed it is almost certain that the original images or sacred stones representing particular gods (or ghosts) lost their funereal distinctive origin by being gobbled up by subsequent more powerful deities. Apart from the evolution of the temple and the idol, what has given the supreme importance, power and dignity to the gods would seem to be the evolution of the priesthood since it is upon the importance and majesty of the gods whom they tended and worshipped that the importance of the priests themselves depended. The evolution of priesthood presents an astonishing spectacle. The temple attendants, originally employed for the purpose of tending to or caring for the supposed material requirements of the deity and the relevant sacred rites, grow into "priests" who alone know the habits and requirements of the presiding deity and the hidden signs of his pleasure and displeasure! They are thus gradually seen to acquire, as intermediaries between the deity and the worshipper, some of the sacredness of the deity himself. Indeed the priests in course of time lay down what soon develop into customs, rituals and "divine" traditions which only they can interpret and execute.

Where God abides let us hasten - When the saint says "where God abides" it would seem he does not refer to the god in the temple, although as an apostle of Bhakti (a personal relationship between God· and the devotee), Lord Vithala of Pandharpur (a town in Maharashtra) was his special deity, in whose temple Tukaram sang his devotional songs, the Abhangas. The saint exhorts his listeners in the Vithala temple itself to hasten where God abides, and it is clear that he does not mean that his listeners should hasten to the temple. In his singing he has lost his individuality and is obviously exhorting the listeners to hasten to *That* which *thou Art*, the source of all beingness. In another Abhanga, the saint sings, "wherever I go you are there with me." Nisargadatta Maharaj used to ask his visitors, "what is it without which you would not know that you are present here,indeed without which you would be only a dead body?". The answer, of course, is : Consciousness. In the absence of consciousness, as in deep sleep or under heavy sedation, there cannot be any existence of any kind because in the absence of sentience (an aspect of consciousness), none of the senses would work and the manifestation would not be sensed or cognized. Therefore, as Maharaj used to say, there is no power on earth that is greater than consciousness, the source of sentience and of all thought, and that, therefore, it is to consciousness that man must direct his appeal and prayers for all that he needs. In other words, where God abides let us hasten: Consciousness is where· God abides — indeed as Maharaj asseverated, consciousness IS GOD.

There let us seek our restful haven - The saint implies that it is only in consciousness itself that we shall find our restful haven. The immediate question to be investigated is : Who is to seek the peace and rest and from what is the rest to be sought? In other words, we must be clear about the relationship between consciousness and ourselves. Essentially, what does consciousness mean for the individual? The briefest answer would be that *Consciousness is the sense of presence*: the feeling of being alive and present, a conviction for which no one needs any confirmation from someone else. Consciousness is obviously formless, and a human being or any sentient being, although it may have a form, depends for its aliveness on the formless consciousness. The sense of presence — the knowledge of being alive — arises in consciousness which is in fact nothing but the mere thought "I am" as far as the individual is concerned. Therefore whatever arises in consciousness and appears as a thing or an object or a feeling or an event can only be *of the nature* of thought. Every individual is only an appearance in the consciousness of another individual and can have no substance or nature as such of his own. In other words, a human being is in fact only an image, an illusion which is a part of the total phenomenal manifestation, and whatever seems to happen to him as an event is only a part of the total functioning of this manifestation. It is for this reason that Nisargadatta Maharaj used to call the entire manifested universe (including, of course, all human beings) and its functioning "the child of a barren woman."

On this basis, let us proceed to consider who is seeking rest from what. It would seem that we as individuals seek rest from all struggle, conflict, fear, sorrow and grief — with an occasional sprinkling of pleasure — that represents life for us. What happens however is that inspite of a realization of this fact we continue to go on with it, suffering, grumbling , grabbing and hoping for a better tomorrow or at least a better chance in the next life. The whole situation is based on the concept of a permanent "me", different and separate from a permanent "you" and "him" — a separate permanent entity trying to survive in a difficult society against the onslaught of enemies, hoping for a better life in the time to come. What is this separate, independent, permanent entity that the mind clings to with such persistence and determination? When we examine the situation closely and thoroughly, especially in the perspective of the consciousness and the totality of phenomenal manifestation reflected therein, do we not find that the entity is the result of thought, of conceptualizing and objectifying, of accumulated and repeated conditioning through tradition that there is "something" in us which survives through time? The conditioning starts at home from parents and elders from the earliest moments of the dawn of intellect, then proceeds through the educational institutions and through organised religions and traditional religious texts that the human being is a separate entity who must strive with all his might to improve himself into a better individual not only in this life but in the lives yet to come. But if one goes into this matter very deeply with an open and enquiring mind, one cannot but come to the conclusion that the "me" which considers itself a separate, permanent, independent entity is nothing but the creation of thought, merely an objectivization of the mind which can exist only so long as consciousness exists. There is no "me" in deep sleep when consciousness holds itself temporarily in abeyance; how can it last when individual consciousness leaves the body permanently (when the body dies) and *merges* with the universal consciousness? When this fact is apperceived — the fact that we are all intrinsic part of the totality of manifestation that is the universal consciousness — then we abide with God and find our restful haven.

To him our weal and woe we must surrender — What Tukaram conveys in this line is a sort of extension of what he has said in the previous lines. Only an object can suffer. Only a "me" can suffer. But, as we have seen, the "me" is merely thought, an image in consciousness with which consciousness has identified itself as a separate entity. Like the "me-entity", the suffering and its opposite, both pleasure and pain, are what appear in consciousness and are of the nature of thought. This is easily verified and confirmed by the fact that when one thinks one is happy or unhappy, either feeling suddenly disappears when some other more powerful thought interferes and superimposes itself on the earlier feeling. It is therefore clear that both pleasure and pain that are usually thought of as happiness and unhappiness, are apparently experienced by what-we-are-not with which what-we-are has identified itself. What-we-are is the eternal subject and therefore cannot suffer; as such it cannot even know anything. We seem to suffer only because we have identified ourselves with a phenomenal object. We must understand very clearly what we really and truly ARE. *All there is* is the universal consciousness, which is what we all are in the phenomenal manifestation. When this universal or phenomenal consciousness objectifies itself as subject and object for the purpose of the phenomenal manifestation, it becomes identified with each sentient object and thus is created the concept of a separate "me" with supposed volition and choice of action: In this process of the creation of the "me"s we objectivize what is pure subjectivity and call it "we", and we call our thoughts and concepts our "mind". It is this "me-concept" or ego that experiences suffering and seeks the peace of liberation. In other words, what-we-are is sentience or the sense of presence, extended in space-time so that the phenomenal objects may be recognized; what-we-are-not is the individual being or object that is imagined to be suffering any experience, pleasant or otherwise. Then the question arises: What does Tukaram ask us to surrender? The saint asks us to surrender the mistaken identification with an illusory entity, the stifling sense of separation from the totality of manifestation. The surrender of such illusory identification would signify a sudden and enormous relief totally beyond intellectual comprehension. One enjoys bathing in salt water because it brings about a feeling lightness; when an obese person loses a substantial amount of weight, his immediate reaction is one of relief because a certain amount of burden has been relieved, but when he had it he did not feel the excess weight as a burden. We are so used to our identification with the body as a separate entity that we accept it as a normal condition and would not like to give it up. Phenomenal living with such entitification could thus well be an unconscious but nonetheless a heavy burden. Living through sequential time with its pains and losses, and the remorse and regrets of painful memories combined with the hopes and fears of the future could thus presumably constitute an unbelievably heavy load suffering that could be considered as negative merely because we have been unconsciously carrying it all the time. A total surrender of this phenomenal living through sequential time along with all its inherent burden is what the saint suggests. Why then should such a surrender of the entity appear to us as unthinkable and ludicrous? Because we are so enormously conditioned to think of ourselves as the phenomenal apparatus itself, and because we know and recognize happiness only as the opposite of unhappiness, and the perfect serenity that would result from the proposed surrender — and which is our normal state — is unknown to us as "me"s.

   It is he who will remove our hunger — The saint uses the word "hunger" here in a most expressive manner inasmuch as it encompasses a meaning far beyond the normal one of "need for food". It is used in the sense of "desire" generally, a desire not only for sensual gratification but a desire to change "what is" into what one thinks it should be, a desire to become what one is not. Indeed, the word "hunger" in the present context would include the desire even for spiritual enlightenment because the basis of any desire is volition on the part of the supposed entity. It is important to understand that the saint does not say that God will "fulfil" all our desires continuously as they arise, but that He will "remove" our desire (hunger). Removing desire presupposes the removing of the *cause of desire;* for removing the cause of desire, it is necessary to see how desire arises. There is no desire as such in the fact of perceiving and cognizing something; the appreciation of something beautiful is a perfectly natural sensation. It is only when thought interferes with this natural sensation that desire arises. In other words, perceiving something by itself does not cause desire — in the hiatus between the perception and the relevant thought there is no desire. It is thought that creates an image out of that sensation, an image that thought makes desirable because thought is based on memory. The desire that is thus born becomes also the cause of fear and frustration because thought combines desire with the possibility that desire may not be fulfilled. As Maharaj often pointed out, thought, desire and fear are all based on time or duration — they are not part of the present moment. All thought is spontaneous and any effort at controlling thought would only make matters worse. It is for this reason that the saint says that it is only He who will *remove* our desire, and He will do so — indeed, can do so — only when the "me" is surrendered to Him. This surrendering of the "me" happens naturally and spontaneously when the understanding dawns that the "me" has no nature of its own, that it is only a thought, a concept, an illusion. With the surrendering of the "me", the hunger (the desire) gets automatically annihilated because then there is no "me" to think and respond to external situations, and then thought does not interfere with the natural sensation of mere perception.

In what way does the understanding of our true nature remove desire? Understanding of our true nature comports an understanding of the nature of the relationship between the unmanifest noumenon and the phenomenal manifestation. The totality of the phenomenal manifestation is merely the objective expression of the subjective unmanifest — the duality is merely in the form of the manifested and the formlessness of the unmanifest, while there is a basic and essential unity between them. Indeed, they are not two at all. The totality of the manifestation and its functioning is the objective aspect of the subjective absolute, and depends on spacetime as the necessary conceptual condition for the manifested phenomenon to be cognized. All sentient objects (including human beings) are part of the total manifestation, the sentient beings the instruments for perceiving the objects as each object becomes the subject in the other's consciousness. In other words, sentient beings arise directly as phenomena *like all other phenomena*, but the apparent universe is made known to sentient beings indirectly through their sentience expressing itself by means of their cognitive faculties. The functioning of the manifestation — the events involving the various phenomena including the sentient beings — is, therefore, necessarily independent of the sentient beings who are merely instruments for perceiving the events which depend, for their happening, on the law of   causation. One event would be the effect of a cause, which in its turn would be the cause of another event. Therefore, the sentient beings are merely instruments for the course of events and, being objects like any other phenomena, could not possibly have the *subjective* authority and power to interfere and introduce a new element into the apparently inexorable chain of causation. In other words, the question of a sentient being to have a desire and the volition or the will to want something or become something, and to make efforts to achieve it, is an absurd notion. Volition or acts of will in order to achieve a desire on the part of an imaginary entity are not only illusory but can only be inevitably ineffectual. All that can happen is that the effect of the chain of causation ("Destiny") would cause an apparent feeling of fulfilment or pleasure if it is in accordance with one's desire or intention, and a sense of defeat or frustration or pain if it is not. One might add that events will take their course, and what causes the infamous Karma is not the event itself but the ineffectual psychic impulsion conceptualized as "hunger", "desire", "purpose", or "intention". Is not a *truly deep* undesrstanding of this fact capable of removing the illusory hunger?

In regard to the identification with a phenomenal object, the cause of all the misery and "bondage", it needs to be emphasized that such phenomenon has no essential nature of its own, and so the mere identification with one such object would not necessarily constitute bondage. Even a disidentified sage very often lives, like Nisargadatta Maharaj, as any other ordinary person. Although some pseudo-sages do use the affectation of referring to themselves in third person by their names to show that they are disidentified, most genuine sages like Ramana Maharshi and Maharaj, continue to use the personal pronoun "I" when they talk to other people even when they actually regard that "I" as "IT", for they obviously have no concern with what others might think of that "IT". The sage does not consider that phenomena have any volition at all and thus all his actions are spontaneous and phenomenally noumenal actions. What is responsible for the "Karma" and "bondage", and the conflict and misery in this relative life, is not mere identification with a particular body (which is clearly necessary to live as an intrinsic part of the total manifestation) but the *superimposed* concept of an independent and autonomous "me", or "self", or ego which causes *the separation from the rest*
Phenomenality as such is as much integral in noumenality as are

the waves in the ocean water; what causes the rift, the conflict, the misery is the discrimination, the fragmentation of phenomenality into separate components each assuming personal subjectivity as"me" *vis-a-vis* all others. This is the "original sin": a phenomenal object — the human being — assuming the subjectivity of the noumenal Absolute. When volition is abandoned or surrendered, mentation or mental activity by way of objectivizing lessens or ceases, and then this disidentification enables our noumenal centre to operate. Then, all action originates as direct, spontaneous and noumenal — as "God's will". To put it more accurately, God's will inevitably prevails, but what will cease is the misconception that it is our action; and we shall carry on not as the doers but as instruments for God's actions that we (as consciousness) merely witness without the interference of thought. Therefore, if we live without the misconception of any volition on the part of an illusory entity, how can there be any worries, and for whom? There will be realization that we do not live but that we "are lived."

On Him we shall rest our cares and fears.

For He is the Ocean of bliss and cheer:

What Tukaram is saying in these lines is not that we should retain our cares and fears, and continue to think about what we want and keep worrying and fearing that we may not get it — and, then appeal to God to grant our wishes because he is the only one powerful enough to do so. This would in effect mean the same thing as appealing to God to take our side in our war against others. What the saint means is that we should abandon conceptual thought and forget our anxiety altogether — on Him we shall rest our cares and fears — and surrender ourselves to Him in the faith that He knows best; our individual view would necessarily be a narrow and limited one which may not in the long run be in our own interests. Much as a parent would love to indulge a child, he would not give a bottle of poison to the child to play with inspite of all the fuss that the child might make. An excellent illustration of the limited view of the split-mind of an individual and the whole mind of the Jnani could perhaps be found in the fact that at a certain level of magnification the individual cells of an organism would appear to be engaged in a fierce and ruthless battle for individual survival, but if the organism were to be observed as a whole through a different level of magnification, it would be clearly noticed that what appeared as conflict at the lower level was indeed harmony at the higher level.

The sculpted figure of the Dancing Shiva — with its four arms and their gestures, so dynamic and yet so superbly balanced — very beautifully expresses the rhythm and unity of Life, personifying as it does the continuous and ceaseless flow of energy passing through infinitely different patterns merging into the totality of the phenomenal activity of the Brahman through the ceaselessly changing myriad manifestations in the phenomenal world.

When Tukaram says "on Him we shall rest our cares and fears", what he in fact tells us is that at any given moment, "what is" is an indisputable fact which could not have happened without God's knowledge and will, and if we wanted it changed because we thought it did not suit us, it would clearly indicate that we were not prepared to accept God's will. If we leave it to Him to do what He considered right and proper in the circumstances we shall be resting our cares and fears on Him who is the ocean of bliss and cheer. In other words, we accept the fact that the duck's short legs cannot be lengthened without discomfort to the duck just as the crane's legs cannot be shortened without hurting it. And in accepting this fact as right and proper, we accept our imperfections too as right and proper in the larger perspective. Such a wider vision automatically restrains our conceptualizing concerning our narrow cares and fears, and becomes conducive to a surrender to the totality of the manifestation and its functioning — not an abject surrender of our freedom but the elevating surrender of our pseudo-subjectivity as an entity which leads to the real freedom from cares and fears. In throwing the burden of the cares and fears on to Him, we throw away also the illusory individual — the ego — who had quite unnecessarily assumed the burden, so that not only the existing worries but the very problem of life simply ceases to exist. When conceptualization ceases, the concept of time — the conditioning of the past and the fears about the future — on which it is based also vanishes and we actually experience the present moment in which the whole world is Brahman, in which we see ourselves as mere units for perceiving the universal functioning and not as distinct and separate organisms with supposed independence of choice and action.

Conflict and, its inseparable other side, anxiety are inherent in the very nature of the intellect which distinguishes man from the animal. Any action through instinct is spontaneous and therefore has no room for thought or anxiety, but in any action based on intellect there is never any total assurance that the decision cannot be wrong, even apart from the imponderable factor. Action based on intellect causes to come into being the twin factors of anxiety/responsibility together with fear and hostility towards people and circumstances beyond our control, both being based on the illusory ego. In other words, conflict and anxiety — our cares and fears — are inseparably bound with the concept of the "me" against the

"other, and when Tukaram says "on Him we shall rest our cares
and fears", he expects us to understand that we must give up the
burden of the ego, the burden of the identification with a separate
entity that just does not exist other than as an illusory concept,
what Wittgenstein called "a little man within".
Abiding at his feet let us ever be found,
For are we not his offspring beloved.
How are we to give up this burden of the ego? Tukaram says, with
infinite innocence, let us ever be found abiding at His feet. These
two lovely lines bring out the inseparable bond between Bhakti
(devotion to God) and Knowledge. "Abiding at His feet" obviously means "surrender". To the Bhakta surrender is easily understood to mean "thy will be done". To the seeker of Knowledge
surrender would mean the understanding that the conceptual individual entity, being only an infinitesimal but nonetheless intrinsic part of the totality of manifestation, cannot possibly have
any independent existence with volition. At the same time the
understanding would include the fact that the entire phenomenal
manifestation, being the objective expression of That pure subjectivity, cannot be anything other than the supreme Absolute. In
other words, to both the Bhakta and the seeker of Knowledge,
"abiding at His feet" should mean the surrender of the identification with a separate entity, not by one someone to another someone (because that would at once imply the continuation of the
separation) but merely the witnessing of the dropping off of the
affliction of the ego and its desires — so that there is no longer any
separation between the devotee and his God, between the seeker
and what he is seeking.
    The question that would arise at this stage is : Assuming that
such surrender of the entity had been effected, how does one
conduct one's daily life in the world? How does one carry on one's
business and live one's life. The Chinese sage Huang-Po says : "If
you were to practice keeping your mind motionless at all times
with the object of not creating any thought, the result would be no
dualism, no dependence on others, and no attachment; if you
would allow all matters to take their own course throughout the
day as if you were too ill to bother, without the specific desire to
be known or unknown to others, with your mind like a block of
stone that mends no holes, then the universal law would deeply
impregnate your understanding. And, very soon you will find
yourself firmly unattached, and your reactions to phenomena
rapidly decreasing and your ceaseless flow of thoughts coming to
an end."
    In the state that follows the absence of conceptualizing and the

relevant fabrication of objects in the mind, all thought and all action assumes noumenal nature. With the understanding that all events are pre-determined parts of the totality of functioning, actions take place without any anxiety since all thought about success or failure of actions is absent. In other words, when the understanding that subject and object are one is clear and deeply entrenched in the psyche, all actions become spontaneous and natural without the taint of the dualism and separation between the self and the other. What is more, the purity and the naturalness of one's actions cannot but evoke a sympathetic response from others concerned even though they may not in fact be in their immediate interests. In other words, a deep understanding, working mysteriously, would make life less complicated and more pleasant.

An important point is that a clear understanding of "what is" does not make us shut out the phenomenal world as an illusion because then we would be making a false distinction between the real and the unreal, between the substance and the shadow, between the noumenon and the phenomenon. All there is is reality, and any illusion, any appearance, any shadow cannot but be a reflection of that very reality. To consider that the phenomenal universe, being an illusion, is other than reality would mean that we are making reality something less than the totality it is. The true understanding accepts the position that noumenality is at once both transcendent to and immanent in phenomenality, and, therefore, all distinctions are seen to be void. In other words, nothing is seen as acceptable or not acceptable, existing or not existing, with the result that dispassion is cultivated through the realization that neither the attractive nor the unattractive attributes of things have any absolute existence. And, most important, rivalry in the world becomes a game — a Lila — rather than a strife and conflict. In short, the immediate result of the deep understanding is that *man frees himself from the world and its ills and sufferings and chaos by seeing the absurdity of it.* He sees that what he had considered and labelled as desirable or undesirable, and based his ideals and aims in life on such illusory distinctions, merely constitute the diversity in the course of life which otherwise would have been an unbearable bore. An apperception of the basic meaninglessness of conventional values in terms of reality lifts man out of the apparent strife and conflict of life so that he now sees it as a game in which he must participate according to the rules but which he need not at all take seriously. How does this happen? The man who has, through the understanding of "what is", freed himself from conventional standards of judgment, considers it stupid either to accept the suffering that is imposed by those very standards, or at the same time to immerse himself in what are usually considered great joys. He does not in any literal sense withdraw and hide himself from the material world of people and events, for to do so would at once mean a confession of having passed a judgment upon the world based on the same conventional values. As Nisargadatta Maharaj would say, he continues to remain within society but refrains from acting out of the prevailing motives that make the ordinary man struggle for wealth, fame and security, the very same motives and intentions which create the karma for the individual. Cheerfully accepting whatever comes his way, without any judgment, as part of the totality of functioning, he remains within the underlying unity that encompasses man and nature in the totality that is the universe, and wanders through life enjoying all experiences without ever becoming attached — either positively to the delights or negatively to the sorrows — in any way.

Sant Tukaram puts all this so innocently by saying, "Abiding at His feet let us ever be found, for are we not His offspring beloved?" What this means in effect is that we are asked to surrender all our individual desires at His feet and live with the pure confidence that God as the parent of all living creatures could not possibly be doing anything that would not be in our *ultimate* interest although sometimes certain events may seem like suffering. Such a surrender in effect means the surrender of volition, whether the understanding is in terms of the separate entity being a mere illusion and therefore incapable of having any independent or autonomous existence, or whether the understanding takes the shape of relying on the kindness of God as the creator of all beings, who would always protect us in that capacity. With the surrender of the concept of an independent entity and its supposed volition, the very source of desires dries up and, simultaneously, the bondage which is inflicted by desires and the efforts to attain the objects of those desires, also gets annihilated. Thereafter what remains is a sense of total freedom because the very source and cause of the bondage has been demolished. It is necessary to clarify this point. It is not that thoughts and desires do not arise. The arising of thought-desire in the mind is as spontaneous and natural as the arising of waves on an expanse of water. It is the nature of the mind to produce thoughts-desires and any efforts to supress this natural phenomenon will not only be a failure but will intensify the trouble. What does happen after the dawning of the understanding is that *the thoughts-desires are not pursued;* they arise and when they are ignored without being followed up, they disappear. In other words, the understanding results in mere witnessing of the process of the arising and disappearing of the thoughts-desires without any involvement. And then gradually, the arising of the desires itself lessens both in its intensity as well as its frequency and to that extent increases the sense of peace and the feeling of contentment.

This problem of how to live at the lower level of everyday life with its continuous problems of decision-making and human relations when one's understanding of "what is" reaches the higher level is one which demands a successful answer. The problem specifically boils down to the question: Will not the understanding that the supposed entity is merely an illusory concept (and that as such it cannot have any kind of volition or independence of choice and action) upset and weaken the will to live life effectively? This problem is so persistent and is the cause of so much confusion and frustration that it needs to be dealt with in depth. The most important point in this matter is that *the problem does not exist for one who is firmly established in the understanding.* The obvious answer from Nisargadatta Maharaj to the seeker whom this problem pesters so persistently is, "establish yourself firmly in the understanding and see if there is any problem". But this answer would not satisfy him and it would be interpreted to mean that the question is not being met in a forthright manner. Let us then consider the matter in its various aspects--

(a) Let us see what Lao-Tzu has to say in the matter particularly because he did not deal with the principles of any philosophy but was essentially concerned with practical results. Lao Tzu wrote his Book TAO TE CHING (Pronounced Dao Dir Jing, meaning "The Classic of the Way and the Power") more than two thousand years ago, at a time of troubles when war led to more wars, treachery was answered by more treachery and as armies from different factions roamed all over the land and "thorns and brambles grew". He came to the firm conclusion, based not on any religious tenets but on firm, impeccable logic and actual experience, that "he who acts harms, he who grabs lets slip". What this means is that where human relations are concerned, force can only defeat itself because every action must produce a reaction, every challenge a corresponding response in a never ending cause-effect relationship. Every event or action that tends to alter the existing position produces a resistance. This applies to every object and every arrangement, and in all walks of life whether it is personal relations or business or politics. Even a stone resists crushing and, naturally, a living creature resists more actively and in more diverse ways. Hence the advice "let sleeping dogs lie." In the more rustic society snakes are known to live peacefully enough with human beings until they fear danger through interference. The fact about resistance is that so far as human beings and their organisations are concerned, resistance grows more and more articulate and effective unless, of course, it is totally destroyed beyond a certain point; and until that point is reached, resistance is highly reciprocal to any challenge and, therefore force would be definitely counter-productive. It is for this reason that we see in all human affairs a cyclical pattern. Mere passage of time cannot explain this pattern which is actually governed by the cause and effect relationship. This was one of the significant points in the Nisargadatta teaching.

It is generally considered that what human beings do is due to an act of volition on their part, an act that they choose to do. What really happens, however, is that living as such is conditioned so much by instinct, habit and what is considered at the time as the "in-thing" that one's way of life is essentially a series of reflexes and far removed from the deliberate and purposeful action that it is supposed to be. The truth is that "volition" can be no more than an illusory inference because there is no entity as such who could exercise such volition or will. All we find by way of volition is an impulse, an expression of the· "me-concept" that could by no stretch of imagination be considered powerful enough to affect either the relentless and inexorable chain of causation or the totality of the functioning of manifestation; all it can be is an integral element of one or the other.

I am tempted to narrate an incident that is apt in this regard concerning a bank executive I knew personally who was more than ordinarily endowed with a powerful ego and the concomitant sense of volition and personal effort and achievement. He had never realized that he had a job because there were customers whose needs had to be satisfied in order that the bank could prosper. He came to know one day that a customer, whom he had not only neglected but had often insulted and antagonized, had suddenly·come into a position where he could influence and direct considerable amount of business to any of the several banks with whom he had dealings. He knew fully well that he would lose this business if he himself did not approach this customer, and knew equally well that the customer would not accept his approach. He was in a difficult situation because he himself was not prepared to go to the customer in person and risk being insulted in turn. Finally, with great difficulty the public relations officer, an officer who was very popular and particularly liked by the concerned customer, was sent to call on the customer with a special invitation to visit the bank's executive. The PRO succeeded with considerable difficulty in persuading the influential customer. An appointment was fixed, and the P.R.O warned the haughty executive of the consequences if he failed to keep his temper in dealing with the customer this time. On the day of the appointment everything seemed to go well, the executive welcomed the customer with unusual warmth and unaccustomed humility and the P.R.O. with a sigh of relief went to arrange for refreshments. However, by the time he returned after a few minutes, he could hear angry voices inside the room, and almost immediately the customer came storming out of the room, threw an accusatory glare at the bemused P.R.O. and went away without uttering a single word. When the PRO went into the room he found the executive mopping perspiration off his face with his handkerchief. He motioned the PRO to a chair, and it was some time before he could compose himself and begin to talk. He was utterly dejected. Apparently everything had started well, the customer had appreciated the reformed attitude of the banker and was preparing to reciprocate his feelings, but at some indistinct moment, the banker said, inspite of all his prior good resolutions, he had found himself shouting at the customer (of course, *the customer* was a very difficult man!). Finally, in utter desolation, the bank executive confessed, "I really don't know how it happened - I certainly *did not intend* it to happen". How often we hear similar heart-rending pleas from people! Volition, then, would seem to be merely an illusory inference, a mere demonstrative expression on the part of an energized "me-concept" which resulted in frustration in this particular case, but which could easily have resulted in a false sense of achievement if the result had happened to be different. In other words, human beings—whatever they may think—do not live and exercise volition but are entirely "lived" as such. Could it not be that the importance of an individual life—and even the fact of living itself—has been overestimated and exaggerated? And then there is the notion of the "sacredness of life" (for all practical purposes presumably only human life!) when Nature itself exhibits the strongest possible tendency of treating "life" as purely incidental to the totality of manifestation which even the physicist today admits is "of the nature of thought". And the metaphysician says it all by saying "this, which is all that sentient beings are, itself is not."

(b) To get back to the question of the capacity of the man of understanding—or the devotee who chooses to ever abide at God's feet—to live a normal life in this world, we must first consider what is to be understood by the words "a normal life." Inordinate

ambition cannot make a normal life; nor could excessive aggressiveness be termed a trait that could make for a normal life. The
anxiety about the man of understanding being able to lead a normal daily life may then specifically be taken to refer to a sense of
balance in his relations to other human beings in the world, to his
ability to keep a job or run a business reasonably efficiently. If this
is clearly understood, much of the confusion would disappear. In
any case, the man with an excessively aggressive ambition would
not even be interested in either the understanding or the devotion! In regard to normal conduct and progress, whether at a job or
a business, understanding or devotion should prove to be a considerable help rather than a hindrance because the man of understanding will have naturally and unconsciously developed "virtues" like tolerance and patience which would certainly help his
human relations while the absence of conceptualizing or infructuous thinking about the success or failure would very definitely
bring about great improvement in the efficiency of his working
since he would not be wasting energy in useless worrying. Lao-
Tzu therefore calls this "soft" attitude (as opposed to the positive,
hard attitude of aggressive force) the most effective technique of
getting people to do what we want. Why? Because, he says, "To
yield is to be preserved whole ...Because the wise man does not
contend, no one can contend against him." He calls such action
actionless activity which succeeds by BEING rather than doing, by
ATTITUDE rather than an act, by COMPASSION rather than compulsion, by HUMILITY and TOLERANCE rather than force and
aggression. This is precisely what Nisargadatta Maharaj meant
when he said - "Once there is understanding, you may do what
you like." The basis of this technique of human relations is the
determining factor, the undeniable fact, that *people intuitively sense
our attitudes.* An insincere attitude will generally be seen through
just as quickly as an attitude of yielding that is based on fear and
insecurity. It is only the genuine attitude of compassion and
humility that is firmly based on the understanding that the good
and the bad, and all the traditional opposites, are polaric in relationship - and therefore totally avoids any judging, which would
evoke the appropriate response. Indeed, even when the man of
understanding uses force, it becomes transparently clear *through
his attitude* that force has been used as an unavoidable and regrett-
able necessity. This response to the genuine non-aggressive attitude (the essence of which is not to make the other person feel
inferior) of humility and compassion comes about because in man
there is an implicit intuition of concord and harmony in the functioning of the phenomenal manifestation of which man forms but

a part, inspite of the explicit display of discord and disharmony that he finds in life.

In this beautiful Abhanga which has been interpreted here, the saint places in perfect perspective the problem of living life naturally, spontaneously, noumenally. What we should understand by it could be summarized in terms based on the Nisargadatta teaching, as under :

The basic understanding is that all manifestation — including all human beings — is what *appears* in consciousness (HERE and NOW), and it transcends the concepts of space and time and therefore motion too; these concepts arise in sentient objects (including human beings) as a necessary condition in order that the manifestation and its functioning may be cognized. In the course of this process, consciousness, the Absolute potential, becomes identified with each sentient being as a supposed autonomous individual with freedom of choice and action; but in fact the sentient being continues to be nothing more than the phenomenal object that had arisen as part of the manifestation with no independent nature of its own. This ego, the result of the dualism of pseudo-subject and object, is the cause of the suffering in the world. It is this that the saint wants to be surrendered so that when the pseudo-subjectivity is given up the "me" is given up too, and then what remains is the eternal subject "I", along with the apparent manifested universe which in *its totality* is nothing other than the "I-subject", the manifestation is merely an illusory structure like a shadow that is "in-formed" by the I-subject and therefore not different.

If this understanding is well and truly entrenched in the mind, if the sentient being is very deeply convinced that as an *apparent* individual he does not live as an entity but is merely "being lived" in the dream-structure of this manifestation, his volition drops off naturally. In other words, independence and autonomy of the individual entity with its volition or choice of decision and action are seen for what they really are, i.e. utterly illusory. The sentient being who has realized that what he is is not an entity at all now understands that he cannot possibly be an individual subject of other sentient objects, and that, therefore, it is pointless to harbour any desires or intentions — all that he can do, or all that can happen, is the choiceless witnessing of the manifestation and its functioning through the psychosomatic apparatus. Indeed, the surrender of volition means accepting "God's will" because the surrender of volition truly means not only the absence of conscious doing but also the absence of deliberate not-doing.

Then there is the problem of control with which the ego and its supposed volition are intimately involved. Our entire life seems to be nothing but a wasted effort to control our natural responses and reactions to events. The basis of any control is the dualism of the one who controls and that which is controlled. We hardly ever bother to consider who this supposed controller is and what he is supposed to control. The controller is clearly the suppositional entity that intends to change "what-is" to suit what he thinks are his requirements; and the whole point is that this controller has no identity other than the concept created by thought, by the past and by memory. And what this ego-controller is trying to do is to control something that is also the product of thought. For instance, suppose one is angry about something. The immediate reaction is to suppress the anger or at least to rationalize it; but the fact of the matter is, as Maharaj repeatedly pointed out, that one is not separate from the anger (or any other emotion) because the one who tries to suppress anger and the anger itself are not two separate things but are both appearances or movements in consciousness - *the controller is the controlled.* Living life without control, however, does not mean indulging in whatever you crave for, since the whole point of living naturally without control is living non-volitionally, living without wanting anything consciously or not-wanting anything deliberately, living without mentation (reacting mentally), merely witnessing the events as in a dream-play without any involvement. Then, the mind becomes not vacant like that of the idiot but extraordinarily alert, with the brain recording only the facts necessary for practical purposes. Then, the mind becomes free of the usual constant chattering neither because of any conscious control nor due to any chemical action but easily and naturally through the mere understanding of "what-is". Then, the mind (which is the content of the personal or individual consciousness) becomes one with the impersonal or universal consciousness, and inspite of all the activity without, remains within in that silence which is not related to either time or space or sound which are all concerned only with the suppositional entity.

Against the background of the understanding we have thus arrived at, this lovely Abhanga of Tukaram could well be paraphrased as under:

Let us understand our true nature and abide therein. Such understanding would comport the necessity of surrendering our false identification with an illusory entity that is supposedly independent and autonomous. The surrender of this ego will remove all volitional desire that is the hunger. Then, thereafter all action will be spontaneous action without personal responsibility or guilt. Thus, in this abiding in our true nature will arrive perfect serenity.

Our true nature? The universal consciousness, of course, - the sense of Presence which prevails in each and every sentient being without any distinction or discrimination, not as an individual entity but the sense of Presence *as such*. It is to this universal consciousness that, in another significant Abhanga, the saint addresses as God and sings, "Wherever I go, you are my constant companion, leading me by the hand; and taking over all my responsibilities and worries you provide constant support for me."

15

O, Death Where is Thy Sting?

In order to understand the fascination which the phenomenon of death has exercised on man's mind since time immemorial, it is necessary to éxamine and understand the very structure of the human being. Before doing that, however, it might be rather interesting to go briefly into the matter of the concept of the "life of the dead", perhaps the earliest belief on which religion would seem to have its basis.

The belief in continued life, like all human concepts, has naturally been subject to various stages of evolution, imperceptibly sliding smoothly into one another; but it is possible to discern three main stages in the development of the concept of the continued existence of the dead. In the first or lowest stratum, the idea of death itself or the difference between life and death was not too clearly perceived; in the second stratum, while the phenomenon of death was accepted as a physical fact, it was not regarded as anything but temporary and therefore, the resurrection of the body was expected; it is only in the third stratum that death was regarded as the final end of the body, the survival being related to a separate somewhat airy, intangible entity called the soul.

In the first stratum, the primitive man intuitively felt his real immortality, and his way of life based on the low level of his intellect gave him the feeling that life was interminable; this feeling, of course, was strengthened by the fact that no man has a personal experience of death. Death, as a phenomenon, referred only to being killed by violence, natural or otherwise, like being drowned in a river in spate or being struck by lightning, or being killed and devoured by a wild animal. In other words, the idea of the inevitability of death could not be imagined. What is more, to the primitive man the occurrence of the intermittance of consciousness during sleep or during accidents or through being stunned, was a common enough experience. The savage was used to seeing his fellow men being rendered unconscious either by natural factors or through accidents or fights, and thereafter recovering their consciousness and their full vigour after a certain length of time. During such a period of unconsciousness, he naturally kept the bodies safe and looked after their physical needs and comfort. To the savage, therefore, any loss of consciousness was always temporary and the body of the injured man had in the meantime to be cared for.

The primitive psychology played a definite role in this attitude of the primitive man in regard to his wounded and injured friends and relatives. Quite early in the development of the human mind there must have been an intuitive feeling that apart from the tangible body, there has to be some invisible being which dwells within the physical body, which quits the body together with the breath when death occurs, and which, even when the body is alive, wanders away from the body when dreams occur. Therefore, the primitive man, from a very early date, regarded consciousness (or life, or soul) as something allied to the breath which could leave the body and return at certain times, in certain conditions. It is this intuitive realization, coupled with his own daily experience regarding himself and others, which became the basis of the primitive man's conception that the dead man was a man whose invisible soul had left the body but could quite possibly return to the body; and, therefore, the dead body had to be preserved — such a concept would naturally eventuate ultimately in mummyfication, particularly in the drier climates as in Peru and Egypt.

During the first stage, therefore, the attitude of the primitive man was clearly that of an affectionate regard for the dead, which expressed itself in the dead body being kept and tended at home — either in the cave or the hut or whatever — and food being kept beside the body. The first stage would seem to have gradually merged into the second stage which is that of burial in one form or another. The second stage, however, would appear to have gradually transformed the affection for the dead into a certain kind of fear of the dead, which began with the concept of the possible return of the body itself to pester the survivors and which later on gave place to the concept of the return in the form of a shadowy spirit or a ghost. The third stage sees the practice of burning the dead body, and it would seem that with this practice of burning the body arose the idea of immortality of the soul. This refined notion of immortality, however, became gradually acceptable even to the more modern European nations although they continued the practice of burying their dead and although their avowed belief continues to be the Resurrection. There seems to be no doubt that in most cases where a race now burns their dead — like the Hindus — the earlier practice was indeed to bury them. The Vedas clearly speak of burial as the usual mode of disposing of the dead body and it would appear even otherwise that burial was the practice in India till about B.C.1300. Then came cremation with the ashes being buried, and much later, came the practice of the ashes being thrown in some sacred river.

The early cremationists certainly hoped, by reducing to ashes the bodies of their dead and burying the ashes, to prevent the corpse from returning to the homes of the living; but they surely could not prevent the recurrence of the ghosts in the dreams of the living, nor could they stop the minds of the living from weaving fantacies regarding the ghost. In other words, while the resurrection of the body was out because burning utterly and irretrievably destroyed the body, what came in was the doctrine of the immortality of the soul; while the body was destroyed the spirit still survived, giving rise to ghost and revenants. The process of evolution of the concept of survival, however, seems to have continued on to a stage where the fire is conceived as the means of releasing the spirit from the bonds of the flesh, and the ghost gets liberated from the solitary life in the tomb to a world of shades and spirits. Indeed, ancestor-worship has, it would seem, played such a large part in the genesis of religious emotions that a systematic anaysis of the existing gods or divine personalities would reveal them to have been deified human beings long dead and gone. Sir Alfred Lyall has said somewhere, speaking of India in general, that the best-known minor provincial deities are usually persons of past generations "who have earned special promotion and brevet rank among disembodied ghosts.".

This very brief account of the development of the concept of death through the ages presents a perspective to consider the problem which the phenomenon of death presents to us today. To the primitive man, death was not really a problem because he would have been perplexed if he were to be presented with a truism that "all men are mortal". Life was to him a perpetual affair unless he was killed by a natural phenomenon or in battle either with his enemy or with a wild animal. Death becomes for the modern man a problem because he is stunned by the sudden "disappearance" of a loved one who is dead, and whose death brings home to him the undeniable fact that he himself would have to die one day. This poses for him the problem: my organism, the physical body will disappear, but what about the "me" who used to own the body and preside over its functions before breath and consciousness left the organism? The fact of the matter is that the problem is a problem because while on the one hand man sees himself as the presiding principle — the functioning element — in the physical organism manifested in space-time, what he does on the other hand is that instead of keeping this functioning element as the intemporal element, distinct from the physical apparatus, he personalizes it and conceives it as being endowed with a perpetual duration. In other words, as Nisargadatta Maharaj used to point out so very often, instead of correctly conceiving the self or the soul or the functioning element as intemporality itself, he conceives it incorrectly *as an entity* separate from the psychosomatic apparatus but nonetheless existing in space-time perpetuity whose end is pushed back into *an infinity within the temporal duration.* Thus arises the problem where do I go after death? In order to understand this problem in total clarity, it is necessary to examine the structure of the human being in totality, and not merely as a phenomenal manifestation, a physical appearance.

The Illusion Of Death

"Infinite dynamism" is how the totality of the cosmos could be described with tolerable accuracy, all phenomenal manifestation being the ceaseless play of the primordeal energy, wherein things appear and disappear, integrate and disintegrate continuously, but all within the eternal stability of the absolute intemporality. Indeed, the entire cosmos is an illusion appearing within the consciousness when it is in movement, an illusion which disappears and merges into consciousness when the energetic movement ceases and consciousness goes into its eternal state of rest. In its state of illusory movement, the cosmos presents a picture of innumerable phenomenal objects (which appear and disappear continuously) which form a holistic hierarchy from the initial hydrogen to the human being gifted with intellect — all together forming wholes of more and more complex, and more and more individualized organization, within the total hierarchy. While in perspective, this phenomenal hierarchy may present in its functioning a certain continuity, a closer view would reveal two definite quantum jumps, the first being the distinction between the inanimate and animate things (the presence of sentience), and the other consisting of the appearing of intellect (its manifest expression being the word) which differentiated between the sentient human beings and the other sentient animals. The important point in this analysis is that inspite of this *notional* distinction, the various phenomenal objects are not *basically* different: the animal (and the vegetable) are inanimate matter plus something more which makes them grow and live; man is both inanimate matter and animal matter plus something more by way of intellect.

Subject to this basic understanding that the two quantum jumps do not make for a complete break to establish totally different phenomenal objects, it is possible — and even necessary — to see how the three categories differ from one another in their respective functioning in the totality of the manifestation.

(a) *The inanimate object* is integrated by the use of certain materials in certain circumstances when it makes its appearance. This structure of the inanimate object enjoys a relative stability until it disintegrates either through the inherent radio activity or through outside influences. This disintegration is final and total in the sense that no corresponding reconstruction or reintegration takes place in it.

(b) The structure of a *sentient object* — the "living" thing — does not have the relative stability of the inanimate object. Unlike the inanimate object, it is not born once, to die once but is subject to and *depends on sustenance in order to remain alive*, and even when it receives sustenance, it disintegrates and integrates — dies and is reborn — continually until it disintegrates ultimately into what is known as death. Every living thing is a whole composed of various sub-wholes, individual cells which are in a continuous state of altering, disappearing and being replaced by new cells. In other words, the sentient object — the living thing — is an unstable equilibrium (as opposed to the relatively stable equilibrium of the inanimate object), being the combination of two opposing metabolisms, one of disintegration and the other of integration. In fact this polaric duality is the very basis of what is conceived as life, of the very appearance and existence of the universal manifestation. All phenomenal manifestation is the result of the balanced play of the interrelated polaric opposites—the integration and disintegration represented by the Vedantic Purusha-Prakriti, and the Chinese representation of Yang and Yin.

(c) The third category, differentiated by *the appearance of intellect* as manifested by the "word", is represented solely by the human beings. It is through intellect that man has evolved to the higher plane of general ideas — pure ideas, symbols — which go beyond the things symbolized by comprehending them. Not only does man perceive things like the sentient animal but *he is aware of that perception and is able to think about such perceptions.*

The jump between the inanimate objects and animals is denoted by the appearance of "life" and the will to live : The plant naturally turns towards the elements which provide its sustenance,i.e.light, air and water. This will to live, expressed in terms of special effort, is more clearly demonstrated by the animal in its struggle to preserve not only its own existence but that of the entity with which it has identified itself i.e. to family, its master etc. In other words, the animal, as notionally distinguished from the man, is concerned with, and represents, the primordial or cosmic aspect of integration while being unaware of the interrelated aspect of disintegration. It is not that the animal is not concerned with death as the manifestation of disintegration. In its efforts to preserve its existence, it fights disintegration but the point is that *the animal disintegrates inspite of itself* — the animal is concerned only with one aspect of the duality of existence i.e. integration or life. The absence of intellect prevents the animal from *thinking* about death — it can only be intuitively aware of the imminent danger to life. In other words, while consciousness — the universal or impersonal consciousness — does function within the animal (and thus makes him a sentient being like man), the animal cannot, in the absence of intellect, *perceive* the functioning of his individual or personal consciousness. The individual consciousness certainly functions in the animal as the "me" in opposition to the "other", and the animal consciously divides the other animate things in the outside world as friends and foes. But that is all — *the mind is not aware of this duality of feeling or emotion* because this consonance and dissonance, this affinity and antipathy, are intuitive and in-built; *it is the conditioned reflexes of the animal that regulate its behaviour and not reason or ratiocination.* The animal, therefore, does not have to face the kind of problems which oppress man and which are created by the operation of the intellect.

In answer to queries , and otherwise, Nisargadatta Maharaj always pointed out that it was the presence or absence of intellect which differentiated man from animal, though both were sentient beings. Although man, like the animal, does everything possible to preserve his existence, this is not man's true or primary objective. Man's will to live becomes, with the appearance of the intellect, not an end in itself as in the case of the animal, but the means to a totally different end i.e. "to be", as totally different from "to live". While the animal affectivity stopped at the reaction of his physical organism to the happenings in the outside world, human affectivity goes beyond the affinities and antipathies of the reactions of his physical organism, and *comprehends and evaluates these reactions*. The result of this comprehension and evaluation by the intellect of the consonances and dissonances of the reactions to the outside world is that man longs for the perfect or ideal harmony which he has only conceptualized but not actually experienced. This gap between the conceptualization and the actualization of absolute harmony or, what might be termed, true immortality is the perpetual problem from which man cannot free himself. Indeed this is man's "bondage" from which he seeks "liberation". The real cause of this gap is the fact that the intellect dangles before man this ideal of perfect harmony, but intellect itself can work only at the level of the animal affectivity, at the level of the "me" and the "other", at the level of the friend and foe, at the level of the acceptable and the unacceptable. In other words, conceptualization of the ideal state is based not on the actuality of the interrelated dual aspects of joy and suffering, but on the illusory aspect of unalloyed joy in this very phenomenal existence. What is more, man goes to the extent of imagining his joy and happiness as his normal and rightful state *in his existence as a phenomenal object*. All that man wants is to be integrated in a superior state, the culmination of which would be total bliss. *It is in these terms* that he would evolve and progress and strive to attain that superior state or heaven or whatever. Underlying such conceptualization is the basic fact that, instead of *being* the universal consciousness or the Absolute Principle (by whatever name called), man *endeavours to become something*. This endeavour to "become" is the result of a complete misconception by which man, instead of realizing that he is merely one object among "the ten thousand things" (as the Taoist says) representing the objective noumenon, considers himself as an independent, autonomous entity, the subject of all his objects. To put it differently, man has imbibed both the aspects of integration and disintegration (unlike the animal who has only integration in its make-up) because of the appearance of the intellect, but the unfortunate fact of the matter is that disintegration is not seen as an autonomous factor but merely as a step towards a better state: man wants the disintegration of an unacceptable state (in which there is a continuous struggle for integration or happiness) in order to attain the more acceptable state where there would be no need of disintegration. In a word, the "beingness" of Absolute Reality is confused with the "becoming" in the relative duality. Man is not prepared to give up the relative "me" so as to be the absolute "I". He wants the "me", a phenomenal object, to become the absolute subject. As Nisargadatta Maharaj said, it is like the case of a drowning man who is not prepared to let go of his heavy hoard of gold. Man is not prepared to accept death as the final disintegration of the object "me" so that he could be the eternal and only subject "I" — he wants and expects death as a temporary disintegration that would bring for the "me" unalloyed and perpetual joy and happiness.

When a man witnesses the death of another, what he sees is that the organism stops functioning, and because his intellect tells him — and his deep-rooted intuition convinces him — he *knows* that is the body that is dead and that he himself — the one who was there a hundred years ago and who will be there a hundred years hence — cannot die. He also knows that this one who survives the physical death does not have the form that he had when he lived. But he cannot envisage the possibility that *THAT which has always been eternally present does not need a form* in order to be present — visible or invisible, material or immaterial — because he cannot give up the idea of a separate entity as a "me". His instinct of eternal presence is indeed true but his intellect cannot give up its conditioned reflex to personalize that eternal principle. The result is that he sees the eternal principle as a "me", leaving the existing body on death but continuing to "exist" phenomenally somewhere else. Man finds it extraordinarily difficult to accept the total annihilation of the phenomenal object with which there is identification as a separate entity. Such identification persists beyond his concept of the death of the physical apparatus, expecting the "me" to exist in some other world. In other words, he cannot give up the idea of space-time representation for the "me", and he asks: where does one go after death? The problem and mystery of death is thus based firmly on the concept of a "me" (as opposed to the "other" or "not-me") who will some time or the other reach the point of departure called "death" which is known, and who will presumably go to a destination *in space-time* which is not known. In point of fact, death poses a problem which is not truly a problem at all because this problem is based on false and illusory conceptualization. There is truly no "me" at all to go anywhere. A deep understanding of this fact alone, as Maharaj used to say, would constitute enlightenment.

Why is there no "me" at all? All that the "me" is, is a manifestation, an appearance in consciousness, which totally disappears in deep sleep when consciousness holds itself in abeyance. All the "me"s are part of the total manifestation which is the objective expression of the subject "I". Once this is clearly apprehended, the problem is seen in all its falseness and absurdity — it is something created by the mind and is meaningless and totally misconceived from the point of Reality. Since what I am is the subjective, Abso-lute Reality, the question as to what happens to an appearance in consciousness (which is all that a "me" can be as a phenomenal object) when it disappears (dies) is ridiculous because any hap-pening can only be in relative duality, and what I am — what we all are in Reality — is Intemporality. Seeking stability and perma-nence of BEING in the state of relativity (the very basis of which is incessant movement) is what the problem amounts to, and death is part of the series of movements (which began with birth), the last change which marks the disappearance of one phenomenal object among millions.

Considered in this manner, the problem does seem indeed absurd, but the fact remains that it is a very "real" problem. Why does the problem arise at all? That is the question. The answer is that it is our memory which plays a trick by giving events a sense of continuity, a beginning and an end, the appearance and dis-appearance of a phenomenal object. This illusion of continuity brings about the illusion of changes happening to something or someone that seems permanent. We know that changes keep on happening to everyone from birth onwards during the process of "growing". All the cells composing a body are in the continuous process of dying and being replaced — the process of disintegra-tion and integration — and in this process the new cells group themselves in the same old plan; *the re-grouping of cells in the same plan is what gives the sense of continuity* and the illusory impression of permanence underneath all the changes. Every tree in the forest will have died and been replaced over a period of time, but the forest will continue to be regarded as the same forest; the water in the river keeps flowing all the time every moment, and yet the river continues to be regarded as the same river.

The "reality" and the "permanence" of an object that one im-agines until that object dies or is annihilated — the basic perma-nence within the apparent impermanence of changes — is entirely illusory. The "reality" (and the basic sense of permanence that goes with this reality) of any object — as near as a chair or as distant as a star, whether animate or inanimate — is nothing but an image in mind which is the content of consciousness. An object is "sensed" or "perceived" in mind because of an impression which gathers body and form by unimaginably quick repetitions. Each repetition is a separate quanta and a series of such quanta constitutes what is known as "time". Thus what we imagine as the reality of an object is nothing but a continuous series of impressions in a succession of quanta which we consider as duration in which "changes" take place. It should be clear, therefore, that integration and disintegration takes place so quickly that *we are in fact dying all the time,* that both the reality and the permanence (the survival of which is the basis of man's problem of what happens after death) are both totally illusory, and finally, that all phenomenal manifestation is "mind-stuff".

It is now possible to arrive at the root of the problem as such. One can only have a concept of what happens in deep sleep. One can witness the approach of sleep till the very last moment but one cannot actually have the knowledge of deep sleep; it is only someone else who might time the very moment when one actually fell asleep. It is only when one is awake again that one can say one had good sleep. So it is with death: one can see only someone else's death. This is the root of the problem inasmuch as the problem is purely conceptual, entirely imaginary and illusory. It is only the illusory ego, the "me" who is concerned with the problem of death. As Nisargadatta Maharaj used to put it I do not know either of any birth or of any death so far as I am concerned. The knowledge of a "me" arose only when two persons stated to me that they were my parents, that I was their son, and that a particular name was my name. What happens when I "die"? I shall obviously be back where I was before I was "born", back where the sound goes after it disappears. Death is an event whereby the body disappears in one way or another — buried or cremated — and the breath in the body ceases and mingles with the air outside, and consciousness which had trapped itself within a body (and had identified itself with it) is released and becomes the universal consciousness like a drop of rain water falling in the river. A form that had appeared in the consciousness and perceived by the mind has disappeared. Who is dead? What is all the fuss about?

Two incidents concerning the Chinese sage Chuang-Tzu would put the matter in perspective:

(i) A friend of the sage went to visit him in order to offer his condolences on the death of his wife, and found him sitting with his legs spread out, pounding on an inverted tub and singing lustily. When he expressed his displeasure at this unseemly conduct, Chuang Tzu said "when my wife died, do you think I did not grieve like anyone else? Then I looked back to her beginning and the time before she was born; not only before she was born, but the time before she had a body, not only the time before she had a body, but the time before she had a spirit. In the midst of the confused jumble of mystery and wonder there was a change and she had a spirit; a second change and she had a body; another change and she was born. Now there has been a further change and she is dead. It is exactly like the progression of the seasons - spring, summer, autumn, winter".

(ii) Writing on the death of his Master, Lao-Tzu, Chuang-Tzu says: The Master came because it was time for him to come. He left because he followed the natural flow of events. Be content with each moment of eternity and be willing to follow the flow. Then there will be no cause for joy or grief. In the old days this was called freedom from bondage. The wood is consumed but the fire burns on, and we do not know when it will come to an end.

Our linear type of thinking includes the grammatical convention that a transitive verb like "know" must have a subject, and a predicate; there cannot be "knowing" without someone who knows and something to be known. Our identification with this convention is so powerful that we cannot grasp the fact that there can be "knowing" or "understanding" as such without the knower and the thing known. This inability to put down the ghost of the individual entity — a creation of Maya — shows the extent to which we let conventions and concepts rule our lives. This is indeed the basis of the obsession "what will happen to me when I die?" 'The answer which Nisargadatta Maharaj gave to such a query was, "you will be precisely what you were a hundred years ago". The question is as misconceived as the question what happens to my lap when I stand up, or to my fist when I open my hand. If nothing else, let us hope that our mental conditioning would be weakened a little by remembering the summary of Buddha's teaching in the "VISHUDDHIMAGGA"

There is suffering, but none who suffer,
There is the event, but no doer thereof
There is Nirvana, but no one seeking it,
There is the path, but none to travel it.

What Is This Thing Called Death (And Life)?

The only certain thing in life is death — and death is the end of everything. This was the perspective in which death was viewed in the West until the early 1970s: death meant the end of everything, so what is there to think about, except perhaps that one must make the best of one's opportunities in this life to achieve whatever it is that one wanted to achieve. The basic view in the East, by and large, was different: life and death have, since time immemorial, been viewed not as separate events but as a series of connected events in the flow of time. In the 1970s, there was a sudden explosion of interest in the West about the phenomenon of death and the process of dying, mainly because of a series of studies made by several psychiatrists, physicians and scientists concerning the process of death. These "near-death" studies have focussed the attention of the Western man on the nature and significance of the phenomenon of death, and have thus brought the East and the West together in regard to the question of individual survival after death. The most important point, however, that has been ignored in most of these near-death studies is the fact that *all near-death experiences are only movements in consciousness,* and can only be of the *nature* of dreaming, and therefore conceptual and illusory. Near-death experiences can happen only to the ego, and it just cannot be denied that the ego has no real existence; the ego is purely a concept, an illusion, and it is only when the ego is totally annihilated that real beingness comes into being. BEING is cognized as "That" which, by its very nature, can never be non-being. In most cases, the interest in this subject is not to know the process as such and the principle behind the phenomenon of death, but to find the key to survival, the survival of the individual entity, the key to achieving the security that will provide such survival the immortality of the individual personality. In this incessant search the basic question that is forgotten is: Who (or what) is this individual entity that is afraid of insecurity? The key to the problem (and the search) is the deepest possible understanding that no individual as such can pull himself out of the perennial stream of life, that he is an inseparable part of the whole manifestation, and that death and life are the inseparable and interrelated duality of an essential whole. And it really is a truism that such deep understanding cannot come out of any intellectual comprehension but only out of a totally different dimension. Intellection is part of phenomenality and the required dimension must be other than phenomenal, that is to say, it must be noumenal. In other words, the individual comprehension must lose itself and merge into noumenal apprehension or apperception in which the individual no longer exists as such and the ego is annihilated

Man wants to know the meaning and significance of life and death. The beautiful flower that blooms in the wilderness for a brief period of time is as much a part of the manifested universe as is man. The flower is not concerned with the meaning of its existence, nor is the wild beast in the jungle worried about the meaning of life and death, although it is as much a sentient being as is man. Meaning is clearly not something connected with things themselves; it is a function of the mind, of the intellect, and therefore different persons find different meanings in the same things, and the same people find in the same things different meanings at different times. In other words, meaning is merely the interpretation of the cognized experience of a particular person at a particular time and place, and consequently liable to considerable range of variation. Meaning is sought, therefore, by the illusory ego regarding an objective experience in space-time which is itself merely a concept.

When existence is accepted and apperceived as an *impersonal* sense of being alive and present HERE-AND-NOW, the concept of space-time disappears, the individual with his mind gets annihilated, all seeking becomes irrelevant, and all that remains is IMPERSONAL CONSCIOUSNESS, which is our true nature as the imperishable birthless (and therefore deathless) infinity and intemporality - the purely subjective "I". The only way such apperception can arise is through the acceptance by the mind-intellect of its limitation — mind cannot locate the source of mind — so that the mind-intellect gives up its search for meanings and totally surrenders itself. Then, the mind becomes a vacant, fasting mind, and lays itself open to and welcomes the arising of that intuitive apprehension which may be called apperception. Such apperception cannot be "achieved" for the simple reason that in such efforts it would necessarily be the individual mind that is concerned, and the individual mind is a split-mind divided into subject/object, separated into the "self" and the "other". Indeed, it is only when this split-mind surrenders itself and merges into the whole mind that apperception can *happen*. It is beyond the capacity of one individual wave to understand its true nature; it is only when it subsides, surrenders and merges into the ocean that it is the ocean.

As Nisargadatta Mahàràj was never tired of reminding his visitors, the individual mind — the ego — naturally fears the very concept of the inevitability of death because it means its own annihilation. This fear takes various forms : the ego may decide that life is short and transient and therefore one must make the most of it by way of wine, sex and song; or it may decide on the acceptance of a partial annihilation by "achieving" so much of this life that he will be immortal by way of fame for generations to come, perhaps for ever. And, yet, deep down, man always knows with intuitive conviction that he really is immortal and it is for this reason that he is always seeking — consciously or unconsciously — his true nature. And such search is bound to be futile until there is realisation that it is the illusory, fictitious ego that is seeking its own source; but the ego — the splint-mind — cannot find the answer until he gives himself up in total surrender and sacrifices himself; the mind cannot transcend mind, the eye can see everything except itself.

Perhaps the most important and the most significant account of the experience of death is that of Ramana Maharshi, the sage of Arunachala. When only a young healthy lad of only seventeen, he was one day suddenly overwhelmed by a sudden and oppressive fear of death for no apparent reason. He just had the conviction that he was going to die. This conviction was followed by an equally powerful conviction that it was something that he had to find an answer for himself — then and there; and therefore it did not even occur to him that he might go to a doctor, or at least speak to someone in the house. The recoil of the fear of death drove his mind inwards to concentrate itself on just one thought: now that death is here, what exactly happens? What is it that dies? And this thought was almost simultaneously replaced by another equally powerful thought-conviction: It is only the body that dies. Then, he dramatized the process of the phenomenon of death: he lay with his limbs stretched out stiff and unmoving, and concentrated on the thought that the body was dead, and that the dead body would be carried to the burning ground and burnt and reduced to ashes — totally destroyed. He could actually perceive the whole process,and such perceiving brought about the sudden and immediate apperception that he was the animating consciousness which transcended the body. Such spontaneous apperception was totally outside the dimension of thinking and conceiving. It was an intuitive conviction which did not depend on thought, reason or logic. What had remained totally separate from the body, transcending it altogether,was the timeless,spaceless beingness — what the Maharshi subsequently called "I-I". From that moment onward, fear of death vanished altogether from young Ramana, and the "I" (not the ego -"me") remained focussed on itself, unbroken from then on.

The significant point in this narrative of an authentic occurrence is the attitude of young Ramana — the attitude of an unconditional acceptance of the inevitable event of death, a total surrender to what was happening without the least resistance or recoil to what was happening, only an awareness of — the witnessing of — the occurrence, the ending of what is called living, without argument, without tension.

Such an attitude of utter self-surrender to a perfectly natural happening should have the incidental advantage regarding the actual process of death inasmuch as the inherent relaxation in such an attitude would make the death-process that much easier and more bearable physically, instead of the tension inherent in the attitude of resistance and recoil that would make the process that much more difficult and more painful. An attitude of relaxed cooperation with what is happening (and cannot be avoided) can only be the result of a deep understanding of one's true nature. It is only the conviction that we are the timeless, spaceless noumenon and not the temporal and finite appearance that this body is, that would make such an attitude possible. The knowledge of our true nature would disidentify us from our bodies and would enable us to witness, with perhaps a certain amount of wondrous curiosity, the actual death-process — the disappearance of what had appeared as a phenomenon in consciousness — without any tension or involvement.

The near-death reports of several persons that have been recorded, which bear a certain amount of similarity, are mistakenly considered to be reports of what happens after death. Such experiences, never mind how similar, how consoling and appealing, are nevertheless only movements in consciousness experienced by the ego, and therefore *experiences before and not after death.* Such experiences are in fact only hallucinations arising from the stimulation of certain centres of the brain *during, but before the completion of, the death process.* It would be just as well to remember that the mystical experiences of most Yogis that are recorded are of the same nature. It is for this reason that Nisargadatta Maharaj attached little significance to Yogic experiences. He used to say "you may remain in Samadhi for a thousand years, but when you come back to consciousness, you would be exactly where you were when you went into Samadhi — that is, without knowledge of your true nature". Man's fascination with occult matters and the reports about near-death experiences is a measure of his identification with the body-mind *as a separate entity* with autonomy and independence of volition. Man is concerned with the security and continuity of his own separate entity, and is afraid of the very idea of death as a finality, because it means the surrender of his separateness as an individual entity. This is really a great pity — a huge joke as Maharaj used to say — because by giving up his miserable individuality man not only gives up the miseries and tribulations that are attached to his individuality, but *becomes not a part of the totality but the totality itself.*

It is important to understand that whilst the nature of the phenomena of sleep, *Samadhi* and death may be different in each case, the nature of *the surrendering* itself is not different inasmuch as when sleep is imminent and almost as inevitable as death, one welcomes sleep (and indeed would give almost anything not to be prevented from falling asleep when sleep is needed) and happily surrenders all physical consciousness and individual identity. Therefore, while the surrender to sleep has essentially a physical base, and the surrender to Samadhi has a psychic base, the surrender to death and, more importantly, the surrender to universal life is essentially a matter of attitude resulting from an intuitive and deep understanding of the inter-related phenomena of life and death. When there is the apperception of the fact that the human being is an integral part of the totality of manifestation and thus a mere appearance in consciousness like all manifestation, the sense of being an autonomous separate entity disappears altogether into a spontaneous surrender to the Totality, both in life and in death. The surrendering of the indentification with the body — the psychosomatic apparatus — could perhaps be "achieved" volitionally through practice and determination, and as in the practice of Samadhi, a sense of energy and sublimity (including certain experiences) attained thereby. It must, however, be remembered that such achievement is without the firm base of intuitive conviction of one's true nature, and therefore cannot but be of a transient and superficial nature. True surrender to the Totality — in life as in death — means not only the mere surrender of one's identification with a body (but retaining the identification with a separate entity) but the giving up of the identification with the body *as a separate entity*, which is the very essence of true surrender, and which cannot be "achieved" by any disciplinary practices, however lofty they may be. All disciplinary practices are necessarily initiated by the ego in order to achieve something, and any supposed success in such efforts can only strengthen the ego. In the starkly realistic work called Ashtavakra Gita, in one significant verse, Ashtavakra tells king Janaka, "your only bondage is that you indulge in the practice of Samadhi."

What is important is to understand and clearly realize the simple and obvious fact that this phenomenal manifestation that can be perceived through our senses is a spontaneous creation in which we form an intrinsically small part; and we have had no part at all in the creation of this universe which is a spontaneous reflection of the noumenon within itself, a reflection of consciousness upon itself when it stirred itself into action by the spontaneous arousal of the thought I AM. It is consciousness that perceives and cognizes the manifestation through the senses provided within the psychosomatic construct known as the sentient being. It is consciousness which perceives and cognizes through one object (the body) all other objects. A "he" sees "you" as an object, and that "he" considers himself the subject that sees "you" as the object. Similarly "you" see "him" as an object and consider yourself as the subject, a supposed autonomous individual with volition and independence of choice and action. This is the whole secret of the conceptual ego and its conceptual bondage. If the spontaneity of the whole process of manifestation in its totality is thus apprehended and the hollowness of the distinction between "self" and the "other" is realized, there cannot possibly be any question of a separate individual to be born as an independent entity, nor any question of the death of that entity. It is only the form (in its millions of variations as sentient and insentient objects) that appears and disappears, that is "born" and in due course "dies". *In principle*, as Nisargadatta Maharaj pointed out, every sentient being experiences life and death at regular intervals during the course of its earthly appearance: every wink signifies birth and death (birth when the eyes are open, death when the eyes are closed); there is birth when one wakes up in the morning and death when one is overtaken by sleep; there is birth when one inhales and death at the end of every exhalation. Maharaj said this fact is not clearly understood. Otherwise it would be realized that death is not something one should be really concerned about. If one was not concerned with the phenomenon of one's birth, why should one be concerned with phenomenon of death? Indeed, there really is no "one" who need be concerned with anything. It is this "concern" which constitutes what is conceived as "bondage". Concern implies a separate entity who is concerned about his security, his material welfare and his welfare in the hereafter. Identification with a form as a separate entity constitutes bondage, and the shedding of such identification is itself liberation — the "individual", his "bondage" and his "liberation" are all conceptual, illusory and therefore non-existent.

The question that would arise at this stage is: Assuming that there is a clear apprehension of the mechanics of phenomenal manifestation, how does it work in practice, in daily life? It is necessary to consider this matter in its two aspects : one, the individual retaining his individuality and viewing his phenomenal existence as a process from birth to death, and the other, as the transcending of the individuality itself. The first is the aspect of comprehension which could lead to Bhakti as a dual relationship between the individual and his personal god, and the other as the intuitive apprehension of the essential unity between the unmanifest Absolute and the relative phenomenal manifestation. These two aspects are not necessarily separate in essence : the persistence of the individual as an entity in relation to his creator could well lead to the ultimate disintegration of the individual. The understanding of the individual that he has no autonomy and independence as such, and that his life is being lived as the objective instrument of the Divine, purifies the psyche and enables apperception of his true nature (as Unicity) to *happen spontaneously* therein. This is what is indicated by Lord Krishna in the Bhagvadgita when he says that "He gives *buddhiyoga* (apperception) to those who love him sincerely."

What happens in the case of an individual who understands the underlying oneness between himself and his fellowmen but retains his personal individuality is that he views the birth-death process as an inevitable "transformation" of his individual personality from one body in one life to another body in another life, and thus proceeding through various lives towards the final "goal" of realizing the divine plan. Such an understanding has, of course the advantage of seeing the phenomenon of death as a less frightening affair but carries with it the burden of the ego trying to improve itself and hasten the process of what is seen as a transformation. The individual, after the understanding, sees death as a stage in an overall process and "prepares" for death in various ways. He prepares to cooperate with death in order to make the death process smoother and less painful even as the woman in the process of delivery is advised to relax and consciously ease the tension in her body to facilitate the birth process; the individual may be advised to settle his worldly affairs and make specific efforts to forgive and be forgiven; to prepare for death by leading the good life: to visit the temple or the church or whatever at regular times, to be kind and generous to his neighbour, and generally to prepare for death while still alive, to use the course of living as the launching pad for the take off of the dying process. Such a preparation for death usually means nothing more than a preparation for an easier death and a more acceptable life in the worldly sense in the next birth. A spiritual understanding in which the individual does not give up his identification as a separate entity could at best lead to ecstatic devotion to his personal god which in turn could lead to the disintegration of such identification in course of time, further leading to a complete surrender to the personal god and a total transcendence of all space-time relativity.

When, however, there is instantaneous and intuitive apprehension (that is totally different from an intellectual comprehension) what occurs suddenly and spontaneously is "apperception" which is noumenal in nature inasmuch as in such apprehension the triad of the comprehender, the thing comprehended and the process of comprehension is absent. There is no individual who apperceives; *there is only the apperceiving.* The situation then is entirely different inasmuch while the individual apparatus continues to function, there is no ego acting as the operating centre or the controlling factor. That apparatus thereafter becomes the instrument of totality of functioning of the phenomenal manifestation as a whole. The apparent individual thereafter becomes part of the total functioning and his living becomes noumenal living. Indeed "his" living becomes nothing more than mere witnessing without any involvement in the actions of the psychosomatic apparatus. In other words, the process of living culminating in the phenomenon of death loses all personal significance and becomes part of the totality of functioning and what takes place from the point of view of the *apparent* individual is just the witnessing. Witnessing then is of the nature of noumenality. The individual psychosomatic apparatus carries on its daily activities as heretofore but the sense of separateness between the "self" and the "other" no longer prevails as the dominant factor in all activities and, indeed, the sense of volition and independence of choice and action; is gradually loosened and finally gets totally annihilated. In short, there is transcendence of individuality and individual volition through the deep apprehension that no entity exists independently which could possibly have effective volition of its own and that any seemingly volitional act has in fact no meaning — it is either like the crowing of a cock to herald the inevitable sunrise or like the frustrated fluttering of a caged bird. The individual, when there has been apperception, apparently continues to live like an ordinary person but his living is truly "being lived" and his dying is merely the disappearance of an appearance because of his awareness that his real nature continues to be the same as it was before the appearance of the body in the course of its duration, and even after the disappearance of the body. Transcendence of individuality means transcendence not only of the fear of the unknown that death represents. Transcendence of individuality — disidentification with an entity as a separate individual — means at once the realization that the process of life-death is but a dream and that the awakening from this living-dream renders all that happens therein truly illusory.

In considering the phenomenon of death in depth, it must again be stressed that the phenomenon of death is not the same as the psychosomatic process of dying — the latter is only a minor aspect of the former. The fear of death is totally different from the fear of the possibly painful process of dying; the former is concerned with the loss of one's individuality, the latter only with the physical pain that the process might involve. The fear of death is the fear of the unknown and the unknowable whereas the fear of possible pain (in the process of dying) is known and recorded in memory. The fear of death itself is generally a fear of being annihilated as an individual and it is therefore the ego that fears death. The only way to transcend the fear of death is to accept both the inevitability and the "unknowability" of the phenomenon of death. Such acceptance is totally useless if it is based on helpless frustration; but it is effective if it is the result of a clear understanding of the mechanics of phenomenal appearance and disappearance because such acceptance comports the surrendering of the illusory ego to the Reality, of the insignificant "me" to the real "I", (the giving up of the non-existent part and remaining in the whole unicity).

Nisargadatta Maharaj used to urge his visitors to see the facts as they are: a simple glance at the phenomenal manifestation in the correct perspective should be enough to bring home to us the utter unreality of the process of life and death. We attach so much importance to the wellbeing and comfort of our individual bodies and to the necessity of providing security for ourselves in the time to come. If we would but think of the normal activities of man during the span of fifteen minutes or even less, we would be shaken out of our identification with what we call our "selves" as against the "others". Are we *essentially* in any way different from the billions and billions of "beings" that get created and destroyed continuously during our very normal activity of breathing, eating, digesting, sexual intercourse — billions and billions of microscopically small "beings" endowed with that same animating consciouness that we are endowed with? While we may have a comparatively longer duration of life, are we any more important in the totality that functions? If we look at the matter in this perspective should we not ask ourselves whether we should be really concerned at all about our future over which in all truth we have no control in any shape or manner? Every sentient object begins to die from the moment it is created. Would it be so difficult to clearly see WHAT IS, and thus to accept it with a depth of understanding that would get translated into sweet surrender to the WHAT IS ? When we see and accept WHAT IS without the intervention of thinking or conceptualizing and surrender our selfish individuality, we begin to enjoy life as it comes — both the good and the bad (conceptual criteria that change according to circumstances) — with a sense of wondrous anticipation, and then living becomes free, natural and therefore noumenal when the "me" does not intrude.

What the whole thing amounts to is that in order to understand
this strange unknown thing called "death" that is so starkly inevitable we must understand life. No doubt, man has always been
thinking and dreaming of the day when he will be *physically* immortal but must find out the real significance of death before one
can even consider physical immortality because one may come to
the conclusion that death is not all that unwelcome after all! Living
and dying necessarily go together because they are not two separate things but the beginning and the ending of the process we call
"life", and it is when we are still living that we must consider the
matter of death in a forthright manner and not try to avoid the
issue by sidetracking it into a discussion whether or not one be-
lives in rebirth or reincarnation. One thing is very clear : when
death has occurred, the body has to be destroyed - the closest
loved one will not be able to remain anywhere near the body after
it starts decaying; when the brain is dead, there cannot be any
thought, the mind is also dead. There is no question therefore of
finding out the meaning of death through the process of thought
and memory after death has occurred. And whatever thought can
tell us now about death is a mere concept. We cannot find out
what death means by merely thinking about it as something we
are frightened of and therefore prefer to think in terms of a continuity like rebirth. It would all be nothing more than conceptualizing. What we must find out is what we are NOW, other than
a form to which a name has been given by people who have told
us that they are the parents, other than the conditioning that that
form has received, and other than the experience of pleasure and
pain that it has undergone over a period of time and on which
conditioning and experience (stored in our memory) we would be
basing whatever thinking and conceptualizing we do.

The fact of the matter is that the permanent soul (if you happen
to believe in rebirth) or the permanent entity that you think you
are is in fact nothing other than the illusory thing that thought and
memory have created as a result of recoiling from the movement
and the insecurity which is the very warp and woof of this life,
this dream-life. So the whole problem of finding out what death
really is, boils down to this: if there is no entity at all, who is then
concerned with death? This is the stage of confrontation where the
mind — which has all along been the villain of the piece — finds
ifself exposed and must therefore slink away in disgrace. Whatever
we ARE — call it consciousness or awareness or witnessing or God
or by any other name — then remains in the NOW, totally free
from all problems and questions. In fact that IS death — *dying to
every moment, every experience.* That is ETERNITY. That is IM-

MORTALITY. And the actual event of death and the process of dying is a minor formality because *appreciation of the Truth means dying every moment to your present attachments, your past experiences and guilts, your future fears, hopes and ambitions.* Then, you forget about life and death, and LIVE — or, more accurately, ARE LIVED — with love and humility, accepting what comes every moment with willing surrender. In this way one becomes an infant again with its sense of unicity and it's universal oneness with all that it sees and hears and feels.

The significance which the phenomenon of death has when viewed in the framework of the relative duality of life and death of the individual entity is quite different when considered as an intrinsic part of the totality of the functioning of the universal manifestation as the objective expression of the absolute subjectivity. Sage Vasishtha has an uncommonly pragmatical approach to this matter: While it is true that no one really KNOWS what happens after death, there are only two possibilities — either the dead just cease to exist or they exist in other bodies. Sage Vasishtha says, "Death would denote an exceedingly happy consummation if it means the total extinction of the one who is dead because that would necessarily mean the end of all the vexatious restlessness of living and the freedom from all the everchanging uncertainty of pains and pleasures of living. If, on the other hand, death means not the end of life but merely a change of body, would it not be foolish to fear the phenomenon of death which provides one with a new body?" The sage then proceeds to elaborate in the Yogavasishtha that death is not really total extinction but that life is experienced in a different space-time framework because desires, hopes, and ambitions were not given up in the earlier life: "A person who is dreaming may in that dream experience his death but he would continue to keep on dreaming other dreams; similarly an individual sees another waking dream (living dream) after his death in one waking dream... The phenomenon of death is like fainting when there is a temporary withdrawal or ceasing of the activity of the mind". It would seem that what the sage has said about the phenomenon of death is merely one speculation among many, but it needs to be pointed out that sage Vasishtha has specifically stated that what he says about death is from his own experience inasmuch as he could through his Yogic powers, observe the phenomenon of death — and its process — with the same clarity with which the ordinary person could see the objects in the world. Nonetheless the point must be made that both life and death are movements in consciousness, appearances in the space-time framework which is itself only a concept. To the extent that the matter is considered in this context of what happens in the space-time manifestation and its functioning, the authoritative statement of sage Vasishtha has tremendous importance and value insofar as the individual is concerned.

It is intriguing, however, to consider the matter in the space-time context of relativity, not from the point of the individual but from the view point of totality. So long as the manifestation continues, there must be an *apparent* cause for any event to occur. For the large number and the vast variety of people to exist in the world at a particular time, there must be specific causes. For the theory of relativity to "occur" to an Einstein, which would lead to the most revolutionary theoretical and practical aspects of atomic and sub-atomic physics, there must be an *apparent* cause. For a Jesus Christ and a Hitler to be born at specific points of time, there must have been appropriate cause from the point of view of the totality of the functioning because otherwise manifestation would be static. For the Lila of "Life" as such, there must be a script and the script must bring in causes which lead to certain effects which in turn would become causes for yet further effects in future, and such causes and effects must, of course, function through individuals as the characters in the life's drama. But then in these circumstances the various individuals as characters in the drama of life merely perform their roles and then disappear. Where is the question of the one individual *(jiva)* going through various characters at various times, each new character being based on the facts of his "independent" actions in his life as the previous character? Does the individual really have such independence and autonomy in each of his lives? This is an interesting and intriguing aspect of the phenomena of life and death when considered in the space-time duality in which the universe manifests itself.

It would not be inappropriate at this stage to consider what sage Vasishtha has to say about *the process* of dying which is generally considered to be a painful one. The sage tells us that this is not necesarily so, and that every dying person does not necessarily undergo unbearable pain and agony. It would seem that those who are inordinately attached to the material world and all that it offers *resist* the process of death and thereby create a conflict; it is this conflict which is the cause of any pain and agony that the process of death might entail. On the other hand, "those who are wise and have practised discrimination regarding what is real and what is illusory" accept death as a natural consequence of life and merely witness the process as they would witness any other event in life; and therefore, there is no conflict but only a sense of floating through the process easily and smoothly. In this context, I

might relate the incident when a relative of mine — and a very
dear friend — died of a massive coronary a few years ago. There
was no history of any of the causes which generally bring about a
heart attack; he was a man of uncommonly regular habits with an
easy and relaxed attitude to life which was supported by an official
position in a service that did not entail any unusual physical demands or mental tension. Nonetheless, he had a sudden massive
heart attack and died within a few minutes inspite of prompt
medical attention. The electrocardiogram clearly showed that death
was imminent, and yet the patient, who was himself a doctor and
certainly must have known what was happening, was calmly de-
scribing the process of death - he said there was numbness in the
extremeties, that the numbness was creeping upwards gradually
towards the heart and the brain. Within minutes he was dead,
with a perfectly calm and restful expression on the face as if he
was enjoying the experience! I might add that he was during his
lifetime undoubtedly what sage Vasishtha describes as a man of
discrimination who had accepted with equanimity whatever life
had to offer at any time with a smile.

There is a parable about Lieh—Tzu, a chinese sage who lived in
the fourth century B.C. Lieh—Tzu was on a journey to a place
called Wei and while on his way he was having a meal by the
roadside, he saw a skull lying some distance away obviously the
skull of a person who had died many years ago. He picked a stalk,
pointed to the old skull, and said to his disciple Pai Feng, "Only he
and I know that you were never born and will never die. Is he the
one who is truly miserable? Are we the ones who are truly happy?"
In this statement Lieh—Tzu of course, assumes that the "owner"
of the skull was not an enlightened person when he experienced
the process of death and that he himself, having apperceived the
nature of death, is now aware that only a body can be said to have
been born and is subject to decay. Only a thing or an object can be
born and only a thing or an object can "die" and thereafter, when
consciousness is no longer present to provide the animus in the
body, it is to be burnt or buried and thus irretrievably destroyed.
With the destruction of the body, the concept of the ego is also
destroyed because the individual consciousness, which created
the ego when it identified itself with the individual body, merged
with the universal consciousness. It is in this sense that Lieh—Tzu
refers to the skull and says that "he" knows that you were never
born and will never die, because you are not really the body that
was born and will die in course of time. In regard to himself he
does not have to wait until his body dies to know this same fact
because apperception has already occurred. Then Lieh—Tzu pro-

ceeds to ask his disciple: Is he the one who is truly miserable? Are we the ones who are truly happy? The answer has been provided by sage Vasishtha from the point of view of the individual: in death the dead man is free from all the vaxations of life whereas those living have to continue to face them.

It is interesting to note what a warrior-writer of the seventeenth century Japan had to say at the very outset of his book called a "Prime of Bushido", containing advice to the budding Samurai warrior. He suggests that since death is the most dominating idea to the Samurai, that notion should never be lost sight of at any waking moment, so that the Samurai would constantly remember what a frail thing life is for him and thereby would consider each day as his last and *would never let his thoughts linger* on a long life and the many enjoyments that life might offer; such an attitude would always keep the mind on the efficient performance of one's immediate duties. Another piece of advice offered to the Samurai is that it is only when a mind attached to life and death is abandoned that the finest execution of the undertaken deed takes place; in other words, *it is only in the no-mind state that the nearest attainment to phenomenal perfection can take place,* when there is no thought of success or failure, life or death, because ultimately both are totally irrelevant, their relevance being only in relativity. Another Zen master used to tell his disciples that for any serious study of Zen, it was essential to give up one's life and to "plunge straight into the pit of death."

This would seem to be the kind of spirit Zen built up among its warrior followers : not to argue about the ethical conduct or the divine way but to go ahead with determination with whatever was considered as necessary in the circumstance, however irrational it may seem to be—in other words, to wield your sword (whatever the word "sword" may represent in the circumstance) and go straight ahead, not to give way to lingering irresolutions — precisely the advice Arjuna received from Lord Krishna. Such determination comports the idea that death is an inevitable and logical culmination for any phenomenal object in duration. And, when in life, the thought and fear of death no longer exists in consciousness, the fluidity of the mind continues unobstructed and unhindered like the free flow of water, and *the activity which such fluidity of mind directs is intuitive both in conception and execution.* In other words, death represents the fear of the uncertain and the unknown (while death is a certainty, the time of its happening is not) which restricts, inhibits and almost strangles the natural functioning of the instinct and the intuition.

It is not intended — it would indeed be foolish to do — to be little the achievements of intellect, reasoning and logic in material utilitarianism where the basic and essential driving force is necessarily conceptualization. It is, however, in other areas which are beyond the scope of the intellect that the intrusion of intellect and conceptualization has created the most unfortunate and disastrous situations of modern life—mental instability and spiritual insecurity—that are threatening to destroy the very formulation of human existence and culture. Indeed in almost all moments of crises, it is the intellect which causes panic while it is instinct and intuition—one might call it faith in the unknown—that transcends the circumstances and restores the dignity of the human being to its true nature or *suchness*. It is only when there is no mediatory interference or conceptual trespass that intuition and instinct point to the true position—the "what is"—essentially in their ontological capacity.

One final question: Since the fear and horror of death is so instinctive how is it possible to "accept" the phenomenon of death? How is it possible not to resist the very idea of death? Suicide must be regarded as an exceptional aberration, otherwise every living thing seems to resist death until it has to surrender to it out of sheer lack of strength to resist it any longer. The answer to this questionable doubt is that it is only conceptualization that brings about the worries and fears about death or anything else that is uncertain and unknown. It is only human beings who seek security in a life the very basis of which is insecurity because they think, they imagine, they conceptualize and they objectivize. It would seem reasonable that if this conceptualization is stopped — as do the sages, the spiritual adepts or masters — we would remain in the natural stream of life like plants who live and grow and die normally and naturally in the totality of phenomenal manifestation. What happens after death? We would obviously be in the same state that we were in before life started in the womb; we would return to the source, the perennial potential. Nature would proceed in any case along its normal course, but, if intellect is prevented from conceptualizing and thus interfering with the natural fluidity of the mind, we would be freed from the unnecessary harrowing anticipations. It is possible, therefore, to erase the horror of death from consciousness, but it would be almost impossible to do so deliberately and purposefully because the mind (which is the content of consciousness) is notoriously persistent about something which it is asked to avoid. Nisargadatta Maharaj used to narrate the parable of the king demanding of his prime minister, on pain of death, the secret of physical immortality. The wise minister brough a packet of some powder and told the king that he had managed to get the entire stock of the immortality powder for the king. It was to be taken only once a year but there was only one condition: when the dose was swallowed, there should be no thought of a monkey. And, of course, whenever the king tried to take the dose of immortality the monkey was already present in his thought. The only way to get rid of the monkey of conceptualization is to realize our true nature. What we truly are is the dimension beyond the space-time in which the manifestation *appears:* the formless, intemporal PRESENCE which witnesses the appearance and disappearance of the phenomenal manifestation (including ourselves as part of it) as one would witness a dream. It is only after a deep understanding that THIS total manifestation, which spontaneouly arises in THAT formless potential and in due course merges therein — which is our real nature — that conceptualizing will cease to bother us with its imagined horrors, including that of death.

Perhaps the fitting conclusion for this chapter would be the lines of the Japanese poet Kenko: Were we to live forever, then indeed people would not feel the pity for things. Truly the beauty of life is its uncertainty.

16

Understanding is all

True understanding - apperception - comports the understanding that there is no separation between understanding and action. When there is true understanding there can not be any question of further conscious action as separate from the understanding. This can be clearly seen when one watches an expert at his task - whether it be trade or industry or sport - because he is never seen to hesitate or "wobble" between the principles he has learnt and the application of these principles; only a learner or a beginner is seen to hesitate because he has doubts about his understanding. An expert works smoothly, naturally, without thinking because for him the "what" and the "how" of the doing have been absorbed in the very understanding, in the perfection of his understanding. This is what Nisargadatta Maharaj obviously had in mind when he declared "Understanding is all". Maharaj had added in response to a relevant query that, once the understanding is true and perfect, "you may do whatever you like". Again, obviously what Maharaj implied by the words "you may do whatever you like" is that all action that follows true understanding would necessarily be spontaneous, natural action in which the individual "you" would be not only absent but irrelevant. The principle is that if nothing is prevented or obstructed from going its own way - "doing its own thing" - the established harmony of the universe would not be disturbed because all the processes in the universe are interrelated. This may shock people. It may be taken to reflect Kropotkin's anarchist theory that a social order will emerge of itself even from a possible anarchy if people are left alone to find for themselves what pleases them and are allowed to follow their nature and bent of mind because individuality is intrinsic in the community and the order of nature is not a forced order. Perhaps a deliberate oversimplification in order to underline and impress the point he is making, but the Chinese sage Lao-tzu puts the following words in a ruler-sage's mouth:

I take no action and people are reformed.
I enjoy peace and people become honest.
I use no force and people become rich.
I have no ambitions and people return to the good and simple life.

The trouble, of course, is that Maharaj's visitor thought in terms of an individual entity with which he is identified and his own relative happiness whereas Maharaj was thinking in terms of the totality of manifestation and its functioning.

Precisely what Maharaj would have had in mind when he asseverated that "understanding is all" would depend on the nature, and the manner in which the understanding would translate itself into practical action. To the best of my knowledge, Maharaj did not go into the matter in such critical details at any one sitting, and it would therefore be necessary to reconstruct the structure of such understanding from various statements that he had made at different times in different circumstances. I remember a particular incident when I was doing the translation one morning. There was one regular visitor who used to take down notes in a thick notebook inspite of hints from Maharaj that the understanding of what he was talking about could not be had from taking down notes and studying them at leisure : the understanding had to be sudden and spontaneous so that it was wholly free from any intellectual bias of any kind regarding the meaning of his words. Maharaj had said something that morning that was rather cryptic but extremely significant. When I had translated that into English, Maharaj must have noticed the confusion in the visitor's face because she had stopped writing and was looking at me questioningly. I was about to explain further, when Maharaj almost shouted at me "No, don't explain." Then he had added that with any further explanation the understanding would lose its depth. It is said that the Buddha was apparently not in favour of setting forth a system of philosophy that would be consistent enough to satisfy intellectual curiosity on conventional lines. When he was pressed for answers to certain questions which he considered irrelevant from the point of view of actual experience, he would maintain a "noble silence". Ramana Maharshi , too, would look over the shoulders of a visitor into distance when the latter kept repeating questions which the Maharshi had earlier indicated as being not relevant and therefore of a distracting nature.

Nisargadatta Maharaj always laid great emphasis on the fact that a man with a dull intellect would never be able to understand even vaguely what he was talking about, and that he would ask such a person to do *japa* or some other *Sadhana* so that his psyche could gradually become purer and enable him, perhaps in due course, to get the necessary intellectual capacity that could lead to that direct understanding beyond which there was nothing to aspire for or work for. He also made it absolutely clear that the intellect he was talking about was not the kind of intellect that enabled people to pass examinations and earn university degrees but the kind of intellect that has a large content of intuitive insight. What Maharaj had in mind regarding the type of intellect that was necessary to absorb what he was trying to convey is beautifully illustrated by the well-known story of the Chinese sage Hui-Neng, who is said to have had his first enlightenment when, even as a boy, he happened to hear someone reading the Vajrachhedika. He felt so overwhelmed that almost without any further thought he set out for Hung-Jan's monastery for a formal initiation and spritual training. It would, therefore, seem that he had had the original *satori* without the benefit of any formal teaching from any master, and, what is more, he is known to have been at that time an illiterate peasant. It may be recalled that Ramana Maharshi too had his awakening without the guidance of any specific Guru when one day without any warning, he was overtaken by a sudden violent fear of death; he laid himself down and intensely considered the phenomenon of death : what does death mean? What is it that is dying? Out of that intensity of concentration came the deepest possible conviction that it was the body that dies and that he was the spirit transcending the body. In his own words, "From that moment onwards the "I" or Self focussed attention on itself... Absorption in the self *continued unbroken* from that time on."

When Hui-neng arrived at the monastery, Hung-Jan at once recognized the depth of Hui-Neng's insight and immediately put him to work in the kitchen area, perhaps fearing that the majority of scholarly monks in the monastery might reject him because of his humble origins. In due course Hung-Jan announced that he was in search of a successor and that he would form his judgment after each monk had submitted a poem based on his understanding of Buddhism. It was generally assumed that the office would go to the chief monk Shen-Hsiu and so no one really attempted to compete. The chief monk posted the following poem on the board in beautiful flowing brush strokes which clearly proclaimed generations of culture behind them, but he submitted his poem anonymously with the intention that he would claim authorship only if it received the approval of the Patriarch.

The Body is the Bodhi Tree;
The mind like a bright mirror standing,
Take care to wipe it all the time,
And allow no dust to cling.

When Hui-Neng was passing by, he noticed the poem, read it, and spontaneoulsy added below in his rough unlettered hand the lines:

There never was a Bodhi Tree,
Nor bright mirror standing,
Basically, not one thing exists,
So where is the dust to cling?

The Patriarch, who had kept an eye on the board, came out and read both the poems. He knew at once who the authors were, knew also the amount of careful effort that must have gone into the chief monk's poem (and the reason for submitting it anonymously), and the utter spontaneity and conviction with which Hui-neng had carelessly dashed off his words. He sent for Hui Neng quietly that night, conferred the office of Patriarch on him by handing over to him the traditional robe and begging bowl (said to have come down from the Buddha himself) which were the official insignia, and told him to flee into the mountains because when the news was known, the powerful chief monk, Shen-Hsiu, would do him harm. It is said that Shen-Hsiu did pursue Hui-Neng, overtook him at about mid-day, and tried to pull the robe and bowl from his hands. Hui-Neng quietly put them down on a rock beside the path, and said to him "These are only things which are no more than symbols. If you want the things so much, you are welcome to them." It is further said that when Shen-Hsiu eagerly tried to grab them, he could not even move them because "they had become heavy as the mountain." Then he fell at Hui-Neng's feet and said, "forgive me, I really do want the teaching, not the things." Hui-Neng made him sit by his side on the rock and told him gently, "It is really very simple. Stop thinking *this is mine* and *this is not mine* - and then tell me, where are *you-?* Tell me also, what did your face look like before your parents were born?"

Once Nisargadatta Maharaj, in utter puzzled perplexity, asked me why a man renowned for his academic achievements should have asked during the talk that morning, a question which clearly showed a basic lack of apprehension of what he, Maharaj, thought was a fairly simple and straight-forward statement. I ventured the opinion, that seemed to satisfy him, that the academic mind produced a peculiar kind of thought patterns that prevented the apprehension of a subject that was not based on a purely scientific and dialectic approach to life and its problems. Most of the knowledge that is imparted in our schools and colleges for quite some time past is based almost wholly on what might be called conventional standards that can be presented in certain specific symbols and notations which would demarcate black from white and reduce the gray area to an absolute minimum. What Maharaj was talking about belonged almost entirely to the gray area! Identical kind of difficulty apparently faced the older theoretical physicists from clearly understanding the principles of sub-atomic physics whilst the newer younger breed of physicists in their twenties took to the new physics like ducks to water.

Another very real difficulty is that in order to communicate, the use of the transitive verb is so unavoidable that it has become the general structure of a language. Indeed the use of the passive tense gives rise to a certain amount of suspicion that something is being deliberately hidden. And the result is that one generally expects the verb "know" to have a subject who knows and an object that is known. What happens then is that this conventional entity - if it is not a personal noun like "I" or "You" or "He", then there is at least a "one" - interferes with the understanding of something as pure knowledge: and it is extremely difficult for most people to understand a statement from Maharaj that, while he is *apparently* speaking to a visitor, actually it is "a process of consciousness speaking to consciousness". In other words, the subject-object-verb convention prevents the clear perceiving of the fact that *our phenomenal world is more a collection of processes rather than entities, and that things (including human beings) are really events.*Then again,for instance, we at once understand the fact that the sun shines on the various objects in the world but the fact that it is the process of shining (and that shining is the very nature of the sun rather than a deliberate act) that is the more important of the two (the sun and its shining) is not so easily comprehended.

Then there is the greater difficulty of the several conventional roles which every man has to adopt in the process of living together in a community, apart from the fact that such communal living would necessarily involve an enormous amount of conditioning concerning law and order, ethics, conduct etc. The difficulty operates at every step to such an extent that it is almost impossible to live one's life without *a personal identity* in some role or other - husband or wife, father or mother, white collar worker or blue collar worker - apart from the roles depending on a variety of hobbies. The result is that we are so accustomed - so deeply conditioned - to think in terms of an individual that it becomes almost impossible even to think in terms which do not include and involve the individual as *a separate entity* with autonomous choice of action. When Nisargadatta Maharaj was seriously ill with cancer and could not give his usual talks twice a day, he still tried to speak but restricted the queries to those which had really troubled the questioner into a kind of mental block. At this time, one regular visitor asked a question with considerable reluctance: "I understand, at least intellectually, the basis of that eternal state which we all seek, but if that state means the annihilation of the individual, how do I know that, however perfect that state may be, I myself would not have chosen, if I could, to continue to remain in the existing state?" This query from a most intelligent person shows the depth of the conditioning concerning the individual entity, though the point of the query is a separate matter. The point is that this individual entity that seems so clear, so specific, so substantial is really nothing but a concept, a convention, an inference made up of certain selected memories over a certain past period. Actually this seemingly specific identity varies not only as different people see it and evaluate it, but also changes accordingly as the impressions of that particular entity about itself keep on changing!

The significance concerning a person's identity is twofold : one, that different people have different impressions based on past events, and the memories that these events have left in the brain as reactions to those events; two, these events and the reactions and memories relating to them are not all events but only a selection of events determined on the basis of standards that are not absolute standards but relative standards. In other words, conventions would necessarily be based on certain signs, symbols and measurements, with the result that conventional knowledge cannot but be a system of abstractions in which objects and events must necessarily be reduced to their general, hazy outlines. The astonishing but logical fact is that the individual entity thus turns out to be not only the "metaphysical appearance in consciousness", but actually, and in the every day practical experience, *an abstract of general outlines based on certain selected impressions* concerning certain selected events. And it is from the point of view of such an individual entity that knowledge is sought. It is therefore not surprising that *knowledge that is not based on abstractions in which the individual entity becomes not only an irrelevance but an actual obstruction, is not easily apprehended.*

It cannot be gainsaid that abstraction is certainly necessary for communication between people; the word 'tree' brings about a comparatively communicable basis for exchange of information between two parties, otherwise a whole lot of description would be necessary every time one talked about what is known as a tree! But the fact of the matter is that while abstractions and conventional signs and symbols are necessary for comprehending events one at a time on the "spotlight" basis, such a method is not only inadequate but misleading when one talks about a universe in which events are happening not only all together but at one time with incredible rapidity; only a powerful floodlight with a very wide periphery would do in such circumstances for any comprehension to be possible. Trying to understand the working of the universe in terms of linear thought and verbal concepts is a little like trying to see an enormous mural by Michaelangelo in the dark with a single dull ray of a pen-torch! The working of the human body seems frighteningly complex to a medical student because he tries to comprehend it in bits and pieces, one at a time, by this kind of thinking whereas to an experienced physician or surgeon it is a comparatively simple matter because what he uses is a peripheral kind of understanding: his experience has turned the spotlight into a powerful floodlight. This is precisely what happens in the case of the top class artist, athlete, expert workman in every field: he forgets the earlier training he has acquired with great effort and persistence using his limited kind of abstract, linear type of thinking, and allows the peripheral vision of the mind, the spontaneous and intuitive mind to come into operation. Indeed the success of the expert depends on the extent to which he keeps the central, conscious thought into the background and *permits* the general intuitive, unconscious thought to take over. This is precisely what Nisargadatta Maharaj meant when he repeatedly urged his listeners to forget the words and *allow* the deepest meaning in those words to penetrate into their very being, that kind of meaning which would lose all the signifiance if any effort were made to communicate it to someone else (or even to oneself individually) by thinking, by verbalisation. This too is precisely what he meant when he said that any effort would be not only unnecessary but obstructive, and that it was only necessary to *allow* the intuitive understanding to take root without any obstruction so that it could flower and blossom. Knowledge of reality cannot come about by "cumbersome calculations of theology, metaphysics and logical interference" which only serve as the obstructions which Maharaj referred to.

The story is told of a disciple of the Taoist master Lao-Tzu who fell at his feet and declared in exultation, "Master, thanks to you, I have arrived." Lao-Tzu raised him too his feet with great compassion and said, "If you have arrived, then it is certain that you have NOT arived." The disciple was disappointed, but as he had great faith in the Master he continued with his daily routine. Then one day he again came to Lao-Tzu and announced very respectfully but matter-of-factly that the master was absolutely right. Lao-Tzu looked into his eyes with a steady gaze for a few moments, then embraced him very warmly and asked him what had happened. The disciple explained, "When I was told that I had not arrived, I knew that I had already done all that I could have done; there was nothing more I could do. So I LET GO and emptied myself. And then there was an unbelievable and utter sense of total freedom — and the last barrier was broken: there was no longer a me to make any effort, or to arrive anywhere. IT had arrived".

In considering the nature of the understanding which Nisargadatta Maharaj had in mind when he declared that understanding itself was everything, we must understand clearly what such "understanding" is supposed to contain. The essential content of understanding is Reality or Truth or God or any other name by which THAT may be called. The very core of this understanding is what may be termed "non-duality" in the sense that since That-Which-Is is all there is, all that exists phenomenally can only be its objective manifestation. Every thing or object that is sensorially perceptible is an appearance or a phenomenon in consciousness, and in this sense (much as it may seem surprising) human beings, like all things perceptible sensorially, are also appearances in con- sciousness perceptible to one another. Then, if That-Which-Is is all there can be , all human beings must obviously and necessarily be THAT also, along with all phenomena AND consciousness. In other words, manifested, we are phenomenon or appearance in consciousness ; unmanifested, we can only be noumenon or con- sciousness (or, its contents, the Mind). They *seem* separate- neumenon and phenomenon-because one has appearance and the other has not. But they are not separate - how can the substance and its form, gold and a gold ornament, be separate as such except from the point of view of appearance which one has and the other does not have? Phenomenon is the objective aspect of the subjec- tive noumenon — noumenon can *appear* only as phenomenon; and in such a manifestation mind must necessarily split itself into obser- ver and the observed. Thus the observer & the observed are dual aspects of the manifesting consciousness when the consciousness-at- rest arouses itself (because that is its nature) into action so that man- ifestation may occur. And in the knowing — in UNDERSTANDING — that the observer cannot exist apart from the observed, divided mind regains its wholeness and holiness. This is the principle of non- duality within the duality of manifestation.

What this means in effect is that all human beings, all sentient beings, though appearances in phenomenality are, prior to man- ifestation, the infinite intemporal "I": that though "I" am phe- nomenally absent (because my phenomenal presence is through the sensorially preceptible object), what "I" am noumenally (what we all are) is PRESENCE - This - Here - Now - the totality of the unknown from which arises the totality of the known, phe- nomenally the nothingness of the void, but noumenally the full- ness of the potential plenum."I"manifest in objective phe- nomenality through the mechanism of dualistic polarity, a split- ting of my Mind into interrelated opposites — by means of subject and object, observer and observed, male and female, positive and negative — without which the phenomenal universe could not have been conceived. "I" thus manifest as the totality of all objects, and although each object seems to function as the subject of all the other sensorially perceptible objects, "I" alone am subjectivity.

It is essential to understand the relationship between the phe- nomenal universe and the sentient beings. The sentient beings are not directly concerned with the appearance of the universe, but the curious fact is that the apparent universe neither arises because of the sentient beings nor quite independently of them. The sen- tient beings are as much of an appearance as is the universe, and indeed, they arise simultaneously and concurrently. The confusion or difficulty would seem to arise from the fact that, as Nisargadatta Maharaj repeatedly pointed out, the sentient beings have a twofold significance — they are *sensorially perceptible* like all objects in the universe, and at the same time it is their sentience which enables them *to perceive* and cognize other objects, (including other sentient beings) through their cognitive faculties. In other words, if the manifestation (the appearance by itself) is considered the static aspect, the dynamic aspect — the perception and cognition of the manifested objects — would be represented by sentience; that is to say, the cognitive faculties are *able to interpret* the manifested objects and events but they are *not the cause* of their appearance. What this means in fact is that sentient beings, while themselves a part of the manifested universe, form the operating element in the functioning of the manifested universe. A lack of clear understanding of this position is what causes the conflict and unhappiness in human beings. It means in effect that *the duality* which is a polaric phenomenon is in practice treated as *dualism* where the two opposites are sundered into irreparable separation. And separation means conflict and unhappiness. Indeed, separation is based on measurement in the sense of this area (of possession, of relationship or whatever) is mine and this other one is not mine. It is precisely this separation which is called Maya, from which liberation is desired. The Sanskrit root of the word "Maya" is said to be *matr* ("To measure, to form, build or lay out a plan") from which other words like metre and matrix arise. The process of division is essentially based on dividing or separating in one way or another. Thus the Sanskrit word Dvaita or the English word "duality" have their root in the Sanskrit *dva*. Therefore when it is said that the world of objects and events, the phenomenal world, is Maya, it is not meant that the phenomenal world is a separate world which vanishes altogether when there is enlightenment, because this would imply the annihilation of something that was different from Brahman whereas the Brahman being the sole Reality, anything else can only be the dual aspect of Brahman and not something with an independent nature. What is in fact denoted by the word Maya is an *imperfect perceiving* of the manifested world in terms of classification, diversification, measurement - all mere concepts which are considered necessary for the linear understanding of the working of the manifested world, but which have no reality.

In other words, the totality, the Brahman is unmeasured and undefined. But in it is operative a principle that limits and finitizes. This limiting principle is Maya *which* involves *veiling* of the whole and *treating* of the sections or parts. These aspects are known in Vedantic terminology as *avarana* (weiling) and *vikshepa* (treating) respectively.

The whole point of the concept of non-duality is that unmani fested noumenon and the manifested phenomenon are neither separate nor to be joined; they are polaric, interrelated opposites of duality which, when superimposed on each other, disappear into what would phenomenally be a void of nothingness but is in. reality the fullness of the plenum of potentiality. Maya is that which makes people not accept or forget (or not put into practice) the principle of polarity (which is the basis of duality without which manifestation would not be possible) and turns the duality of interrelated opposites into the scourge of dualism and ego. This principle of polarity is against the very basis of Western thought and aspirations which is to get rid of evil altogether and make this world a paradise to live in. Such thought ignores the basic fact of life that there is "evil" only because there is "good", and that the very idea of a paradise would be ludicrous in the absence of a hell. Hindu thought, on the other hand, considers the world as a play (Lila) of God simply because the thought has to be put in a kind of poetic mythology otherwise it would mean trying to make a positive and factual frame work in which to place that Reality which can only intuitively be apperceived as infinite, intemporal unicity. If it is accepted that Reality must necessarily be non-dual (because if we do not do so, there would be an unending regression of subject and object based on the ineluctable query of the child, "Who made God?") then it cannot but be accepted that the manifested universe, of which the human beings are an integral part, is only an aspect (and not a separate creation) of the unmanifested reality. Further too, if it is this same reality that is immanent in all sentient beings, it cannot but be accepted that it is the same consciousness which is within both the saint and the sinner, that good and evil, pleasure and pain are not only the inseparable essentials of the game of life that the Hindu calls God's Lila but that each side of life — both the bright and the murky — must have the upper hand at some time or another, in order that the play may go on. In other words, "evil" as such should not constitute a problem because the conceptual phenomenal world is a relative world of interrelated opposites. The problem of evil and indeed, all problems arise only because this basic fact of life is ignored and people live in dualism (as differentiated from the duality of interrelated opposites), separate in the dichotomy of "self" and the "other", in the perpetual search for happiness and the ever changing concept of the "good", together with the complete banishment of pain and unhappiness and the allied concept of evil. Can such a search end in anything but frustration?

A Tao peom, said to be one of the oldest, begins as under:
The perfect understanding is without difficulty,
Except that it shuns picking and choosing.
Only when you cease liking and disliking
Will all be clearly understood.
A split-hair's difference,
And heaven and earth are set apart!
If you seek the plain truth,
Be not concerned with right and wrong.
The conflict between right and wrong
Is the sickness of the mind.

To put the idea in the words of the Lao-Tzu, "when everyone recognizes goodness as good, there is already evil." To see this is to understand that seeking good to the exclusion of evil, seeking beauty to the exclusion of ugliness is like seeing the stars to the exclusion of space, seeing the print in a book to the exclusion of the white background, seeking to hold water in a sieve, seeking to avoid the left by persistently turning to the right and thus going around in circles. Inspite of the simplest logic in this principle of polarity — or perhaps because of it! — we are inclined to ignore it altogether out of hand because our conditioning clearly indicates to us that unless we constantly keep on trying to improve everything, including ourselves, the only possible end would be sliding back to a lazy chaos : if sufficient and successful effort is not made by "me", the "others" would overtake me. It is astonishing that we ignore our actual experience which proves the contrary inasmuch as, for instance, more and more success, more and more money, better and better cars and gadgets, more and more luxury in qualitative and quantative terms have not brought us a sense of either total achievement or total satisfaction; in fact one finds oneself holding a tiger by the tail. Is there really a choice?

Our conventional thinking and our way of life based thereon makes us take the view that it is one or the other — either the pursuit of the good and the beautiful or wallowing in the evil and the ugly. The fact, however, is that there really is no choice because both are inseparable elements in living. The human situation is not unlike what has been described as that of the "fleas on a hot griddle" : the flea who falls must jump and the flee who jumps must fall! It is not a case of fatalism based on frustration; the inevitability of the duality of interrelated opposites is what exists. The duality of subject and object (both really phenomenal objects endowed with sentience to perceive each other through the cognitive faculties) is not in the least different from any other pair of interrelated opposites. Acceptance of this mechanism of duality as the very basis of manifestation seems difficult because our thinking has been moulded over a long period on conventional linear basis which prevents us from seeihg things and events as they really are. Thus there is no question of escaping from having to use clothes or having to eat food — hunger and food are forever inseparable; heat and perspiration are not a matter of cause and effect; we do not perspire *because* it is hot; heat and perspiration *together* form one event. Human experience does not occur *because* of an external event but it is a manifestation in consciousness, a reaction of the outside stimulus in the psychosomatic apparatus. To explain human experience, the common Zen illustration is the reflection of the moon in the water: neither the moon nor the water is concerned with the phenomenon, nor is there a cause-effect relationship; in the absence of one or the other there is no reflection; also, while the water reflects the beauty of the moon, the reflection of the moon demonstrates the clarity of the water.

The real problem, as Nisargadatta Maharaj used to say, is that almost all problems are created because we think, we conceptualize, we fabricate symbols and images, including images of ourselves. In certain circumstances we feel uneasy and uncomfortable not because the outside world contains any objects that have any power to do so, but only because the images we create of ourselves (and others) at that time are in conflict with the one that we already have constructed on the basis of past experience. And the joke is that no image can have any substance. If conceptualization stops — or is at least clearly seen for what it really is,—an astonishing change cannot but take place without any specific "action" apart from the understanding itself : the "self" and the "me" is seen as merely a concept based on a selection of impressions over a period, and consequently the separation or dichotomy between subject and object is healed. Then the relationship between the knower and the known, between the experiencer and the experience itself becomes not one of ireconcilable opposition but one of polaric mutuality inasmuch as there cannot be the one without the other. There is then not only an intellectual comprehension but an intuitive apprehension of the world being a "net of jewels", every jewel containing the reflection of all the others, a fantastic interrelated harmony which could not possibly have had any outside cause for its existence. Along with this is felt very deeply that what we used to caU our voluntary actions are actually involuntary, and that volition is nothing but an ineffectual and temporary obstruction to such involuntary workings of the universe. Thus when one is hungry and the stomach growls, one is reminded that it is time to eat. When one sits down to eat, the hunger is appeased and if at that moment one does not begin to conceptualize one is aware of the dogs barking and the birds singing. Moments such as these make one intuitively feel that "this is all there is" and that all else is a burden that we create by our notion of a purpose in life, of getting something out of life. Moments such as these make us realize the relativity of time and motion because then there is no "me" flowing in the current of time and constantly struggling to resist the flow of events; there is only the "I" on the shore watching the events moving in the flow of consciousness.

The understanding that thus transcends mere intellectual comprehension, comports the realization that the pursuit of the illusory "good and the beautiful" (as opposed to the bad and the ugly) means in effect the pursuit of an illusory future aimed at prolonging human life because nothing can be more relative than temporality and duration. Duration (time) along with space is only a concept providing the framework in which a manifested phenomenon can be observed and measured. And it is this concept of measuring that forms the Maya, but once the false is seen as false, Maya gets stripped of its powers to fool and enslave the human being. The subjective feeling of an insect that lives only for a few hours or days is not different from that of an animal that lives for several hundred years; inspite of a steady increase in the life expectancy of the human being almost all over the world, there is no change in the subjective feeling of man at the moment of death. The point is that one must, willy nilly, live in the present moment and if one makes a fetish of improving conditions in the future, one lives neither in the apparent present nor in the illusory future. The fact of the matter is that "time" is only a concept, the future moves into the past leaving no "time" for the present. There is only the present moment which is eternity when the relativity of time as a concept of measurement is clearly understood.

When I used to translate Nisargadatta Maharaj's talks from Marathi into English, the usual routine was that at the end of the morning session, my friend Mullarpattan and I would take Maharaj for a drive in the car (at around noon time!). The short interval at the end of the talk was a time when Maharaj would relax (the heat of the noon time did not disturb him) and perhaps discuss a point or two relevant to the talk. Once at such a time, in a mood of utter relaxation he suddenly looked at me and said, "What is the core of the 'understanding' I always talk about?". The answer came like a shot, "Not trying to understand the apprehension because all that effort can raise is only the stink of stale comprehension." Maharaj directed his piercing gaze at me, perhaps to make sure that I was not trying to be clever, and then gave me a big heart-warming smile. As Maharaj would say, nothing is simpler than the Truth, the WHAT-IS, but it must be perceived directly, immediately, not through conceptual symbols which limit and blinker perception. He would repeatedly urge visitors to remember that the understanding that can be verbalized is not THE understanding because the very basis of verbalization is separation between the subject (the "me") who verbalizes and that which is verbalized; *verbalization is the act of the split mind.* What precisely is this true understanding and how can it be achieved? The direct answer to this question is that whatever is submitted as an answer would still be a concept, and further that pure understanding can not be 'achieved' but only accepted when it arises spontaneously! This may seem like a stalemate but it is not. What is to be seen is that anything that is given by the Guru or spiritual guide is to be accepted in the nature of a thorn that is used to remove an embedded thorn and then thrown away. Any advice or guidance concerning true knowledge must be seen as merely pointers or indicators to the Truth so that such an attitude will bring about a state of mind, variously called vacant mind or no-mind or fasting mind in which true understanding can sprout spontaneously. When this happens no doubts of any kind can arise and that understanding is of the same nature as understanding I AM — that I am alive, that I exist, and that I do not need anyone else's confirmation that I am alive and present.

It is essential to see clearly the difference between the true understanding in the whole mind and the conceptual understanding in the split mind. The whole mind or pure mind is not tainted by the separation between a "me" and the "other" and the thought produced in the whole mind is, therefore, also pure while the thought produced in the split mind is first tainted by the division between the "me" and the "other" and then corrupted by the desire of the "me" to score in competition with the "other". The whole thing appears to be an enormous joke when there is the "Great Awakening", the full realization that life is a living-dream, the entire phenomenal manifestation of the universe (including all the "me's" and the "you's") being merely an illusory structure reflected in consciousness, and cognized by consciousness. The illusory split of the mind — the content of consciousness — arises through the attempt of the consciousness to be both itself and the individual psychosomatic apparatus with which it has identified itself, a split between its real subjectivity and the pseudo-subjectivity of the ego which arises from such identification, a split between what-we-are and what-we-*think*-we-are. The illusion ends and the split is healed when there is realization of this fact, and mind ceases to act from the standpoint of the conceptual "me" (in opposition to the "other") making the constant effort to control, to choose, to judge. Such realization comports the understanding that the moon does not have its cool brilliance because of any special outside treatment, that the blue mountains are not blue because they have especially been so painted, that the grass grows by itself and does not need to be pulled out of the ground, that our physical organs work by themselves without conscious direction.

The essence of all spontaneous action that is the genuine consequence of the pure understanding (in which the "me" is totally absent as the one to understand) is a natural sincerity. It is not often realized that there cannot be the slightest trace of intention or planning in an action that is spontaneous and natural. What is more, spontaneity and naturalness cannot be "achieved", either by trying or trying not to try! As the Zenrin poem puts it, "You cannot have it by taking thought; you cannot seek it by not taking thought." This may again seem to be an impossible impasse, but it is not really so. Effort (or an effort not to make an effort) is based on desire or volition, which itself is an aspect of the "me-concept" or the ego. It is the split mind which sees the apparent impasse as such, while spontaneity is synonymous with the absence of the split mind. Spontaneity can arise only when the split mind has been abandoned and trust is put in the working of the whole mind. This does not mean that we must abandon our working mind in everyday life, but that we should not put our whole trust into it, to the exclusion of the whole mind. It is an everyday experience that when our "conscious" mind cannot provide an answer to a problem, the answer comes to us when we "sleep on it" through the "unconscious" mind. There has to be the realization of the limitations of the conscious mind so that we do not force ourselves to be unreasonably careful and only conscious of the illusory "me"; we keep the liberty to have trust in that final authority which makes the grass grow and our limbs and organs to work "by themselves". Otherwise, anxiety and self-consciousness will destroy that minimum sensitivity so necessary for decisions to arise.

As Ramana Maharshi has stated, "to think is not man's normal function" : that is to say, conceptualization, fabricating images in the mind, comparing and judging things according to an abstract

of memories and reflections based on symbols and concepts — all
this can become a paralyzing force if carried beyond a certain
limit. In any case, as a judgement or decision must be arrived at in
all but routine matters, it would be impossible to take into account
all our memories and experiences in the final judgement, and it
must necessarily be a "hunch". And this "hunch" is more likely to
be a right one if the mind has not paralyzed itself into a stupor by
trying to remember everything, but is relaxed enough to trust its
spontaneity based on the *unconscious* record of its own memory
and reflection. Indeed, in such circumstances there is no separation between thought and action, one impinges on the other in
trust and commitment. What really happens then is that action
takes place naturally and spontaneously, without the mind simultaneously and concurrently trying to check whether the action is in
conformity with its own idea of what is best for "me". In other
words, when "thinking" is condemned by the wise, it is this kind
of thinking which restricts and inhibits spontaneous action that is
condemned. The same principle applies to "feeling" in relation to
"action", and it is in this sense that the Jnani is described in
Yogavasishtha as *mahabhogi* (super-enjoyer). One of the misconceived notions about a Jnani is that he is considered to be a stoic
who is impervious to pleasure or pain. The sage Vasishtha in the
Yogavasishtha makes it clear that the Jnani not only enjoys whatever comes his way but that he enjoys it much more fully than an
ordinary person. The reason is obvious : in the midst of his enjoyment *he does not speculate about the enjoyment itself;* he is not concerned with enjoying the feeling of enjoyment, and thus the enjoyment is not diluted by any thinking or conceptualizing. In other
words, the Jnani *is* the *enjoying* (the noumenal function of enjoying)
and not the conceptual entity experiencing the enjoyment; he is
therefore the *mahabhogi.*

    Spontaneity can arise only when mind, which is the content of
consciousness, realizes the absurdity of its trying to grasp consciousness. It is only when mind is silent and dual-thought ceases
that noumenal thought can arise and understanding can translate
itself into spontaneous action. The significance of this point is
that as soon as consciousness has identified itself with the individual body as a separate entity, the ego image is firmly established. Thereafter any effort to relax or let go is only the negative
aspect of the habitual effort of volition and control. This is the
reason for the impasse; if I try to hold on, it is bad, if I try to let go,
it is still bad or worse! The answer lies in the impasse itself : the
positive thought and the negative thought are both spontaneous
in the sense that neither was deliberately intended, and in this

very understanding that the ego, the cause of both thoughts, is itself a spontaneous arising in consciousness, a mere movement in consciousness without any substance, the impasse disappears — the ego gets strangulated in its own trap. *Understanding is all, any effort is an obstruction.* Understanding is spontaneous and noumenal, even the understanding that the compulsive action is also spontaneous. Then the ego annihilates itself because it is exposed as the illusion that it is. This understanding comports the understanding that actions are not those of the ego but those of the "suchness" of a particular psychosomatic apparatus based on the genes of that apparatus and the conditioning it has received.

At this stage a doubt may arise : If that is so, it means that anyone could do whatever he felt compelled to do : Yes, indeed, but then if the understanding is deep and clear, the same attitude would apply to "others" as it does to "me", and there should be no complaints about the damage done to "me" by such actions of the "others". Actually a true understanding would not include any difference between the "me" and the "other" because the very content of such understanding would include the realization that both are illusions and that only the events have any significance as a part of the totality of functioning and the individual "doer" is an irrelevant factor. What this means in effect is that one begins to take life as it comes along in a world which seems to have lost all its previous boundaries and barriers, so that there really is no need to avoid false thoughts or seek the true ones — all thought is spontaneous and without substance, a temporary movement in consciousness that is neither to be accepted nor rejected, but ignored so that it disappears as spontaneously as it appeared.

The other day I had an experience of the easy capacity of a child to see things with a clear insight because the conditioning has not yet taken a firm hold. My daughter-in-law Gita has a daughter who is now five years old, an extraordinarily lively little thing full of restless energy and happy bounce. One evening after an un-usually hectic day, the mother gave her a bath and told her to pray to God and ask Him to make her a good girl. Without any fuss, the child quietly sat down with her eyes closed for quite a while. Later that evening, during supper, Gita asked the girl what she had asked from God. The answer was, "I prayed to God and asked Him to make me a good girl so that I would not harass my teacher in class and that I would not make Mummy angry all the time. I did not ask him to make me work harder at my lessons because I already do and get good marks in all my subjects." When Gita

heard this, her eyes were shining with unshed tears of astonishment and joy at the precision of the child's prayer. However, the
next two days were no different, and the harassed mother asked
the daughter why she continued to be a naughty girl. The girl's
spontaneous answer was, "Mummy, you asked me to pray to God,
which I did. If he has not answered the prayer, it surely means that
either He cannot do anything about it, or that He wants me to be
what I am." Then she went about her way. The mother was flab-
bergasted but had the sense to remain discreetly silent. When Gita
narrated the incident to me, I at once thought of Nisargadatta
Maharaj, how enormously delighted he would have been to hear
the story of the child who had shown astonishing insight into the
fact of being natural without any effort to be natural.

Understanding, as Maharaj used the term and understood it,
would thus seem to be not a fixed idea or concept but a sort of
flow, a fluid process of nature that freely irrigated life by merging
thought and action. It is not so much the scholarly knowledge of
Vedanta as the intuitive apperception of Tao, about which
Chuang-Tzu says, "It may be·attained but not seen". It may be
"felt but not conceived; intuited but not categorized; divined but
not explained." When Maharaj said understanding is all and further added that no further action as such was necessary, he obviously meant it in the sense that no effort is necessary to breathe, to
digest the food that is eaten, in the sense in which the masters in
the art of self-defence can defend themselves against several men
(who could quite easily incapacitate themselves because of their
forced effort) without even breathing heavily at the end. No effort
being necessary obviously meant no deliberate conscious effort
was necessary; it was like floating with the current, or rolling with
the punch; an illustration of the principle is the sturdy tree getting
pulled down by the storm while the lowly grass remains swaying
as usual. Such understanding which includes within itself any
necessary action is much like the innate intelligence of the living
organism, particularly the fantastically intricate working of the
nervous system.

Nisargadatta Maharaj repeatedly stressed the fact that it is difficult, if not impossible, to explain or define such perfect understanding because we ourselves ARE that understanding which is
"like the sword that cuts but cannot cut itself , like the eye that sees
but cannot see itself". Modern science has clearly demonstrated
that we change the behaviour of the nucleus by the very fact of
watching it, and that by the very fact of our observing them, the
galaxies go further away from us. *The impossible obstacle to objective
knowledge is our own subjective presence which is phenomenal abs-*

ence. How can conceiving conceive that which itself is conceivi
ng? We cannot but accept that the perfect understanding is the
source and the field of our own subjective being, which may be
intuitively felt but not objectively observed. This understanding is
the intuitive knowledge we have of our universality, of being the
ground, the field within which appear all the multitude of forms
and experience. It is the consciousness - I AM - the common
ground for every sentient being which gives him the intuitive
feeling of *being,* of which we cannot have objective knowledge
and, therefore, cannot form a mechanical and linear pattern. What
actually happens is that we ignore the field, the background, and
concentrate our spotlight vision on the phenomenal objects and
events and experiences, whereas the only way for the understanding *to occur* is for the spotlight to be switched off and the floodlight vision of the quiet, fasting mind to be allowed to come on so
that the vivid awareness of what-we-are can occur by itself.

The perfect understanding, then, that is the floodlight vision of
the whole universe, shows it as a harmony of intricate patterns, "a
network of jewels each reflecting all the others." It is only the
spotlight vision that sees each pattern by itself, section by section,
and concludes that the universe is a mass of conflict. Indeed, the
biological world is certainly a "mutual eating society" in which
one species becomes the food of another, but then it is part of the
universal intelligence that that should be so if the whole biological
balance is not to be upset by overpopulation and self-
strangulation. Actually, it is again the limited spotlight vision
which would give this perfectly normal universal phenomenon a
sense of horror whereas the broad perspective of the perfect
understanding would see things as they really are, that birth and
death are really nothing but the integration and disintegration, the
appearance and subsequent disappearance, of the phenomenal
objects in manifestation.

It is with reference to this perfect understanding which is itself
the totality of the functioning of the manifested universe, that
Chuang-Tzu describes the "man of perfect virtue", in assumed
contrast to the average man living his life (which science tries to
extend so very enthusiastically) in the persistent hope of a better
tomorrow and in the constant dread of imminent death.

> The man of perfect virtue in repose has no thoughts, in
> action no anxiety. He recognizes no right, nor wrong, nor
> good, nor bad. Within the four seas, when all profit, that is
> his repose. Men cling to him as children who have lost
> their mothers; they rally around him as wayfarers do who
> have missed their way. He has wealth to spare but knows

not whence it comes. He has food and drink more than sufficient but knows not who provides it... (*As a description of Nisargadatta Maharaj, how astonishingly accurate this is!*) In an age of perfect virtue, good men need not be appreciated—ability is not conspicuous. Rulers are mere beacons, while the people are as free as the deer. *They are upright without being conscious of duty to their neighbours.* They love one another without being conscious of charity. They are true without being conscious of loyalty. They are honest without being conscious of good faith. They act freely in all things without recognizing obligations to anyone. Thus their deeds have no trace; their affairs are not handed down to posterity.

The significant point in this narration is that the actions of the "man of perfect virtue" -the Jnani - are not deliberate because they are expected from him, but are his "suchness" arising from that perfect understanding, and therefore, spontaneous and unpremeditated, an intrinsic part of that understanding itself. Therefore understanding and action are not, and need not, be separate. The further significance - perhaps the more important - is that the recognized virtues of uprightness, charity, loyalty, good faith, compassion etc. are not something to be deliberately cultivated with a view to obtaining some merit (material or otherwise) but that they are *the natural consequence* of the understanding itself. The appreciation of this ineluctable conclusion means in effect the suspension of our dialectical logic and leads to a sort of the numbing of the mind because it is contrary to all our conditioned thinking. The man of understanding however, does not depend on his split mind for his understanding, and intuitively accepts the universe as complete every moment and needing no intellectual justifiction — It is the HERE AND NOW.

In other words, true understanding sincerely accepts human failings not only as part of the working of the totality of the universe but as a necessary part like salt is to food. When it is realized that true understanding does not distinguish between proper and improper, right and wrong, but accepts whatever is as the reflection of the noumenal being, it would be clear that any deliberate effort to "improve" anything would be a self-contradiction. As Maharaj would say, any deliberate effort is like "beating a drum to seek a fugitive", or as a Taoist sage would say "putting legs on a snake". In other words the basis of the understanding is the acceptance of the wide variety in the multitude of manifestation, the realization of the futility of trying to iron out all differences into a single concept of what is conceived as right or proper, the realization of the foolishness of trying to place the world on a Procrustean bed of linear regulations by stretching a person who is too short for the length of the bed and cutting off a portion of the legs if he is too tall!

True understanding comports a trust in the essential harmony in the working of the universe irrespective of appearances of good and bad aspects, a trust in the normal process of living concerning the constant changes and transformations, including birth and death. To quote Chuang-Tzu again, "How do I know that the love of life is not a delusion? How do I know that he who is afraid of death is not like a man who was away from his home when young and therefore has no intention to return... How do I know that the dead will not repent of their former craving for life?" It's an interesting thought that if one could have filmed the history of civilizations and geological and biological formations in the last 5000 years and give it a quick run through like a fast moving Charlie Chaplin film, all that we would see would be like crystals forming and dissolving at an incredible speed and this would have no bearing at all on what human beings have considered as life and living during those 5000 years! It is all really a matter of perspective and perceiving that "things" are without substance, that "me" and the "things" are the same process of living, that *not* perceiving this is also a part of the same process, and finally that there is nothing to be done about it and nothing not to be done about it! All there is "is the stream and its myriad convolutions-waves, bubbles, spray, whirlpool, and eddies" - and we are that. What would be the reaction to this? That it "sounds" wonderful, but... And that attitude is also a part of the WHAT-IS. How can that be? How can that not be? The WHAT-IS is all there is, and nothing that happens can be outside that. It is precisely in this sense that Nisargadatta Maharaj stated that understanding is all: Be the centre of the universe and the universe disappears; be *one* of the many sentient beings and you are in hell. Think from the viewpoint of Totality and no problems can arise. Think from the viewpoint of the individual and problems will never cease.

When Maharaj stated that understanding is all, he also used to explain that when the perfect understanding arrives, it does so along with the realization that there cannot be any separate individual entity to do any deliberate action : it includes the understanding that the individual is merely a phenomenal appearance in consciousness and, as such, cannot have any independent or autonomous existence, and that therefore the ideas of an individual entity having any choice of decision and action is ridiculous. This can lead to only one conclusion that, strictly speaking, all action is spontaneous. This conclusion is demonstrated in life by the fact that very many events do not turn out to be according to pre-conceived plans. There is also the fact of life (that is quite often totally ignored) that most of the actions that take place in a living organism are entirely without any conscious direction. The difference between the man of understanding and the ordinary man is that the former has trust in the intuitive floodlight vision whereas the latter prefers and chooses to use his limited spotlight vision which, he thinks, he can direct in any direction he wants. The whole point, is however, that in the totality of functioning spontaneous action will take place irrespective of the conceptual volition or intention. Indeed when such acts happen, the individual cannot explain - and he is puzzled - why he apparently did something that was not only not planned but almost wholly against his nature and temperament.

In regard to spontaneous actions, an interesting happening was narrated to me by my married daughter Jaya who lives in Bangalore, the capital city of the State of Karnataka in south India. It concerned a friend of hers who believed implicitly in the power and efficacy of the practice of chanting the Vishnusahasranama (the thousand names of Lord Vishnu). It happened one evening. Her husband had as usual returned from the club and was relaxing in his favourite chair with the newspaper, awaiting supper. When the doorbell rang, she went and opened the door and was surprised by two men who rushed in and pushed the door shut. One of them had a menacing knife in his hand, and he warned her in a low whisper against raising a hue and cry. They entered the drawing room, and while the one with the knife kept guard on the startled husband, the other one quietly went through the other rooms to confirm that there was no one else in the house. Then she was asked to go into the adjoining room and to remain quietly in the dark. Seeing that there was no point in putting up any resistance, she proceeded to the other room, more puzzled than frightened because all the time she felt that what was happening was wrong : how could this happen to her when she was regularly chanting the Vishnusahasranama? Just then she heard a terrific roar from her husband and when she hurried back into the drawing room she saw that her husband, angrier than she had ever seen him, had smashed a heavy chair into the face of the man with the knife and was loudly berating both of them for the outrage. Seeing this Rudravtar (an angry aspect of Shiva), both men hurriedly disappeared out of the house, with her husband chasing them almost down the road with the chair still lifted in his hands. This action by the gentleman was not only quite spontaneous and unexpected but totally out of character because he was normally a very quiet person, by no means an athlete or a physical fitness enthusiast, playing bridge at the club being his most strenous activity.

While spontaneous activity might seem unusual and a matter of astonishment to the average person, it is the normal procedure for the man of understanding. To others it seems that whatever the Jñani does becomes successful and they wrongly ascribe this phenomenon to his "powers" *(siddhi)*. His success is actually due mostly to a sense of confidence that arises through a lack of self-frustrating anxiety. At the same time he is perfectly capable, by the same token, of doing something that comes naturally in the prevailing circumstances with a total disregard to convention or consequence or a sense of decorum. It is for this reason that he is usually an enigma to most people : his actions are unpredictable precisely because they are natural and spontaneous!

How does understanding translate itself into action in daily life? The answer is: by being aware of life without thinking about it, persistently but effortlessly, so that this "being aware" keeps functioning even when there are thoughts. The true understanding absorbs the realization that, like the clouds that wander through the sky, thoughts floating through the mind have neither any home nor any roots. Once consciousness is seen as the substratum of everything phenomenal (including sentient beings *and their thoughts and actions*), discrimination ceases because no thing can have any independent existence. Virtues and vices are not then seen as opposites but as polaric counterparts which negate each other when superimposed. All action becomes spontaneous, being the operation of virtuality as latent power that exhibits itself in the miraculous fruition of plants, the formation of eyes and ears, the circulation of blood and the reticulation of nerves. Such force or power is generated without any conscious direction; it is natural and spontaneous force, of which electricity (no one really knows its *nature* though its operation is well known) is only one aspect. This is what true understanding translates itself into — spontaneous and uncontrived activity in practical matters of daily life, which is aptly described by one writer as "coincidence control". This miraculous natural force of virtuality (which has nothing to do with *siddhi*) is described beautifully by Lao-Tzu as:

> Superior virtue is not (volitionally) virtuous,
> and thus is virtue.
> Inferior virtue does not forsake being virtuous,
> and thus is not virtue.
> Superior virtue uses no force,

but nothing remains undone.
Inferior virtue uses force,
but achieves nothing.
Virtuality is steeped in ordinariness and anonymity, and is
therefore often not noticed as in the case of Nisargadatta Maharaj. It
is this same force or power that brings out the genius in various-
men in various fields of action which cannot be explained in
mundane terms, through the step-by-step linear method expressed in words. The only way it can be described (but not explained)
is through some pointers, as does Lao-tzu:
When the great Tao was lost, there came (the notions of)
humanity and justice.
When knowledge and cleverness arrived,
there came great deceptions.
When familiar relations went into disharmony,
there came (the notions of) good parents and loyal children.
When the nation fell into disorder and misrule,
there came (the ideas of) loyal ministers.
When action is spontaneous and without the slightest hesita-
tion, there is no room for thought because thought is truly born of
failure, failure to survive. The curious fact is that the chances of
survival are best when there is no undue anxiety to survive (and
this is seen from a number of successful "do or die" actions) because the special force of virtuality is available to those who do not
tire themselves out by their anxiety. The fact, however, that is
even more curious is that anxiety also includes the positive effort
to stop the worry. This is where the true understanding comes
truly into its own: all volition, positive or negative, constitutes a
drag for the simple reason that it is the spurious non-existent
individual ego that does the volitional worrying either way. True
understanding accepts whatever life brings and responds to each
experience wholeheartedly without any resistance or recoil, giving
the mind freedom to think whatever it wants to think including
the freedom to worry. Thus, speaking of the death of his master
Lao-Tzu, Chuang-Tzu says, "The Master came because it was time.
He left because he followed the natural flow." As Nisargádatta
Maharaj used to say, "it is only the psychosomatic apparatus that
reacts to an experience, and it can only react according to the way
it is made (i.e. according to its genes) and shaped. What is more,
different body-minds will react differently and the same body-
mind may react differently in different circumstances. So why worry? In other words, the senses, feelings and thoughts must be
allowed to operate in their natural way because any attempt to

control them can only result in worsening the disturbance. As Lord Krishna says in the Bhagavadgita, "the man who is one with the Divine and understands the Truth believes 'I do nothing at all' for in seeing, hearing, touching, smelling, tasting, walking, sleeping, breathing, in speaking, emiting, grapsing, opening and closing the eyes, he holds that it is only the senses that are concerned with the objects of the senses." It is only through true understanding that any change may occur in thought, emotions, appetites and muscular effort at controlling them would necessarily be futile to a large extent because the nervous system is essentially electric circuitry and not muscle.

One of the most daring pronouncements in this matter is made by a Chinese sage, Yang-Chu:

> Let the ear hear what it longs to hear, the eye see what it longs to see, the nose smell what it likes to smell, the mouth speak what it wants to speak, let the body have every comfort that it craves, let the mind do as it will... What the body desires for its comfort is warmth and good food. Thwart its attainment of these and you cramp what is natural and essential to man. What the mind wants is liberty to stray whither it will, and if it has not this freedom, the very nature of man is cramped and thwarted.

It must be remembered, of course, that this advice is given to the seekers of knowledge who may be misled into disciplinary practices which would turn out to be hindrance. Nisargadatta Maharaj also repeatedly warned his listeners against trying to control their thoughts, emotions and appetites. "Whatever has to go", he said "must fall off by itself. Any effort at controlling thoughts, appetites would only strengthen them and along with them the ego. All that you are concerned with - all that you ARE — is the impersonal understanding. Let that understanding work through mere witnessing without judging".

One final question: What is the basis on which spontaneity works so effectively. The answer in one word would be HUMILITY, but not in the sense in which it is generally used. What is usually called "humility" happens to be in fact nothing but inverted pride or negative pride, whereas the only implication of true humility is the utter absence of any entity either to be proud or not to be proud. What we interpret as suffering is really the negative form of happiness and, by the same token, happiness is the positive form of suffering, both respectively the negative and positive aspects of what we understand as "experience". Similarly, humility is the negative form of pride, and pride the positive form of humility, because both are in essence the same and different only in their interpretation. By true humility is meant the absence of an ego-entity to experience either.

Thus the sequence is clear : the deep and clear understanding (not the intellectual comprehension at the linear level) of WHAT-IS leads to true humility and the annihilation of the ego-entity; the absence of the ego-entity leads to the absence of self-conscious effort, which means in effect natural and spontaneous action. This spontaneous action reflects the fact that human intelligence is not something of an outside agency implanted into the sentient being, but that it is very much an inherent aspect of the whole organism of the phenomenal universe that maintains the functional order in dynamic balance through the operation of the consciousness which is the substratum of the entire phenomenal manifestation. This balance is maintained through the natural mechanism of polarity between apparent opposites; therefore, conflict based on stark, irreconcilable opposites of good and evil, subject and object, "me" and the "other" would necessarily be not only superficial and of temporary significance, but basically unacceptable to the essential culture. What this really boils down to is that this entire phenomenal show of the universe — the Lila — has no real purpose and it is really futile to seek a goal in life in open competition against all comers. Most "successful" men would readily admit this in their heart of hearts but the conditioning over the years is so powerful that most human beings, especially in the West, would not dare to accept it and admit it. And, of course, as soon as a goal is conceived, spontaneity is at once destroyed and the self-consciousness of the ego-entity takes over. From then on, the vision is pinpointed on the goal, thus missing everything worthwhile in life. The "purposeful" life indeed misses the purpose of life which is to enjoy the unity in the duality and multiplicity of life. When the true understanding brings about true humility and gets rid of the ego-entity, then springs the sense of total freedom and then comes the floodlight of true vision which misses nothing and enjoys everything. Then, spontaneous action, not being in conflict with the natural course of events, enables the man of understanding to be fully receptive through his senses to the entirety of the world. He takes it easy, is relaxed and free of tension because he is not self-conscious about the results, and he enjoys the game of life to the full without any inhibitions.

It is interesting to see how understanding — and the spontaneous action that goes with it — relates to the virtues which almost every organized religion exhorts man to cultivate. Let us take the case of the phenomenon of anger with which one is no doubt painfully familiar, and which one is supposed to control.

From the point of view of tension, it is debatable who is more susceptible to the ravages of tension — the one who freely gives vent to his anger and gets it out of the way, or the one who is conditioned to the necessity of controlling his anger and finds that every effort at such control only suppresses the tension until very soon it explodes into a heart attack or something similar. During the process of getting angry, the average person's thinking is on the lines of: "I am getting angry, and I should not get angry." Such thinking is done by the ego, the "me", and the anger arises because the "other" says or does something which the "me" considers against its interests. In other words, this kind of thinking takes place in the split mind of dualism, and so long as the separation between the "me" and the "other" exists, anger and the allied phenomena must necessarily occur. On the other hand, what happens when there is understanding? So long as the body, as the psychosomatic apparatus exists, it must necessarily respond, through the senses, to an outside stimulus in various ways in varying degrees. When the man of understanding gets angry (it may be assumed that such occasions would be considerably fewer than in the case of the ordinary person), he does not say to himself, "I am angry" and try to justify his anger. The anger is witnessed, and the relevant thought is "there is anger". The difference thus between the anger of the average person and that of the man of understanding is fundamental. The man of understanding merely witnesses the phenomenon of anger and does not try to justify it; *he does not get involved* in the phenomenon of anger as the "me" against the "other". What happens then is that anger does not receive any more fuel to keep it smouldering and naturally therefore must annihilate itself — and such annihilation is also witnessed. In other words, when there is understanding, the occasional arising of anger as a spontaneous reaction to an outside stimulus is almost instantaneously followed by its demolition. As Nisargadatta Maharaj put it, "thoughts—desires—emotions do arise, but they are not pursued."

A similar pattern can be seen in regard to the "achievement" of virtues like tolerance and compassion. There is hardly any extant religion in the commandments of which these virtues do not take the pride of place, and such commandments have been made continuously over the last two thousand years or more, without the slightest improvement in human nature or conduct — if anything, matters have gone from bad to worse, and now almost every man fears for the very survival of mankind! While the present situation is undoubtedly a most tragic one, with the constant threat of a nuclear holocaust, the fact remains that it is not without a certain comic element. Every "me" is worried sick about the situation but continues to compete fiercely for the slightest material gain (whether he really needs it or not) against every "other"! There is a story that illustrates the present condition of the world. The army chaplain at one Sunday service announced "I am going to preach this morning on the serviceman's misuse of the word 'hell' ". Then he proceeded to discuss at great length the absurdity and poverty of expression betrayed by such everyday expressions like "Get the hell out of here", or "What the hell do you want?", or Where the hell have you been?" He explained how easy it is to get out of this sickening habit by making only a little effort to use more specific words instead of the all-encompassing 'hell'. It was a good sermon. Standing at the door after the benediction, greeting the worshippers as they emerged, the chaplain received from a senior officer this sincere compliment : "Chaplain, that was a hell of a good sermon. I hope the boys will keep it in mind all the time".

As Nisargadatta Maharaj repeatedly reminded his visitors, when there is understanding, the concepts of tolerance and compassion take an altogether different turn: they lose their perversity of compulsion as commandments and, instead, become the natural consequential aspects of the understanding itself. Tolerance and compassion follow as a matter of natural course in the conduct and behaviour of the man of understanding because understanding essentially comports the realization that the human being is basically only *a part* of the total phenomenal manifestation, that the sentience with which man is endowed (and which makes him think he is *apart* from the rest of the world) is only the mechanism of nature with which the perceiving of the phenomenal universe takes place, and therefore, the separation of the "me" from the "other" constituting the ego, being totally illusory, has no essential nature of its own. In other words, understanding presupposes the demolition of the separation between the "me" and the "other" which is the root cause of all intolerance and conflict. Therefore the virtues that are generally recognized as something to be deliberately cultivated with the aim and object of achieving some merit — material or otherwise — in this world or hereafter, are in reality the natural consequence of the understanding itself, and, as such, the man of understanding does not specifically attach any value to them. So far as the man of understanding is concerned, virtues are merely one part of the pair of interrelated polaric opposites; the moment one accepts the concept of any virute one cannot reject its interrelated opposite.

The very essence of understanding is that *nothing in the phenomenal manifestaion can be rejected.* "Who" is to reject what? The "who" is himself a part of the totality of manifestation, and the totality of phenomenal manifestation is the objective expression of the subjective noumenon. The essence of true understanding, therefore, is the unconditional and willing acceptance of all the variety in the manifestation and its functioning. Who does the acceptance? "I" of course, — not the "me" — the subjective noumenal "I" whose objective expression is the phenomenal manifestation and all that there is in it, the good and the beautiful together with the bad and the ugly — the "I" who has lost its temporary phenomenal aberration of the "me". In other words, the "who" is irrelevant because the understanding which includes the acceptance of "what is" IS the impersonal, subjective "I".

17

Conclusion

Nisargadatta Maharaj in his talks referred so little to the traditional scriptures that the chronic visitors to the various Gurus at once noticed this fact which some of them even held against him. There are many such people who have made it a practice and habit to visit as many Gurus as they possibly can, and they make it a point to mention this fact with a certain amount of pride. In fact I recollect one particular visitor from upcountry who mentioned to Maharaj that Maharaj was the eighty-sixth holy person he had visited. Maharaj, with his lively sense of humour, had not only listened to him with a straight face but with an expression of admiration which had surely made the visitor's day. Each to his own pleasure, one supposes. Several of such visitors, satisfied with Maharaj's *darshan*, used to be content with one visit and then go on their way to some other Guru, the next one on their list.

Some others wanted, in addition to *darshan*, to listen to a talk or a discourse by Maharaj; and they were the ones who knew all the stock words, the various formulas in the many traditional writings, and who wrote Maharaj off because he showed no familiarity with, and did not quote liberally from, these writings; they did not realize that Maharaj spoke from experience and not from scholarship. Perhaps it is for this reason that Maharaj's relatively few visitors could generally be accommodated in his small attic room, and they were the ones who intuitively sensed greatness in Maharaj and they were the ones who could instinctively throw into background any familiarity they might have had with the hallowed writings in order that they could directly absorb Maharaj's teachings.

The real danger of an undue familiarity with the key words, phrases and formulas is the tendency to retain and repeat such formulas indiscriminately and consider it to be the end in itself. How many pseudo *pandits* and pseudo-saints and pseudo-gurus there are who pride themselves on their ability to recite the entire Bhagvadgita. The danger is that the real significance behind these key words and phrases is likely not only to be pushed into background but even totally ignored; the danger is that the formula E = MC² might be taken to be the comprehensive Theory of Relativity. Actually, the birth of these formulas could easily be imagined in a scene in the hoary past, at the end of a series of enlightened talks and dialogues and discussions with a group of highly trained and naturally gifted aspirants, when the ancient, enlightened sage was most respectfully requested by the disciples to condense the entire teaching in one sentence or formula that could at once rekindle the joyous spark of enlightenment or at least empty the mind into a state of vacancy. Thus could have arisen a beautiful sanskrit formula like "Tat Twam Asi" — That Thou Art. But what happens very often is that what must have come as the ultimate crowning glory of an extremely deep lesson in mysticism, the Mahavakya is now treated as the starting point, without the substantial content of preparation that must have originally gone into it. A superficial familiarity with the mystical teaching which breeds "a kind of reverential insensibility, a stupor of the spirit, an inward deafness to the meaning of the sacred words," is therefore the result.

It is surely in order to discourage such a "deafness to the meaning of the sacred words" that Nisargadatta Maharaj preferred to base his talks on his own experience, rather than the words of some other enlightened being of earlier ages, to construct his talks on the self-validating experience of his own direct awareness and not on the ancient shruti or inspired writings.

Maharaj's teaching primarily concerned the one Divine Reality substantial to the totality of the phenomenal manifestation, the one without which no manifestation could at all be possible, let alone the perceiving and cognizing of it — that is to say, the universal consciousness or, as the Chinese philosophers called it the Mind. Indeed, as Maharaj used to say, consciousness is both the manifesting of the manifestation and the cognizing of it. In other words, consciousness is all there is, the manifestation and everything therein being an appearance within the consciousness. Human beings — and all sentient beings — are in fact mere appearances forming a   part of that total phenomenal manifestation and, other than that, they have no autonomous or independent existence. This is the Truth whether human beings like it or not, whether they accept it or not. Indeed, the apperception of this truth is all the enlightenment that can be expected to happen. Such understanding, of course, must be not merely on an intellectual basis but an apperception in sheer depth and utter conviction. The most pertinent point is that such apperception can only take place in a mind (the content of consciousness) that is not already fully occupied by the fears and hopes of the self concerning the phenomenal sensual world, in a mind that is therefore in a vacant or "fasting" state and thus capable of receiving such apperception. Such a vacant or fasting mind (that is not only not an idiotic mind but an extremly keen and alert mind) has been described by the Sufi poet Jalaluddin Rumi in terms of scientific metaphor as one equipped with the moral "astrolabe of God's mysteries". The ordinary sensual mind is only concerned with the moving, changing process of *becoming* whereas That-Which-Is is the perenial state of being. The individual self can be concerned only with the process of becoming; it is only when the individual entity is annihilated that the state of being can be apperceived and realized in noumenal dimension. The other basic point concerning the apperception of the Divine Ground is that this state being basically unchangeable, is not to be "attained" or "achieved". All that is necessary is for the condition of becoming or changing, which has superimposed itself upon the perennial state, to be removed. The process — if it can be called that — is not one of creating or achieving something by positive effort, but truly the negative one of removing the obnubilation or covering (Maya) that has imposed itself on the original state, through the negative effort of an understanding in depth. Nisargadatta Maharaj was never tired of repeating the words: *"understanding is all"*. As Eckhart has put it, "The knower and the known are one. Simple folk imagine that they should be able to see God as if He stood there, and they here.

This is not so. God and I, we are one in Knowledge."

The futility of making positive efforts to grasp reality has been beautifully expressed by Young-Chia Ta-Shih as under:

It is only when you hunt for It that you lose It;

You cannot take hold of It, but then you cannot get rid of It;

And while you cannot do either, It goes on in Its own way.

You remain silent and It speaks; You speak, and It is dumb;

The great gate of Charity is wide open, with no obstacles before It.

As Nisargadatta Maharaj used to say, an unnecessary mystery concerning the essential nature of things has been made over the years by those who have not really realized the Truth. Those who have, say how truly simple the whole thing is. The only condition is that the knowledge must be desired with a tremendous intensity. Maharaj used to laugh at the irony of it all. You cannot see It, you cannot feel It, only because you really do not want to; you do not want to, because you are either too busy enjoying the many "good" things of life or too busy feeling sorry for yourself at the sorrow and unhappiness which the many "bad" things of life are causing you. If you would only sit quiet and silent, Maharaj would say, you cannot but *feel it*. Without It — the consciousness — you would be a dead body. Even when consciousness is in abeyance — as in deep sleep — you are not aware of either the world or anything in it. In fact *you are consciousness* if you want to see Reality as unicity. If you want to see Reality as God distinct from yourself as an individual, you would still see consciousness as never separate from you. Saint Tukaram sang in one of his immortal Abhangs: "Wherever I go you are always with me (as a friend, philospher and guide)". What is more, as Maharaj used to remind his visitors, consciousness is at work all the time, directing the subtle physiological intelligence to work the ceaseless processes of breathing, assimilation etc. What can it be but consciousness that causes the insignificant seed to develop into a fully formed fetus or a mighty tree? Indeed, if someone talked about "my" consciousness, Maharaj would laugh and remind him about the tremendous strength of the conditioning that makes people speak of "my" consciousness, when actually, the fact was that it was consciousness which had the many sentient beings as its manifold physical mechanism — "Ten thousand Things", as the Taoists say — through which it functions and operates the world and the rest of the manifestation. Maharaj would constantly tell his visitors to carry on their normal daily business and routine as usual, except that they should get

into the habit of remembering that the entire show was consciousness — the totality of the phenomenal manifestation being an
appearance within the consciousness. The totality of the functioning of the manifestation was consciousness, perceived and cog-
nised by consciousness through the psychosomatic mechanisms
known as human beings and other sentient beings. The one who
has deeply apperceived this fact is bound to see the totality of the
functioning of this universe as a Lila, with a certain sense of
amusement and a great deal of tolerance. Such a person is bound
to see that the consciousness, or (in Eckhart's phrase) God, the
creator and perpetual re-creator of the world "becomes and disbe-
comes" in the totality of the phenomenal functioning; that the
Divine Ground, in which the entire phenomenality and the multi-
farious time bound psyche are rooted, is truly, as Maharaj said, a
simple thing that is no-thing, a simple timeless awareness that we
may call consciousness; and that we are indeed that totality of
phenomenality which is identical to the noumenality within
which it has appeared, the Absolute Unicity. All that is necessary
is to disclaim and annihilate that separation which has eclipsed
our noumenality by our identification with a separate entity as the
"self" in opposition to the "other".

To a certain extent, the simple truth is made mysterious because
of the limitations of the word and the language. Language is like a
single beam of light that has to be used to light up an enormous
scene, and then the entire scene becomes almost impossible of
comprehension if it can be shown only small piece by small piece.
It is therefore repeatedly asserted by the masters that Reality can
only be apperceived by a sudden illumination like lightning. What
the artist visualizes as the finished piece of sculpture, the ordinary man can see only a piece of stone. It is only by removing the
unncecessary portion of the stone that the sculptor produces the
final image. In an extremly apt and lovely extract, the fifth-century
author known as "Dionysius the Areopagite", explains this situation thus "— for this is not unlike the art of those who carve a
life-like image from stone, removing from around it all that obstructs clear vision of the latent form, revealing its hidden beauty
solely by taking away. For it is, as I believe, more fitting to praise
Him by taking away than by ascription, for we ascribe attributes
to Him when we start from universals to the particulars; but going
up from particulars to universals we remove things from Him in
order that we may know openly the unknowable which is hidden
in and under all things that may be (sensually) known."

The human languages have evolved and developed with a single
purpose, and that is to deal with the universe as it appears to the

human common sense; a world which consists of innumerable events that concern a number of separate individuals and things spread across a large area, as seen according to human intellect based on the space-time limitation. But in dealing with something that is not only a continuance but totally unrelated to space-time concepts, languages based on space-time semantics at the traditional level are found to be wholly inadequate. Even at the level of the sub-atomic physics, the traditional vocabulary of mathematics is found to be so inadequate that almost an entirely new vocabulary has had to be developed which only the modern scientists seem to be able to understand. Indeed, some of the statements made by the sub-atomic physicists make one wonder whether they refer to physics or to metaphysics. The problem of semantics in regard to the noumenon and its objective expression as the phenomenal manifestation is very real indeed. Hence, in dealing with this subject, the inevitable frequency of paradox and parenthesis, which has perhaps made one editor comment that the author of the book * "has to seek support from parenthetical clauses which, for a while, distract the reader's attention from the main premise". Hence too, the difficulty in the direct understanding of the Divine Ground, which was expressed by a Taoist master as "Knowing is false understanding; not knowing is blind ignorance."

Hence also, the description of it as "it may be attained but not seen". In brief, what it all amounts to is that the only way to understand Reality is to *be* the Reality, which is the same as saying "You won't understand It until you have It".

In dealing with the subject of the Divine Ground or Truth or Reality or God (or whatever), the question that often gets buried under the avalanche of words and emotions is the one which comes from a sincere person: "I am quite content to lead my life as I have always done, in a law-abiding manner, and with an attitude of reasonableness towards most things and concepts. I am, in other words, a nice, ordinary unregenerate person. Why should I concern myself with the ultimate Reality ?" If the answer is, to know God is the basic and ultimate purpose of life, the question would again be asked in all sincerity, "why"? The question must be faced with equal sincerity. The point really is that the personal individuality - personality or self- is for all practical purposes entitled to consider that he is free to identify himself with almost an infinite number of possible objects: food, drink, sex, wealth, power, fame; wife and children, friends, relatives; hobbies, collections, clubs; profession, politics, ambitions, pains, illnesses, hopes,

Editor's Note: Experience of Immortality, Chetana — 1984.

fears, or various combinations of these things. *Why should a nice ordinary person be interested in God or Reality?* The answer that life is not a bed of roses and that a succession of illnesses or failures would make him think of God is not a true answer because it would only mean a sort of spiritual blackmail. The teaching of Nisargadatta Maharaj is extraordinarily simple. His answer to this question would be a simple and direct, "You are quite right — there really is no need for you to concern yourself with religion, God or Reality or whatever." This answer would be based on certain inalienable facts or truths: (a) The individual entity just does not exist and can therefore have no *real* problems other than what the mind might conceive; (b) When in the totality of the phenomenal functioning there is need for a particular psycho-somatic apparatus to think in terms of God or Reality, it is consciousness by whom the need will naturally be translated into the appropriate thought-pattern (c) since there is no such thing as an individual self or entity with autonomous or independent existence, the very question of an individual self seeking union with Reality is ludicrous; (d) all that exists is consciousness functioning in totality through the mechanism of the multitudinous sentient beings; and all events — "good", "bad" or "indifferent" from the point of view of the fictitious ego or the divided mind — are part of the totality of functioning according to its needs in order to maintain the equilibrium of the phenomenal manifestation (until it ultimately merges in the absolute noumenon in which it first arose when the noumenal consciousness became suddenly aware of itself (I AM), and spontaneously and concurrently brought about the phenomenal manifestation). In other words, the individual entity or ego is a purely fictitious creation that arose when the universal consciousness identified itself with the individual psychosomatic mechanism. It is universal consciousness, the energy immanent in all sentient beings and everything that is phenomenally manifested, that truly functions in totality. And a particular"individual's"thoughts will turn towards God or Reality only when the totality feels the need, not a moment earlier or later.

This part of Maharaj's teaching — that the individual, being a mere fiction and therefore without any independence to act on his own initiative independently — is the purest Advaita, and is generally too deep to be acceptable to many people because, for them, free will and volition is the very basis of their life. To treat individuals as mere dream figures means for most people the very bottom being knocked out of their existence and being thrown into an unimaginable pit of sheer, impenetrable darkness. Even those who are genuinely and sincerely interested in the Divine

CONCLUSION   235

Ground as formless Reality, find it extremely difficult to let go of
their individual indentity altogether, and prefer to think of their
individuality as something to be ultimately merged with the
Absolute Reality through personal efforts. They cannot and do not
dispute the inescapable logic behind the illusoriness of the individual ego, but they just cannot "let go". Once, however, they let
go of their identity with an individual ego or entity, the thing that
they could identify themselves with would only be the universal
consciousness which we all truly ARE. But it is this "letting go"
which they cannot do. And this is easily understandable because
it is the ego itself (with which they have identified themselves)
which is supposed to let go, which is supposed to annihilate itself.
And this is impossible. It is precisely for this reason that Maharaj
used to repeat ceaselessly that it is only deep understanding, deep
conviction - apperception - which can bring about the sudden
transformation   or metanoesis; an understanding which is not of
the dimension of space time intellect which is merely a divided
mind, that came about   when consciousness identified itself with
each individual body-mind for the specific purpose of perceiving
the manifestation as the perceiver perceiving a   perceived object. Apperception is of a totally different dimension — timeless
and spaceless, the whole mind of the universal consciousness; and
such understanding being timeless, happens suddenly and spontaneously — and in this moment of eternity, the individual ego
gets annihilated.

   How difficult it is even to understand intellectually this concept
of sudden enlightenment, in which the fictitious ego connot possibly have any part, can be seen from the manner in which the
subject is understood - or misunderstood - even by a well-known
and presumably sincere writer on the subject. He deals with
"metanoesis". He describes it as a sudden   convulsion or complete
revulsion of consciousness, and says that it is the realization of a
"no-mind" state, free from "an intellectual attachment to the ego
principle". So far so good - the fictitious individual is absent. But
then, so very unfortunately, the author goes on to say that this
"no-mind" state exists, as it were, on a knife-edge between the
carelessness of the average sensual man and the strained over-
eagerness of the zealot for salvation. To "achieve" it, he continues,
you must walk delicately and to "maintain" it, you must combine
tremendous determination with a total submission to the promptings of the spirit. Thus he describes what is in fact a *happening* as
a prescribed process of "conscious" discrimination between the
personal self and the self that is Brahman, between the individual
ego and the universal mind. One might well wonder "who" is to

do this conscious discrimination between the ego and the Brahman. This is the difference between the intellectual philosopher and Nisargadatta Maharaj who spoke from experience. The philosopher understands - and speaks - from the point of view of an individual, understanding something, with the object of achieving something. The Jnani speaks from the point of view of understanding *as such* -indeed it *is* the understanding itself which speaks. Eckhart, a mystic (in addition to being a philosopher) has put the matter as under:

> A man must become truly poor and as free from his own creaturely will as he was when he was born. And I tell you, by the eternal Truth, that so long as you *desire* to fulfil the will of God, and have any hankering after eternity and God, for just so long you are not truly poor. He alone has true spiritual poverty who wills nothing, knows nothing, desires nothing.

And here is Huang-Po :

> The Mind (consciousness) is no other than the Buddha, and Buddha is no other than the sentient being. When Mind assumes the form of a sentient being, it has suffered no decrease. When it has become the Buddha, it has not added anything to itself.

With the totality of the phenomenal functioning as the perspective, difficulties cannot arise, but when anything is considered from the viewpoint of the fictitious individual, difficulities will never cease. This is because the individual entity does not have an autonomous or independent existence, and therefore cannot have any free will or volition even though the ego considers that he has. With the dawning of apperception, the ego is exposed as the empty myth that it is, and by the very exposure is instantly annihilated. If the enlightenment is a happening in totality and not something which the spurious entity achieves — the individual psychophysical mechanism being merely the instrument for such happening — in what circumstances does enlightenment occur? Although enlightenment could occur anywhere at any time — as Nisargadatta Maharaj used to say, Totality or Nature is not bound by any laws or regulations of space-time duality — it can be seen that wherever enlightenment has occurred, the ground had already been prepared for it, although in certain cases this fact may not be apparent. Enlightenment can happen in the case of any type of the psychosomatic apparatus. Even though our conditioning all the time demands that an individual should improve himself constantly to reach a certain conceptual ideal, the fact remains that every human being has a more or less specific physical constitu-

tion combined with a specific temperament — that is not susceptible to any substantial change either way — on a scale which can
extend horizontally from a genius to an imbecile (even between
two blood-brothers), from a saint to a satyr, from overpowering
strength to shrinking meekness, from open sociability to mis-
anthropic antipathy.

While any classification system can never be rigorously accurate, it is possible to devise a system of classification based on a
certain criterion. Thus there is the zodiacal system of classification
according to Astrology, based on the twelve signs and nine planets,
by which an individual is supposed to have certain physical, psychic
and temperamental characteristics. Any system of classifications
accepts the inevitable fact that there is bound to be a certain
amount of overlapping of the characteristics from one class and
another (besides the possibility of inexplicable exceptions) but
nonetheless a classification does get general acceptance over a
period of time by the mere fact that by and large the system does
work, for the purpose for which it was devised. There is the
medical classification in Ayurveda according to the proclivity of a
particular body towards diseases of acidity, arthritis, phlegm (Pit-
ta, Vata, Kapha). Then there is the classification in the Bhagvadgita of the paths to salvation — devotion to a personal God or the
divine incarnation (Bhakti), action without attachment (Karma),
and knowledge of the self (Jnana).

It is rather interesting that Dr. William Sheldon and his associates worked out many years ago a comprehensive and well-
developed system of classification, which synchronizes remarkably accurately with the three ways in which enlightenment could
occur, as described in the Bhagvadgita. Dr. Sheldon's classification
is based on the fact that each individual is an amalgam in varying
proportions of three physical and three correlated psychological
elements — endomorphy, misomorphy and ectomorphy. The three
components are fairly evenly blended in most people to make a
generally complex character but the fact remains that, although
cases showing the extreme dominant characteristics of any one
component may be relatively uncommon, nevertheless it is indeed
the existence of these disparate instances which has enabled the
classification to be created. Indeed, the term Dhrma, used so
effectively in the Bhagvadgita, to denote the cardinal characteristic, the innate nature of one sentient being which clearly distinguishes him from another, is considered the basis of his very being,
the *raison detre* for his active life. To this extent, the Dharma of an
individual provides, to a reasonable extent, the basis and reason
for the way in which he is expected to live his life. He thereby at

once provides the explanation and the justification for his actions — and also the base for cooperation in the smooth working of a social system. Indeed the social reputation of a particular group or community of people may well depend upon the predominance of a particular component in this classification.

Dr. Sheldon's classification is that (a) the high endomorph's essential characteristic is a soft roundedness, (b) the high meso-morph is big-boned, with hard, strong muscles, while (c) the high ectomorph is comparatively slender, with small bones and weak muscles. The endomorphic physical constitution built around the digestive tract has a corresponding temperamental pattern, based on love of food, comfort and luxury, that Dr. Sheldon calls viscer-atonic temperament, projects an indiscriminate extroversion and emotionality which makes a member of this class prone to a craving for affection not only from the closest family members but also from the entire world, and, of course, he is a compulsive lover who loves the whole world and greets everyone with a sincere open smile; and these characteristics become exaggerated when the vis-ceratonic expects reciprocity when he is ill or in trouble. The mesa-morphic constitution is correlated to a temperament that is termed Somatotonia, depicted by an intense love of physical activity and restlessness, an aggressive and almost uncontrolled lust for power; an unusual capacity to bear pain, coupled with, sometimes shock-ing insensitivity amounting to callousness towards the feelings of others; a strong competitive instinct coupled with uncommon physical courage and intrepidity; and the Somatotonic prefers to bear his pains and travails in solitude. The temperament allied to the ectomorphic physical construct is cerebrotonic, characterized by an over-sensitivity coupled with an over-alertness of the brain. The typical cerebrotonic is an incorrigible introvert con-cerned more with what is behind the apparent scene than the scene itself, concerned more with the essential core than the appa-rent matter; not concerned with domination and power over others, therefore not interested in competitive affairs; the cerebro-tonic is quite content to be allowed to live his own life peacefully; a remarkable characteristic of the cerebrotonic is that while he is not unduly interested in food and drink, he can be intensely sex-ual in a most possessive way.

The logical conclusion of the analysis of this classification is that while the visceratonic endomorph and the somatotonic meso-morph are relatively well adapted, in their own ways, to the world they live in — each will naturally tend to "create" his own social world — the cerebrotonic ectomorph is generally not very well adjusted to the people and things which surround him, for the obvious reason that his inherent love of solitude prevents him from actively and consciously creating his own social world. In other words, while the visceratonic goes on his merry way in his rollicking world, and the somatotonic pushes and muscles his way in the competitive world — both accepted as normal and average citizens in their respective worlds — it is the cerebrotonic who often achieves the unscaled heights and unplumbed depths in his sheltered world of imagination and research. From the uncommonly high number of geniuses in almost every field among the cerebrotonics, it may well be assumed that Nature has somehow provided for the survival of this over-evolved and not very viable, comparatively rare human being, in one way or another. This analysis lends itself smoothly and easily to the three paths to salvation according to the Hindu tradition. The visceratonic's natural propensity towards externalizing his emotions would make him almost automatically take the path of devotion to the personal God (Bhakti) with its inherent component of universal goodwill accompanied by charity and compassion towards all sentient beings. The path of action (Karma) would obviously suit the Somatotonic with an abundance of physical stamina and energy which makes him be "on the go" all the time. Similarly, the path of Knowledge (Jnana) would be clearly marked out for the introverted cerebrotonic.

From the astonishingly wide range of cases where enlightenment has taken place in different parts of the world in different times in the history of mankind, it is clear that Nature or Totality does not restrict the occurrence of enlightenment to any particular type of human being. It must be remembered, of course, that the three types are rarely exclusive among the milions of human beings. An average or normal person could possibly be categorized as belonging to a particular type insofar as certain basic characteristics are concerned but these characteristics would generally be found to be very generously overlaid by those of the other two types. In fact, the three paths to salvation are themselves purely conceptual and are rarely so exclusive as to keep out the other two; indeed to consider and approach God in a particular, restricted manner is to invite a distorted view of both the Totality and the Reality, and would mean viewing the matter purely from the viewpoint of the individual and not from the true viewpoint of the phenomenal functioning as a whole. The real question is: is there a common ground in the various cases of enlightenment that happen in the widespread spectrum of the human personality — whether basically visceratonic or somatotonic or cerebrotonic — overlaid profusely with the many different shades of the other two types. It is thinking along these lines that is likely to give us an insight into the happening known as enlightenment that transforms the human being from phenomenality into noumenality. There is indeed such a common ground and, what is more, this common ground is so obviously open to see that it is only the spiritually blind who can avoid seeing it. The common ground for all the three types, and innumerable combinations of the characteristics of each, is the effacement of the "me" or the "self" in opposition to the "others". As one Zen Patriarch puts it, "One in all, all in one — if only this is realized, no more worry about not being perfect." Nisargadatta Maharaj used to say, once the mystery that is no mystery is fathomed, once the open secret is realized that all that is, is Unicity — whether manifest or unmanifest — one returns to the source and remains where one has always been without the other.

The annihilation of the "me" or the "self" cannot be "achieved". This is so because the one who wants to "achieve" this is none other than the "me" or the "self" or the "ego" or the mind; and mind cannot destroy mind. The mind is the creation of time and space, and it is only that kind of understanding which is not of time that can annihilate the timebound mind or ego. This is for the cerebrotonic. For the exuberant visceratonic and the restlessly active Somatotonic, the mind can be annihilated into the no-mind state only when the emotional energy of the one and the physical energy of the other get channelized into realms in which the "self" is barred. This can happen only when the emotions are directed not towards sensual pleasures for the "me" but towards the embodiment of the source of all "me"s; this can happen only when the physical energies get directed not towards the personal sucess for the "me"against the "others", but towards excellence in performance as such, irrespective of results. So long as the devotee's devotion is purpose -oriented and the worker's work is result oriented, so long will elightenment be obstructed in its happening. It is only when the devotee's devotion is pure and free of any premeditated purpose can elightenment take place; it is only when the worker does his work without any thought of personal reward, does work become worship and enlightenment can occur. Similarly, it is only when understanding is freed of "the one who understands" and "that which is understood", that enlightenment might happen. In other words, it is only when the very intention, the volition, the desire of something personal to be achieved by personal efforts gets thrown out, that enlightenment can come in.

The barrier to perfect results is always the intrusion of the "self". That this is so has been repeatedly confirmed in the history of mankind by the most successful in every field of life—service, art, business and even fighting. Indeed, what is meant by "inspired" effort in any field is that effort where the "self" has been absent. Perfection is unicity and perfection cannot happen when there is separation, conflict, fears and anxiety, that is to say, when the "me" is present. When the "me" is present, perfection cannot be present. We are, however, so thoroughly conditioned by the concept of personal effort for personal results that the idea of any effort or work not motivated by results is just not acceptable to us. The truth, however, is that all events are predetermined. This truth is not acceptable to us; the doubt is thus expressed: all effort is the result of thought and thought is personal - how can the thought, the effort, and the correlated result be impersonal and predetermined? The answer is astonishingly simple. As Nisargadatta Maharaj used to ask, "where does the thought, that precedes a particular action, come from?"It is true that thought is based on memory, but the point is: out of hundreds of thoughts that could have arisen at a particular point of time, why should a *particular* thought have arisen, the one that gives rise to a particular action.? Obviously that particular thought, or thought-pattern, could have come only in consciousness, and universal consciousness is where the totality of functioning in the phenomenal manifestation takes place. In other words, when a particular event- momentous or otherwise - is to take place in accordance with the totality of functioning, would it be so difficult to imagine that universal consciousness would direct a particular thought-pattern to the individual consciousness in a particular psychosomatic apparatus which would lead to the particular event or events envisaged in the totality of functioning.?

All one need do is visualize just one scene in 1944 when the whole of Europe had been brought under the heel of the mighty Nazi armed forces, and Adolf Hitler stood on the shores of Calais, looking into the distance at the white cliffs of Dover and the one little country not yet crushed by the German Army — trying to decide whether or not to invade England. Every General without exception had predicted that with one mighty attack England could be brought to its knees within the week. But, of course, Hitler finally decided not to attack. What caused the thought-pattern in his mind that led to a decision which cost him not only his own life but the most amazing victory in the history of Europe that was utterly within his grasp ? Destiny ? God ? The universal consciousness within which takes place the totality of the phenomenal manifestation and its functioning ?

Whether from the viewpoint of devotion or knowledge or whatever, the basic idea is only one : the individual entity, "me", the "self" is merely a concept and not something with an autonomous existence with independent choice of decision and action. The unchangeable fact is that there is no human being as such who can act on his own, whatever he may believe. The idea may seem too revolutionary to be acceptable. But it really is no more revolutionary than was the idea that the sun was stationary and the earth (and the other planets) moved round the sun, at a time when it was very firmly believed—why, they could see it with their own eyes— that the sun moved during the day from east to west. Because people would be shocked by this revolutionary idea, Coppernicus had to wait several years before he dared put forward his proved theory for fear of reprisals from the Church, but ultimately truth had to be accepted. And, inspite of the revolutionary idea, people remained people, and life went on as before. It was gradually accepted as a true fact that the sun was indeed stationary, but in the common parlance people continued to talk of the sun as rising in the east and setting in the west. Nisargadatta Maharaj used to warn his visitors that his teaching would be considered revolutionary even among those who were interested in non-duality, and that, therefore, it was not to be discussed with all and sundry. If a hundred people were told that they had as much independent volition as a character in a dream, at least ninety would laugh at the "silly" idea, nine might admire its quaintness, and perhaps only one would seriously consider   it in depth. But a fact is a fact whether any human being believed it or not. The sun would remain stationary and the planets would move around it, whether anyone believed it or not. But the more significant point of the idea of the individual entity being a mere illusion is the result of the understanding and acceptance of the idea.

The immediate reaction of one who accepted the idea would be a sense of total loss of identity and the question would at once arise, how he was to live his life in future if he accepted the principle of non-volition. He did not see the incongruity in the question, and if a visitor put forward this problem, Maharaj would laugh and answer, "you may do whatever you like". Maharaj obviously meant to convey by this answer, "You may do whatever you *think you* are doing". The question itself exposes the fact that the principle of non-volition has not been understood in depth. There are two aspects to this problem. One, whatever actually happens would have happened in any case, irrespective of the fact that the individual considers the decisions and the action (and the guilt) to be his own — in which case, he continues to think as if he has independece of choice as an individual, and therefore has not really understood the principle. Two, he considers that as he is not the doer but merely the instrument of the Totality, he could do anything which he would not normally consider ethical. Here again, it means he has not truly understood the principle. This second aspect has been well brought out by John Everard who puts it thus: Turn the man loose who has found the living Guide within him, and let him neglect the outward *if he can.*Just as you would say to a man who loves his wife with all tenderness, "you are at liberty to beat her, hurt her or kill her *if you want to".*

The real significance of the principle of non-volition is that the one who has truly understood the principle no longer "acts" — either positively by doing something or negatively by ceasing to do something. Chuang-Tzu describes the acts of such people as follows: "they are upright without being conscious of duty to their neighbours; they love one another without being conscious of charity; they are true without being conscious of loyalty; they are honest without being conscious of good faith; they act freely in all things without recognizing obligations to anyone." In short what actually happens is that having understood the principle very deeply, they truly "let go" of their individual identity and merely witness the actions that take place following their understanding. In other words they let the Dharma of their individual psyche take over with such modifications as the understanding may have made. This is the real point. Such modifications may take the form not only of smoothing the edges of the personality within its own type but even the superimposing of certain traits from a different type altogether. Thus the basic gregariousness of the visceratonic may be smoothened out into a genuine kindliness and charity (not in the sense of almgiving but in its original sense of the highest form of love) and general goodwill; similarly, the aggressive lust for power inherent in the typical somatotonic may be softened into a capacity to work for the general good of the society with nonattachment; and in the case of the cerebrotonic, reason would almost certainly be greatly tempered by love and an intuitive perceptiveness. Even more important is the fact that a particular type, while he continued to function with the basic characteristics, may, as a result of the understanding, be so generously superimposed by the characteristics of the other two typs that *the distinction between the three types may well turn out to be extremely hazy.* The essential point of the analysis is to be clearly aware that the proper understanding of non-volition pushes the "me" so far back into the psyche that an extraordinary sense of freedom comes about: when the identity with a single individual disappears, what takes its place is the identity with the universal consciousness.

The ultimate result of the understanding of the principle of non-volition is the acceptance of all events cheerfully as the "will of God," and living freely, freed of all affective attachments, in the "state of life to which it has pleased God to call us", playing one's role in this dream-play that is called life, without taking anything too seriously,with a certain amount of amusement at the apparent absurdity of it all.

Nisargadatta Maharaj was an occurrence in the functioning of Totality. Those who were drawn to him — some by their own *apparent* volition, others through the force of circumstances beyond their control — were a part of the happening that Nisargadatta Maharaj was. The extent to which each apparent individual "benefited" from his association with Maharaj, being a part of the process of evolution, depended upon the extent to which the ground had been prepared in each case to receive such benefit. The understanding, or apperception of what is — the nature or *suchness* of things being noumenal, must necessarily be spontaneous and sudden, while the effect of it, if any , on the individual mechanism, being of the dimension of space-time relativity, would be not necessarily sudden but gradual over a period of time depending upon the Dharma (the natural type) of each psychosomatic apparatus. It is futile to seek reason and meaning into the events of life. It can only lead to entanglements into the briars of space-time duality which made even Einstein exclaim that he could not accept that "God is playing dice with the universe". Neils Bohr gave the necessary explanation that it only *seems* that God is playing dice with the universe because we do not have the full information which God has! It is only the apperception (of the nature of the universe and its source) that can give the noumenal insight to see God's plan as a whole, but then no "one" would then exist who would have any curiosity about it!

The philosopher moans the fact that modern man has totally forgotten the divine element in Nature or *nisarga* and has been behaving towards her like an arrogant and presumptuous conqueror and tyrant, as if man himself is not a part of the natural manifestation as a whole. The intention may have been wholesome but the results otherwise: he tried to turn dry prairies into wheat fields and what he actually produced was deserts; he intended to make every person not only literate but educated to think for himself, by producing books on a vast scale, while all he has done is not only to annihilate forests to provide the necessary newsprint but to use that newsprint to produce mass literature to corrupt young minds; he intended to use unimaginable inventions and discoveries to provide vast energy and magnificent technological improvements to make life easy for the "common man", but all he has succeeded in doing is to put mankind itself in danger of being wiped out. The common man on his part points his finger at the scientist and the multinational industrialist as the villains of the piece, and piously hopes that they will mend their ways before it is too late.

When this messy situation was sometimes referred to by some visitor Nisargadatta Maharaj would laugh — and laugh somtimes so heartily that the visitor would be flabergasted—and ask him to view the same situation in perspective by going back. Is it one man's mind or will that has brought about this situation or are many "experts" in various fields concerned? How many minds or will are there who brought this about? Would you really believe that the divine ground immanent in the total manifestation would totally delegate its functioning to the relatively puny split-mind of man? Maharaj would explain that it is through the primal elements that the grand Divine Design works, and that man is but an insignificant instrument in that Design. What is man anyway? At any moment, man is only that part of the human body which he can see, plus a complex bundle of thoughts and feelings (which keep on changing from moment to moment) — in other words, space containing all these things without any assurance of any duration. This is what man is even from his own "commonsense point of view". The outside view of man as an object is that of a conglomerate of cells, molecules, atoms and particles. The human body comprises billions of semi-autonomous beings called cells, each competing fiercely with the others for the available nourishment for its own survival, ignoring all others; and steadfastly following its own characteristic behaviour pattern (dharma) - and yet managing to maintain a being of a higher order, the human being. Actually, this is only the middle level view and we could go further back. The actual progress may be said to start with the atoms as unitary organism being integrated by the higher level molecules who are themselves controlled by each cell - the cells being integrated by the whole apparatus known as man. But why stop at the organism of the human being? Surely, the process must continue upwards culminating in the entire universe as the ultimate whole, and then on to the immanent Divine Ground of all manifestation - the universal consciousness, the one Mind, the one Will: Thy *will be done* (the Totality of functioning).WHAT-IS is the ineluctable perfection, the Truth, which is man's real nature. Man forgets his real nature, the WHAT-IS, and tries to achieve what he thinks "should be", and becomes unhappy. All that man can do is to forget his individual separateness and witness the functioning of the Totality, as in a dream. And, truly, even this is not in his hands as an individual, but becomes a part of the totality of functioning, which, ironically, is his own objective expression, not as an individual object "me" but as the Absolute Subject, what Ramana Maharshi called the "I-I", the throbbing formless beingness or presence.

Action Learning

[Reproduced from a paper submitted to the ICR conference on Education, held in Bombay, 27th - 30th December 1984 (with suitable minor changes) with the kind permission of the Convenor, Dr. M.L. Dhawale.]

I am writing this paper on my SixtySeventh birthday - and it suddenly strikes me with a tremendous impact that "I" do not feel the slightest change over the years. I was the same "I" fifty years ago or five hundred years ago or even before TIME ever was, and I shall be the same fifty years hence or five hundred years hence or even after TIME ceases to be. This is not a play on words; it is the firmest possible conviction: "I" remain changeless while time passes by.

Is there one single outstanding lesson that I have learnt through action over these sixty-odd years? Yes, it is that while I thought that it was I as an entity that was living my life, in actuality I was "being lived" as an infinitesimal - yet highly significant - part in the functioning of the totality of universal manifestation. And I am not now thinking in terms of any conceptual father-figure as an over-lord God with his heaven and hell. I am thinking clearly and purely on the basis of personal experience. I was recently presented with a small volume by Prof. C.E.M. Joad, published many years ago, with the title *"The meaning of life"*. The immediate thought that came to my mind when I read the title of the book was that the meaning of life is that life has no meaning other than the living of it as a dream-play, over which one has really no control. When I was born I had no choice; no control. When I was born I had no choice; when I am faced with death I expect I shall have no choice either - I shall not be able to tell death to come back after two days as I have still some unfinished work to complete. In between the two phenomena of birth and death, however, I consider myself the master of my own destiny; I have read a number of books on the power of positive thinking and allowed myself to be brainwashed by "miracles through will power and mind control", and yet I find that at every stage in my life almost every significant event has had an enormous element of "chance" or "coincidence" in it. If something turns out to be successful, we consider it the result of our concentrated effort; if not we blame it on bad luck or a lack of adequate "influence in the right quarters".

Nothing in life seems to have any stability. Quite early in life, I recollect, my mother, who was a voracious reader, used to tell me that my propensity to eat small meals at fairly frequent intervals was a bad habit and that medical opinion was clear on the point that the stomach must be given adequate rest between a limited number of meals. I tried the system and found that it did not suit me—it made made me definitely ill—and so I went back to my unhealthy way and kept quite fit. Many years later, medical opinion veered around to the system of smaller and oftener meals because the stomach was then spared the strain of digesting heavy meals. Then, I was told that I would come to a bad and early end if I continued to have aspirin at regular intervals for my hereditary migraine headaches. While I tried every available system of medicine—over periods which were long enough in all conscience— I could not possibly have given up aspirin and still continued to put in my usual long day at the office. And now, for the past several years, aspirin is, I believe, prescribed in regular doses for certain heart conditions. At any rate, at least in my own case, aspirin has allowed me to live and work for over forty years without any apparent serious ill effects. And it has so happened that my migraine headaches were ultimately relieved and cured by the manipulations of an osteopath! What have I learned from this episode in my life? It is that each one of us is to a certain extent different from perhaps every other human being. Every finger print is different from every other finger print, and every leaf on the same plant is different in some respect or the other from every other leaf. I have learnt to admire the miracle that is NATURE which provides such diversity and multiplicitly in what is really unicity - unicity in universe, which the mystics have been talking to us about from times immemorial and which the sub-atomic physicists have recently proved in their laboratories. I have learnt that I must never forget that I am an intrinsic part of the manifested universe and must always think on this basis; and at the same time, as a separate individual in the multiplicity of the universe, I must not accept anything generally advised without carefully considering whether what is recommended suits me as an individual. This would refer to all areas of human existence, subject of course, to the law of the land and the basic social courtesies towards others.

Life: Who controls?

During the school years, I have had two incidents which have remained firmly in my mind, and therefore, I would presume that they have had a certain amount of influence on my thinking and behaviour.

(a) It was in the final year of the school during a history class. The teacher was an excellent one who loved teaching, and he was summarising a whole period of 200 years of Indian history, without referring to any textbook or notes. He was in fact taking a sweeping look at the historical era. And at a certain juncture it struck me that the one thing history proves is that nothing is stable in life, which is in fact a passing show, and that the wisest thing in life is to regard it as such. It was British rule in India at that time in 1932 and it seemed that it would go on and on for ever, and yet only after 15 years the British left and India had independence. What did I learn from the incident in school? Perhaps the foolishness of expecting anything in life—happiness or whatever — to remain for any length of time; perhaps the foolishness of expecting anything at all, as the due reward of our actions; perhaps how right Dryden was when he said, "all human things are subject to decay and when fate summons, monarchs must obey".

(b) The other incident concerns a class in physiology when the teacher was explaining that the eye is like the lens of a camera and that the object creates an image on the retina of the eye exactly as on the lens of a camera. At that point my mind went off at a tangent. The teacher happened to notice it, walked over to my desk and asked me to stand up and repeat what he had just explained. In fact it was precisely because I had listened to him so attentively that I had a query, so there was no problem in repeating what he had said. He was rather taken aback, but asked me why I was gazing vacantly in space. My query was: the cameraman "clicks" the camera in order to retain on the film the picture on the lens—who does the clicking of the picture on the retina of the eye? For a moment the teacher was startled but he recovered quickly and told me not to ask a stupid question like that. And, but for the fact that I was a reasonably good student, I am sure I would have had my ear well cuffed that day! I really did not think it was a stupid question; my point was that the eye is as much a part of the body, as is the lens a part of the camera. The camera needed an extraneous agency — whether human or an automatic mechanism — in order to preserve the image on the film. The image of the object would surely be there in the eye of a dead man but it would not be registered on the brain; therefore, there must be something which differentiates a dead man from a man who is alive.

It was many years later when I met a self-realized jnani that the point was cleared up. I understood from him that the human body as such is a mere psychosomatic apparatus which consciousness turns into a sentient being: When consciousness is not present in the body either permanently because of death, or temporarily as in sleep or under sedation, the universe does not exist for that psychosomatic apparatus. What did I learn from the incident in the physiology class? Surly, that we spend far too much time studying matters which have only an outward or apparent significance while neglecting their real significance, that we are busy studying the tip of the iceburg while ignoring the heavy mass underneath.

Life: Effortless floating

After passing my B.A.(Hons) examination in Bombay, I went to London to join the London School of Economics. There was an entrance examination in which I had to appear for a paper in Economics for which there was no specific curriculum. So there was nothing really to cram or mug up except to go cursorily through a book on the subject. When the question paper was distributed, I found that there was a fair amount of choice and I selected general topics where the principles of economics could be applied and not much relevant information as such was required. Also, the answers would be more in the form of an opinion arrived at by applying the principles of economics in a logical, rational manner. At any rate, I happened to write the answers in a relaxed frame of mind, perhaps because I had gathered that the test was more to weed out the sub-marginal applicants rather than to test the calibre of each applicant. I had also come to know, that for those who, like me, had applied for entrance to the B.Com. (Bachelor of Commerce) cource, having previously done a B.A. (Bachelor of Arts) course and therefore had not done any course in Accountancy, the usual standard marking was "partial exemption" from the first year course (prior to the B.Com.) so that one could carry on for the B.Com. course subject to appearing successfully for the Accountancy paper at the next examination. Then the results were ready, and I was supposed to see one Professor Plant about my result. When I met the professor and gave my name, he went through the list and said "full exemption". I was taken aback and thought there was some mistake. I explained that in India I had done a B.A. and not a B.Com. He referred to his list again and repeated "full exemption". He held out his hand and we shook hands. I came out of his room rather dazed and told my friends that I was given "full exemption". They would not believe it, and said there would probably be a correction in due course. But there was no correction, and I am probably the only B.Com. in the world who never appeared for a paper in Accountancy! I did, of course, study accountancy later on but not for appearing in any examination relevant to my B.Com. degree. I gathered subsequently that my answer papers for the entrance test were considered so outstanding that the council had recommended full exemption. What did I learn from this incident? First, that there is such a thing as being in exceptional "form" which happens at odd times when one cannot do anything incorrect or put a foot wrong, that at such times one finds oneself in complete tune with the universal pulse, the body and the mind work in total relaxation, there is no thought (let alone anxiety) about what might happen; there is only Sheer Joy in the performance itself.

A similar thing happened when once I played a round of golf with the club professional. It was the first day of my vacation and I had left all my worries at the office, and when I stood at the first Tee, I had the most fantastic feeling of being at the peak of my physical condition. There was of course, no question of winning or losing — either losing face or losing money. When we returned to the clubhouse, I had had my best round ever, and the Pro. did not have to tell me that he had to play quite seriously so as not to lose face by being defeated! Later, on reviewing the game, I found that I had learnt a lot that day. First, that the best results come about (not "achieved") if there is concentration on the work itself, that is to say, what is being done, whether it is a ball being hit or a report being prepared or whatever; that concentration does not mean tension; that on the contrary, concentration means utter relaxation, that relaxation comes about when there are no disturbing thoughts about the results of the effort being made; that, in fact, if there is real concentration and relaxation, the actual effort turns out to be effortless like the winning effort of a champion or an expert in any field; that such effortless effort denotes joy being experienced in the effort itself irrespective of the success which such an effort might or might not result in.

Life: View from below

On my return from England after acquiring the B.Com. degree

of the London University, I had the good fortune to join a leading Indian Bank - as a clerk! It happened to be the bank's policy
at that particular time not to recruit people, however highly qual-
ified, direct into the officers' cadre, but to promote people from
within the clerical grade. I sat at the counter, and did all the
work that was expected of a clerk. I was promoted to the officers' grade as soon as there was a vacancy; and, although at
times I could not help wondering if my joining as a clerk was
not an unwise step, on the whole I became reconciled to the fact
that it had certain advantages. In the event of any disagreement
or difference of opinion between the clerks and officers on any
matter, the argument could not be thrown at me that I could
only see one point of view. I could take a dispassionate view.
Apart from this inherent advantage, what did I learn from this
incident? Most important, I learnt that one must accept in life
the bitter with the sweet, that every fact usually has both advantages and disadvantages, that this particular circumstance gave
me an opportunity to test myself about the quality of my clerical
work; that, in short, one must play to the best of one's ability
any role allotted to one on the stage of life. It is not likely that
life would be one long continuous road with roses all the way!

Life: Creativity

There is one other episode in my career that I feel I should
refer to. At one juncture, it was decided by the Board of Directors that the bank should start advertising in an aggressive sort
of way. Until then, bank advertising was known as the type of
"tombstone" advertising — a list of figures concerning the Bank's
capital, reserves, deposits etc. followed below by the names of
the Bank's directors. I was a little disconcerted when I was asked
to deal with the matter in its entirety because at that time I was
already putting in very long hours almost everyday. But then,
apart from the fact that it meant a definite recognition from the
Board of Directors, it also opened up a new area of work in
which I would have to find out for myself if I had any undisco-
vered resources or talent apart from banking in which subject
was concentrated all my training and experience until then. It
turned out to be the most constructive and satisfying period of
my career in the bank. Immediately, however, I was to find that
the whole thing was not as simple as I had imagined. I had expected that all I had to do was to appoint a good firm of advertising agents and work in cooperation with them. But I soon
found that it was not a simple task to get a firm that would pro-

duce advertising of the type and the standard that I wanted. It meant that for better or worse, I myself would have to undertake the responsibility of doing everything from scratch, from the very visualizing of the advertisements to the completion, and have a small agency for only the technical work of preparing the layout, artwork etc. To cut a long story short, our advertising turned out to be a totally unexpected success, comparable to that of any bank anywhere in the world. I was lucky to get a remarkably energetic man as our advertising agent, and also an excellent photographer who could translate my visualizations into actual photographs with remarkable resourcefulness. I learnt a great deal out of this activity. To begin with, I learnt that perhaps everyone of us has a potential of untapped resources and talent which is always available if drawn upon with a singleminded purpose, that such talent comes to the surface much more quickly and easily if the essential element in the effort is to create something without any specific selfish motive. I must assert that I was honestly concerned with the creation of superlative advertisements and I was perfectly happy that the advertising agent should have the credit, although, of course, people in the bank did know the actual position. My selfish interest lay in the fact that such credit for the work, which followed in ample measure to the hitherto unknown agent from the media circles, encouraged him to work harder than ever before for the success of the bank's advertising. Then there was the question of time. My best ideas seemed to come to me when I sat alone quietly after dinner in a rocking chair in the varandah of our flat, under the starry skies. It was impossible to expect to have any creative ideas in the midst of the heavy work during the day. However, the important point I am making is that although my real working day extended during those years from nine in the morning till late in the night, barring the time for meals, the creative work of advertising was more of a hobby and relaxation than actual work. It was a revelation to me that work which one really likes does not only not tax one's physical or mental resources but creates such a feeling of satisfaction that it actually relaxes and makes for allround well-being. However, perhaps the most important lesson I learned from this aspect of my work was that one really cannot imagine the depth of the potential one has by way of creative resources. I found that work done with a great degree of concentration (which means a great degree of relaxation and not tension which is what is generally misunderstood) releases the kind of unusual energy which works with unbelievable efficacy when really needed.

I would give a specific instance: there was the case of one particular advertisement which was perhaps by far and away our best one, depicting a photograph of four retired persons sitting on a low wall by the sea, sharing a joke and laughing away; every thing was ready except the "copy" which was intended to be short and crisp; this was not an easy task and the right words just would not come to me as I sat in the rocking chair and then all at once the deadline had arrived in the form of a man from the agency standing on the doorstep, in the middle of a working day, with my desk loaded with unusually heavy work. I told the man to wait outside for a little while and I would give him the copy. I took some blank papers and concentration seemed to occur by itself, and I wrote those three or four sentences at the first effort, without a scratch. I sent for the agency man and handed over the paper to him. He read those handwritten sentences. He read them, and he read them again; he looked at me, and then went out shaking his head in perplexity. When such a thing happens I refuse to take credit; it would be stupid to do so. Perhaps this is what is meant when the Tao Master told his disciples: "Do you want to know what Toa is? Go and wash the dishes."

Life: Empathy

There was one particular incident during my career as a banker which had great significance for me. It was when I was the manager of one of the larger branches. One of the borrowers was in difficulties and at my request he was to meet me at a particular time. I had completely cleared my desk; there were no papers on my desk except the papers concerning the particular customer whom I was expecting. My room was on the ground floor, and as I looked out of the window I saw this gentleman sitting morosely in his car, obviously working up the necessary courage to enter the bank premises and see me; my heart went out to him as I could easily understand his state of mind. Suddenly he got out of the car and started slowly walking towards the bank building. I was myself quite worried about the bank's loan but, having seen the utter misery on the poor man's face, I deliberately greeted him as he entered my room, with a cheerful smile which totally belied my inner feeling of apprehension. He was rather startled to see me greeting him so warmly. I showed him to a chair opposite my desk and I was about to go to the other side towards my own chair, when somehow or the other, something made me stop and turn back towards the chair beside the one the borrower was sitting in. There we sat side by side, and I asked him whether he would prefer a cup of tea or coffee. I shall never forget the expression on his face; he had tears in his eyes as he suddenly realized the attitude I had taken: we were not on the opposite sides of the desk! I slipped out of the room for a few moments in order to give him time to compose himself. The meeting went off extremely well, the borrower came out of his mood of helpless panic, and between the two of us the account was nursed back to good health. Why has the incident remained in my mind? Because it taught me a number of things. First and foremost, I could see the actual and immediate effect of demolishing the separation between the banker and the borrower, between "me" and the "other" and establishing a closer relationship towards achieving a common goal. Secondly, the incident gave me the ineluctable insight into the way in which sincere sympathy and a genuine desire to help, intutively communicate themselves. Thirdly, an open and frank discussion with the borrower brought out several factors in regard to how and why the advance got into trouble. And these points were most useful in preventing the possible deterioration in other advances of a similar nature. But the most important of all lessons was the fact that the goodwill with the borrower thus created did no harm to the bank's business! He turned out to be an excellent PRO for the bank.

Life: Ordained

The most important event in my life has been meeting a self-realized Jnani — Nisargadatta Maharaj — in November 1978. It was through reading an article about him in the October issue of the MOUNTAIN PATH (the magazine published by Ramanashramam of Tiruannamalai, South India) that I came to know of him, and knew instinctively that meeting him would be the most significant event in my life. He lived in one of the by-lanes of Khetwadi in Bombay. When I climbed up the steps into his loft room in the small apartment, he was sitting at his usual place on a large thick cushion on the floor, a small old man of about 80. When I made my obeisance to him, he turned his penetrating gaze on me, and said quite distinctly in Marathi (the only language he knew well), "You have finally come, have you? Sit here", and he indicated a place close to him in front. There was no doubt but that in this very first meeting I felt the full impact of his personality and the manner of his greeting — we had never seen each other before in this life. He died three years later and so my actual association with him extended   only for a little less than three years, but the impact of it could not have been more intense if the time had extended over thirty years. It would be an understatement to say that my whole attitude to life changed radically in those three years. The most important thing I learnt from him, so far as this life in concerned, is the supreme importance of apparent ordinariness, the unassuming anonymity which is like the natural protective colouring of an animal or a bird. Such ordinariness is not the assumed humility which is in fact actually obsequiousness but rather what is left after the artificiality of the world is realised and therefore shaken off, a virtue that happens to be virtue because it is based on an inner conviction and not something artificial based on the expectation of a future benefit. Such inner conviction comports the acceptance of the ultimate uselessness of competing against others - if you win you become the constant target of all and suddenly, if you lose, you are termed a failure not only by others but, worse, by yourself.

At this stage I must acknowledge the influence which another remarkable person had on my mind over an extended period of time, and that is, one Shri Hari Vinayak Gurjar, a teacher in my school. One of his teachings which has remained unforgotton is that if one must compete, one should compete against oneself — the best way of shortening a line is to draw a separate one longer than the existing line! When I found what a wonderful thing it is to be associated with a Jnani like Nisargadatta Maharaj, I at once thought of Shri Gurjar who would benefit a great deal by meeting him. Unfortunately, however, Shri Gurjar was then very ill and could not meet Maharaj.

The ordinariness which Maharaj seemed to advocate leaned towards an acceptance of whatever life offered without trying to force anything, which is the basic principle of Judo and Aikido, which is "rolling with the blow" or "swim-- ming with the current", like water following gravity and, if blocked, flowing around the obstacle or finding a new outlet. Such an attitude is healthy because it does not lead to anxiety; because it necessarily involves seeing the universe as a harmoneous whole, with the full realization that looking at it in bits and pieces means avoidable conflict; because it underlines the fact that it is an exercise in futility to seek security and happiness (in the sense in which the word is usually understood) in a world where every species is the prey of some other species, where indeed every incoming and outgoing breath involves the creation and destruction of thousands of "lives" though they may not be perceptible to the naked eye.

Life: Acceptance of "What-Is"

This teaching of Nisargadatta Maharaj is not just something which "sounds nice" but is found to work in practice. I would mention two instances in my personal experience. All experience is necessarily subjective and there is no point in comparing how two persons may react to the same or similar external stimulus. It is useless to say that someone is over-reacting to something which another person may ignore. The point is that there is a reaction which causes what is termed as happiness or unhappiness to the person concerned.

(a) A personal tragedy is something everyone knows and understands. In my own case when it concerned two of my closest relatives, my mental condition became most miserable expecially as it coincided with a very rough patch in human relations at the office. The situation seemed to be getting totally out of control when, suddenly, the simple fact dawned on me that since the matter was totally beyond my control, it was ridiculous that I should worry about it!

The answer was to accept the situation as it was, not with a sense of futility and frustration, but with the awareness of witnessing something that was happening as in a dream, keeping my trust in the basic and essential harmony in the totality of the functioning of the universe, in the unconscious or unpreconceived or natural intelligence of the manifestation, and in the inherent wisdom of adopting the line of least resistance because of the deepest conviction that as an infinitesimal part of totality the purest action is to go along with the process without any sense of volition. The sudden revelation was instantaneous and it was precisely like suddenly relaxing at the highest point of tension, like waking up from a nightmare. I must explain that this incident occurred a few years *before* I met Maharaj, but was, I feel, an essential factor in my quickly apperceiving the truth of what he said, with an unshakable conviction; I KNEW it was so from personal experience. The interesting development in this incident was the extraordinary "coincidence" that as soon as I had adopted this attitude of enlightened acceptance of "What-is" as part of the totality of functioning, everything seemed to click into a new position, everything seemed to improve of its own accord. But the real miracle was that I was able to accept this new changed position of "What-is" with the same attitude of resignation, relaxation and equanimity. The phantom had lost its sting though, of course, there would undoubtedly remain its occasional pricks!

(b) The other incident is a much more mundane one but, nonetheless, I think, of some significance because most people would, sometime or the other, be afflicted by similar circumstances. There is a pack of stray dogs near my flat who hide themselves somewhere between buildings during the day but get together on several nights and make a tremendous din; then they move a little distance away and repeat the performance, and they have several such meeting posts with the result that they keep on disturbing one's sleep for as long as an hour or so at regular intervals. It is a problem for all but the heaviest of sleepers. A neighbour complained to me that he gets into a panic as soon as he is awakened the very first time because he knows the intermittent nuisance would continue for at least an hour or so. I told him about my system of accepting the inevitable and making the best of the situation. The first time I wake up, I told him, I make it a point to lie on my back and deliberately relax the whole body instantly (not gradually, part by part) so that the feeling is of being limp as if in a faint, and also to relax the mind, to "empty" the mind and in a way to make it vacant and free of all thoughts. Thoughts are bound to arise; the trick is not to get involved in them but to ignore them. I find that in this process, one of two things happen: (a) either I happen to fall asleep into a much deeper sleep which is not easily disturbed by the subsequent performance of the dogs, or (b) the condition of the fasting mind continues for quite some time and results in a deep state of meditation in which there is disidentification from the body. The latter is much the more preferable condition for me because I find myself much better rested and seem to fall asleep thereafter into smooth and undisturbed sleep. Either way, the important point is that I do not get myself into a condition of panic when I am first awakened by the dogs. In accepting what the dogs are doing, there is too, a feeling, I find, of an understanding that what the dogs are doing is what comes naturally to them and is therefore an integral part of "What is"

Panic can only create a conflict within oneself which it is possible to avoid.

The acceptance of the situation as "What is" which I have mentioned in these two widely different instances needs to be clarified in order to avoid a serious misunderstanding. The acceptance I have in mind does not have the slightest touch of either compulsion or self-deceit. It may be misunderstood as a fatalistic surrender because there is nothing one can do about it. Such an acceptance signifies a feeling of helplessness which is totally absent in the acceptance I am talking about. Nor does it mean self-deceit in the sense that it is not really an acceptance but weak attempt to ignore it, like that of an ostrich burying its head in the sand, with a hope that the problem if ignored will disappear! The acceptance which I am talking about is, on the other hand, undertaken in the full awareness of all the implications of the situation. But the real and significant factor which makes such acceptance essentially and vitally different from that of helplessness or self-deceit is that such acceptance has an entirely new dimension, a dimension which arises suddenly and spontaneously when the mind-intellect has reached the end of its tether and acknowledges its total defeat in the sense that the problem itself is totally outside its ambit and competence. Indeed, what this really and truly means in its effect is that the surrender is not by the individual but the mind-intellect and in such surrender the individual identity itself gets demolished! What this means when translated into the framework of problem solution is that helplessness arises when the acceptance relates to the inability to find a solution whereas the more basic acceptance related to the full awareness of the entire situation refers not merely to the solution but the problem itself. In other words, the question is not "what is the solution to the problem?", but rather, "Am I trying to find the solution to a problem with which I am not concerned in the first place?" This kind of looking at the problem puts the problem in a perspective which is basically and vitally different enough to be a true one. This kind of seeing is true seeing.

Life: Perceiving

True seeing is seeing a situation in its totality with a whole mind that is not corrupted by the separation of the individual from the totality. The usual or ordinary seeing is with a split-mind; divided between an individual and the rest of the world.

The usual seeing involves a separation or dualism as between "me" and the "other" with the result that the seeing is done with a distorted eye because such a separation can never be realistic inasmuch as all sentient beings together form the totality of the phenomenal manifestation; any separation becomes un-natural and therefore the view of any situation from this view-point becomes necessarily a distorted one.

True seeing — seeing the totality in its inevitable functioning — soon becomes a habit which then transforms itself into true living in which, because of the acceptance of the totality of func-tioning, living becomes freed of tension, work assumes a beauty of its own by being dissociated from the rewards, action becomes more spontaneous and intuitive, and life in general becomes more natural and altogether more enjoyable. When one sees the enormity of the manifestation as a whole, one cannot but under-stand the inevitability of its functioning in accordance with an overall plan which could not possibly fit in with the limited parameters of an individual's intellect. What the individual, as an individual, seeks is basically a kind of security in life, not only for himself and his family but also for his descendents in the second and third generations. Only a little thought on the subject should convince any intelligent person that security as such is a totally illusory concept in a world where the very *raison detre* is constant change. What can an individual therefore do? Actually, all he can do is "to live in the present" in the sense that everything we experience is in reality our reaction to, or in-terpretation of, something that has already passed and gone in the conditioning that we accept as TIME In other words, what we react to at this moment is an event that has already passed through our consciousness some time ago! What this means is that there is really no individual entity which is capable of hav-ing effective volition. All that really happens is that when an event has come and gone (in our consciousness), if our reaction to it is in accordance with what we wished for, it is fortuitous; if not, all that the volition has brought about for us is frustration. The only answer is accepting the inevitable with a sense not of frustration but with a sense of wonderment. And then living becomes non-volitional; living becomes easy and effortless be-cause we see the futility of volition.

Does it mean then that we are to give up living and become hippies? Hardly so! All it means is that we float with the current and do whatever comes naturally according to the make-up of our genes, subject of course to the law of the land and desisting from something that is intutively abhorrent like giving pain to others. In short, my personal experience is that from the viewpoint of totality hardly any problems arise, while from the individual viewpoint problems never cease. This is because perception as such is only mirrorization without any reactionary interpretation; troubles arise because of such individual interpretation. One can easily imagine what would happen if the reflections of our faces in the mirror were to offer us their reactions and comments concerning our faces!

Conclusion

Once there is the clear apprehension that an individual human being is an inseparable part of the totality of phenomenal manifestation and that he cannot pull himself out of the totality as an independent and autonomous entity, man naturally ceases to have personal intentions. When he is convinced that living is a sort of dreaming in which he cannot have any effective control over his actions, all tensions cease and a sense of total freedom takes over, so that he willingly accepts whatever comes his way as proper and right in the totality of the functioning that this dream-life is. This is the ultimate action-lesson I have learnt over the last sixty-odd years.

By Ramesh S. Balsekar

CONSCIOUSNESS SPEAKS. Recommended both for the newcomer to Advaita (non-duality) and the more knowledgeable student of the subject. 392 pages. Paperback.

A DUET OF ONE; THE ASHTAVAKRA GITA DIALOGUE. Here the most beautiful of the Advaitic texts, the Ashtravakra Gita is used as a vehicle for an illuminating look at the nature of duality and dualism. 224 pages. Paperback.

EXPERIENCING THE TEACHING. In this book many facets of Advaita are examined and illuminated through a series of 24 dialogues. 142 pages. Paperback.

THE FINAL TRUTH; A GUIDE TO ULTIMATE UNDERSTANDING. Comprehensive and powerful look at Advaita from the arising of I AM to the final dissolution into identification as pure consciousness. 240 pages. Paperback.

FROM CONSCIOUSNESS TO CONSCIOUSNESS. This wonderful book explores the heart of the guru/ disciple relationship. 80 pages. Paperback.

You may order directly from:

The Acorn Press,
P. O. Box 3279, Durham, NC 27715-3279.
Telephone: (919) 471-3842. FAX (919) 477-2622

Also from the Acorn Press
Books by Sri Nisargadatta Maharaj

I AM THAT; TALKS WITH SRI NISARGADATTA MAHARAJ. Compiled and translated by Maurice Frydman; revised and edited by Sudhakar S. Dikshit. 3rd edition, 9th printing, 1996 (1st published 1973). xxii, 550 pages, illus. Paperback.

Maharaj's unique teaching, in this compilation, regarded my many as a "modern spiritual classic," has been hailed as the direct path to the pathless goal of self-realization.

SEEDS OF CONSCIOUSNESS; THE WISDOM OF SRI NISARGADATTA MAHARAJ. Edited by Jean Dunn; introduction by Ramesh S. Balsekar. 2d ed. 1990 (first published 1982). 215 pages. Paperback. (Selected talks of Maharaj from July 1979 to April 1980.)

PRIOR TO CONSCIOUSNESS; TALKS WITH SRI NISARGADATTA MAHARAJ. Edited by Jean Dunn. 2d ed. 1990, reprinted 1996. ix, 157 pages, illus. Paperback. (Selected talks of Maharaj, 1980-1981.)

CONSCIOUSNESS AND THE ABSOLUTE; THE FINAL TALKS OF SRI NISARGADATTA MAHARAJ. Edited by Jean Dunn. First published 1994. vii, 118 pages, illus. Paperback.

POINTERS FROM NISARGADATTA MAHARAJ. By Ramesh S. Balsekar; edited by Sudhakar S. Dikshit. 1995 (first published 1983, reprinted 1984, 1988, 1990). xvi, 223 pages. Paperback. "This publication is alive with the intensity and force of Nisargadatta Maharaj's spiritual realization, and the fierceness and dedication with which he relentlessly strove to accelerate others' liberation."

You may order directly from:

The Acorn Press,
P. O. Box 3279, Durham, NC 27715-3279.
Telephone: (919) 471-3842. FAX (919) 477-2622